Total Quality Management (TQM)

T0295520

Mathematical Engineering, Manufacturing, and Management Sciences

Series Editor:
Mangey Ram,

Professor, Assistant Dean (International Affairs), Department of Mathematics, Graphic Era University, Dehradun, India

The aim of this new book series is to publish the research studies and articles that bring up the latest development and research applied to mathematics and its applications in the manufacturing and management sciences areas. Mathematical tools and techniques are the strength of engineering sciences. They form the common foundation of all novel disciplines as engineering evolves and develops. The series will include a comprehensive range of applied mathematics and its application in engineering areas such as optimization techniques, mathematical modelling and simulation, stochastic processes and systems engineering, safety-critical system performance, system safety, system security, high assurance software architecture and design, mathematical modelling in environmental safety sciences, finite element methods, differential equations, reliability engineering, etc.

Sustainable Procurement in Supply Chain Operations
Edited by Sachin Mangla, Sunil Luthra, Suresh Jakar, Anil Kumar, and Nirpendra Rana

Mathematics Applied to Engineering and Management
Edited by Mangey Ram and S.B. Singh

Mathematics in Engineering Sciences
Novel Theories, Technologies, and Applications
Edited by Mangey Ram

Advances in Management Research
Innovation and Technology
Edited by Avinash K. Shrivastava, Sudhir Rana, Amiya Kumar Mohapatra, Mangey Ram

Market Assessment with OR Applications
Adarsh Anand, Deepti Agarwal, Mohini Agarwal

Recent Advances in Mathematics for Engineering
Edited by Mangey Ram

Probability, Statistics, and Stochastic Processes for Engineers and Scientists
Aliakbar Montazer Haghighi and Indika Rathnathungalage Wickramasinghe

Total Quality Management (TQM)
Principles, Methods, and Applications
Sunil Luthra, Dixit Garg, Ashish Agarwal, and Sachin K. Mangla

For more information about this series, please visit: https://www.crcpress.com/Mathematical-Engineering-Manufacturing-and-Management-Sciences/book-series/CRCMEMMS

Total Quality Management (TQM)

Principles, Methods, and Applications

Sunil Luthra, Dixit Garg, Ashish Agarwal,
and Sachin K. Mangla

CRC Press
Taylor & Francis Group
Boca Raton London New York

CRC Press is an imprint of the
Taylor & Francis Group, an **informa** business

First edition published 2021
by CRC Press
6000 Broken Sound Parkway NW, Suite 300, Boca Raton, FL 33487-2742

and by CRC Press
2 Park Square, Milton Park, Abingdon, Oxon, OX14 4RN

Library of Congress Cataloging-in-Publication Data

Names: Luthra, Sunil, author. | Garg, Dixit, author. | Agarwal, Ashish, author. | Mangla, Sachin K., author.
Title: Total quality management (TQM) : principles, methods, and applications / Sunil Luthra, Dixit Garg, Ashish Agarwal, and Sachin K. Mangla.
Description: Boca Raton : CRC Press, 2020. | Series: Mathematical engineering, manufacturing, and management sciences | Includes bibliographical references and index.
Identifiers: LCCN 2020018452 (print) | LCCN 2020018453 (ebook) | ISBN 9780367512835 (hardback) | ISBN 9781003053156 (ebook)
Subjects: LCSH: Total quality management--Textbooks. | Total productive maintenance--Textbooks.
Classification: LCC HD62.15 .L87 2020 (print) | LCC HD62.15 (ebook) | DDC 658.4/013--dc23
LC record available at https://lccn.loc.gov/2020018452
LC ebook record available at https://lccn.loc.gov/2020018453

ISBN: 978-0-367-51283-5 (hbk)
ISBN: 978-1-003-05315-6 (ebk)

Typeset in Times
by Deanta Global Publishing Services, Chennai, India

Visit the CRC Press website for Solutions manual and PowerPoint slides: www.routledge.com/9780367512835

Dedication

To

OUR FAMILY MEMBERS

for their unconditional support

Contents

Preface

The objective of this book on Total Quality Management is to provide a learning insight into the concepts related to Quality, Quality Management, Tools of Quality Management, and Quality Management Systems. The book is divided into ten chapters.

The concept of quality is explained in Chapter 1. This chapter illustrates how quality is affected by the expectations of customers and the performance of a product/service. Functionality, reliability, usability, maintainability, efficiency, portability, and service quality are features of product quality which are described in this chapter. The definition of quality, as given by quality experts, is provided along with the evolution of quality management. The chapter includes quality gurus who have worked on quality and defined quality on the basis of different aspects. The chapter introduces dimensions of quality and their measurement. Improving productivity through quality is explained here. For a better understanding, a case study on the Motorola Company is discussed in this chapter.

Chapter 2 begins with the definition of Total Quality Management (TQM). The key principles of TQM are covered, along with elements of TQM. The role of Quality Leaders is discussed. Advantages of TQM are identified. The implementation steps of TQM are described. The pillars of TQM are explained. Obstacles in TQM implementation are identified. The Quality Council is illustrated. The chapter concludes with a case study on TQM implementation at Sundaram Clayton.

The main focus in quality management practices discussed in Chapter 3 is continuous improvement in the field of the products or services. These practices also focus on improving the quality of products or services as per customer requirements. Various approaches to control and to managing quality are illustrated in the chapter with the help of examples. The chapter explains design of FMEA (DFMEA) which provides the possibility of product failure and a decrease in its useful life. Quality Function Deployment (QFD), a process of allocation or assigning the quality-related responsibility to the entire concerned department from design to service, is covered in this chapter. The reader will be able to learn how a house of quality is formed. The application of quality management practices to improve the quality of a ceiling fan manufacturing company is discussed with the help of a case study.

In Chapter 4, customer needs and requirements, the customer satisfaction model, quality of perception, customer feedback, service quality, and customer retention are explained. A customer satisfaction survey at ETDC Chennai India is analysed with the help of a case study.

Chapter 5 is devoted to employee involvement and supplier partnership which are aimed towards organisational development. Improving quality through employee involvement is discussed in this chapter. How to make teams and to assign work is an important activity covered here. A quality circle, which is also known as a quality control cycle, is explained. A quality circle is defined as a group of employees in the workplace who perform the same work or function in their job. An effective recognition and reward system is also included here. Employer involvement and supplier partnership are analysed with the help of a case study at the Tecumseh Products Company.

Chapter 6 starts with defining productivity and quality relationships. Chapter 6 covers the cost of quality (COQ), which is defined as tangible costs which are accounted for based on actual transactions of the cost of production processes. The chapter covers the cost of conformance, defined as the element of cost incurred to avoid poor quality of products. The cost of prevention and various other costs are described in this chapter. The chapter has a case study to explain the cost of quality.

Chapter 7 covers organising for quality. Another theory of the TQM philosophy is the concentration on continuous improvement. The Plan–Do–Study–Act (PDSA) cycle explains the actions that an organisation has to execute for attaining continuous improvement of operations and work culture. The concept of Six Sigma is discussed in this chapter. Kaizen is a Japanese word which means continuous improvement of the processes, work culture, and other aspects of the organisation for continuous quality improvement. Awards in quality management are also explained in Chapter 7. A case study on the School for Quality Education in America is developed and discussed.

Human aspects of management of quality are dealt with in Chapter 8. Here the five steps to increasing commitment are explained. Motivation is the force behind each and every action, willingness, and goal of any person. Key barriers in implementation of employee involvement are identified. A quality circle is a group of workers who do the same or similar work and meet regularly to identify, analyse, and solve work-related problems. This quality circle group is small in size and led by a supervisor or manager. Zero defects is a management tool which reduces defects through prevention; zero defects theory is illustrated here. The cause-and-effect diagram is explained with the help of examples. The concept is analysed with the help of two case studies.

The concept of Total Productive Maintenance (TPM) is illustrated in Chapter 9. Various types of maintenance explained here are breakdown maintenance, preventive maintenance, periodic maintenance, predictive maintenance, corrective maintenance, maintenance prevention, reliability-centred maintenance, productive maintenance, and total productive maintenance. Total productive maintenance is a method used to maintain production with fewer losses or failures and increase the productivity and quality of the product. The pillars of TPM and salient features of TPM are described in the chapter. The steps of TPM implementation are illustrated. The status of TPM in Indian manufacturing industries is discussed with the help of two case studies.

Chapter 10 is on quality management systems. Quality management systems may be defined as techniques/methodologies a manufacturer must follow to ensure that all the products manufactured meet the specifications. The Military Quality System and the ISO 9000 Quality System are two quality systems. The principles of quality management under the ISO 9000 series are explained in this chapter. The phases of implementation of ISO 9001 are described. Case studies based on the adoption of ISO 9001 are discussed at the end of the chapter.

The aim of this book is to understand various concepts of TQM and apply this knowledge to understand the workings of the corporate world. This book will surely help students and practitioners to understand various principles, methods, and applications related to TQM and to apply this knowledge to achieve the best quality strategies.

No matter how hard one strives, no book is ever perfect. There might be certain things that you want to change or correct (in the case of errors). Therefore, we request all our esteemed readers to write us in this regard. Suggestions for the improvement of the book are most welcome.

Dr. Sunil Luthra
Dr. Dixit Garg
Dr. Ashish Agarwal
Dr. Sachin K. Mangla

Acknowledgements

First of all, we would like to express our deep gratitude to all "Honourable Gurus and Teachers" for their constant guidance and encouragement. Their guidance and support were truly inspiring not only to this book, but also to our professional careers. We are grateful to our parents, spouses, and children for their unconditional support.

We wish to gratefully acknowledge the people who have contributed ideas, assistance, and relevant support in the completion of this book. We also wish to thank the anonymous reviewers for their constructive comments and suggestions. Without their support, this book would not have become a reality. We are also grateful to our graduate, postgraduate, and doctoral students for their support.

We are grateful to all members of CRC Press, Taylor & Francis Group, for their assistance and timely motivation in producing this book. We also thank Prof. Mangey Ram, Series Editor, for helping us throughout the project. We hope that readers will share their experiences after reading our book.

We thank the almighty God for giving us strength and wisdom to accomplish this academic exercise.

Dr. Sunil Luthra
Dr. Dixit Garg
Dr. Ashish Agarwal
Dr. Sachin K. Mangla

Author Biographies

 **Dr. Sunil Luthra** is working in the Department of Mechanical Engineering at Ch. Ranbir Singh State Institute of Engineering and Technology, Jhajjar, Haryana, India. He is also working as an Honorary Research Fellow at Bradford School of Management, University of Bradford, Bradford, United Kingdom. He completed his PhD in the National Institute of Technology, Kurukshetra, India. He has been associated with teaching for the last 18 years. In general, his research mainly focuses on developing and validating the different theories, frameworks, and models in the area of sustainability in supply chains, circular economy, sustainable consumption and production, Industry 4.0, cleaner production, and energy systems in the context of emerging economies, especially in the Indian context. He has contributed over 180 research papers in international and national refereed journals, and conferences at international and national level. He has shown his research aptitude by publishing several research papers in high impact factor international journals. He has an excellent research track record with around a cumulative 350 research Impact Factor (IF) points; 68 SCI/SSCI/ESCI indexed publications; more than 20 3* CABS publications; has received around 4300 citations; and has a H-index 33 on Google Scholar). He is a Guest Editor of many reputable journals such the *Journal of Cleaner Production, Production Planning & Control, Resources Policy, Resources, Conservation and Recycling* and *Annals of Operations Research*, etc. He has reviewed papers for more 50 reputable journals. He is on the editorial board of many reputable journals. He has published five books with reputable publishers such as CRC Press, Taylor & Francis Group, LLC and New Age International Publisher (P) Ltd, etc.

 **Dr. Dixit Garg** is working as a Professor in the Mechanical Engineering Department at the National Institute of Technology (Institute of National Importance as per Act of Parliament), Kurukshetra, Haryana, India. He has more than 170 research papers to his credit, published in international and national journals. He has acted as an editor/reviewer in international journals/conferences and short-term training programmed. He has delivered many expert lectures and participated in panel discussions. His specific areas of interest are operations and quality management, just-in-time (JIT), production planning and control, manufacturing processes, supply chain management, educational planning, industrial engineering, productivity, entrepreneurship, and green supply chain management, etc.

Dr. Ashish Agarwal has been working as an Associate Professor of Mechanical Engineering at the School of Engineering & Technology, Indira Gandhi National Open University, New Delhi, India since 1993. He has earned his PhD from IIT Delhi in the area of supply chain management. His papers have been published in national and international journals. He has published his research papers in the *European Journal of Operational Research, Industrial Marketing Management, Supply Chain Management: An International Journal, Work Study,* the *International Journal of Management Science and Engineering Management,* the *Journal of Manufacturing Technology Management,* the *International Journal Intelligent Enterprise, Production & Manufacturing Research,* the *International Journal of Advanced Operations Management, Competitiveness Review,* the *International Journal of Productivity and Performance Management, Productivity,* the *Industrial Engineering Journal,* and the *Global Journal of Enterprise Information System.* He is a reviewer in national and international journals. He has supervised nine PhD students in the area of operations management. He is at present supervising five PhD students. He is a life member of the Indian Society for Technical Education and the Indian Institution of Industrial Engineering.

Dr. Sachin Mangla Kumar is working in the Faculty of Knowledge Management and Business Decision Making, University of Plymouth, United Kingdom. Dr. Sachin is working in the fields of green and sustainable supply chains and operations; Industry 4.0; circular economy; and decision-making and modelling. He is committed to doing and promoting high-quality research. He has published/presented several papers in reputable national and international journals (the *International Journal of Production Economics;* the *International Journal of Production Research; Production Planning and Control; Business Strategy and the Environment;* the *Journal of Cleaner Production;* the *Annals of Operations Research; Transportation Research – Part D; Transportation Research – Part E; Renewable and Sustainable Energy Reviews; Resource Conservation and Recycling; Information System Frontier; Management Decision;* the *International Journal of Logistics Research and Applications; Benchmarking: An International Journal; Industrial Data and Management System;* the *International Journal of Quality and Reliability Management*) and conferences (POMS, SOMS, IIIE, CILT – LRN, GLOGIFT). He has a h-index of 28 and an i10-index of 55. He is involved in editing a couple of special issues as a Guest Editor in leading ABDC/ABD high-ranked journals. Currently, he is also involved in several research projects on various issues and applications of the circular economy and sustainability. Among them, he is responsible for the knowledge-based decision model in 'Enhancing and implementing knowledge-based ICT solutions within high risk and uncertain conditions for agriculture production systems (RUC-APS),' European Commission RISE scheme. Recently, he has also received a grant as a PI from the British Council – Newton Fund Research Environment Links Turkey/UK – Circular and Industry 4.0-driven sustainable solutions for reducing food waste in supply chains in Turkey.

1 Concept of Quality

1.1 PRODUCTS AND SERVICES

Utmost customer satisfaction is a primary need for a product. It is therefore necessary for products and services to meet or exceed customer expectations, resulting in market share improvement. Quality is the expected service being realised. Before a customer makes a purchase, they do a calculation of whether that product and its services are good or not, so the question arises: 'Is the worth of the product/service equal to the money that I am about to give in exchange?'

At any time, when customers buy products, they are convinced that it is worth it or not. They are in a situation where they must or must not buy a product. The operational vision of quality involves getting product/services manufactured/produced to specifications tailored to their prices. The customer receives the value he/she expects only when a functional operation is undertaken that institutes the quality standards into that product/service. A vision of the quality of operations is a shared vision of the concept of quality.

Quality is the effect of a certain customer's view on something as they receive it. Customers indulge themselves in comparing the received product with their own expectation for that particular product/service. This is regardless of the manufacturer's perception of quality for that product/service. Marketing/sales have a great impact on the opinions of customers and their perception of quality. It depends mainly on the product standard and its quality. A customer is dissatisfied when the delivered product is not as good as was promised by the sales and marketing team. The quality is thus not assured. At the same time, it leads to widening of the gap between the operations/manufacturing team and the sales and marketing team. Quality is not absolutely determined by the operations/manufacturing team. Other factors/variables in the fray affecting quality are:

(a) Customer expectations.
(b) Actual product/service received.

So, customer expectations should be fulfilled by the quality of the product or service. Actually, customers also expect that product they are purchasing should be as they want, and the service should be properly carried out by an authentic dealer from where he purchased the product.

1.1.1 PRODUCT/SERVICE FEATURES

New products and services are the cornerstone of every business. Investment in your own growth is essential for profitability and overall growth of the business. But getting involved in the development process is risky. It requires considerable planning and organisation. This guide will describe the main stages of the life cycle of products and services. The best investment decisions happen when the right time to make such an investment is understood. Once that developmental process starts, it proceeds with phased and planned development of the organisation. It will also indicate how to best create a development team and manage a project.

The development process has been perceived as designing a set of product features that improve customer satisfaction. Customer satisfaction is a priority. While a customer may or may not be concerned about adding additional features in the hope of developing customer satisfaction, this is the approach. This approach increases the cost of the product, markets and sales. The justification for these new functions must be compensated with additional costs for the client or a commercial gain as a result of the improvement of the company's brand and the marketing/sales expectations of the clients.

For example, a hotel guest who wishes to stay at a 5-star hotel with per night charge of Rs10,000 would have quite a lot of different expectations to a guest who wishes to stay in a Motel 5 with per night charge of Rs 500. Therefore, the guest of the Motel 5 and the guest of the 5-star hotel may conclude after their stay that they have received quality rooms. Now the question arises as to why Motel 5 and a 5-star hotel can both offer a quality room. The answer is that the 5-star hotel and the Motel 5 rooms are not compared to each other. In each case, the expectations of the clients were met with the room received for the price they paid. The quality of the characteristics of the product corresponds to the expectations of the client.

1.2 QUALITY OF PRODUCTS

There are many various features of product quality:

a) **Functionality**

This refers to the main characteristics of a product and a service. It is defined as a set of alternatives that are related to the existence of a set of functions and their specified properties. All functions have specific properties that explain the quality of the product and its services. The functions are also those that justify the declared needs for the manufacture of qualitative products.

b) **Reliability**

Reliability is also the main feature of a quality product. Measurement of product reliability is done by finding the 'mean time between failures' (MTBF). It is an indicator of durability of products. For example, a car should not break down often, so the MTBF of a car can be specified as 1,000 running hours or 10,000 km.

c) **Usability**

Usability is also a hallmark of product quality. This shows the client's ability to use the product. It is expected that the client can use any type of product without the help of experts. For example, a car may need a mechanic to repair it, but its owner can drive it if they are trained.

d) **Maintainability**

This refers to the ease of a product being able to be kept in its original state without creating a problem. The ability to keep a product for a while makes it expensive, but you may finally use a product for a long time. It may be defective during use and must be repaired to maintain its original quality at the lowest cost. It is measured as 'Average Repair Time (MTTR).'

e) **Efficiency**

Efficiency is the relationship between production and input. It means what we do after consuming sources of inputs. Therefore, a quality product must be measurable by its effectiveness.

f) **Portability**

The quality of the product also has the particularity of portability. It is defined as a set of attributes that affect the ability of the software to transfer from one environment to another. It simply transfers different attributes from one place to another. The environment can be hardware, software or an organisation.

1.3 SERVICE QUALITY

Quality has also gained importance in the service industry. It basically focuses on customer satisfaction. Some of the key performance indicators of service quality are presented here by a model in Figure 1.1.

The quality of the service has additional characteristics; when using a service, the client connects more with the service provider. The quality of the service depends to a large extent on the correct understanding of the client's requirements in such interactions. It provides customers with the right quality at the right time. Each service must be designed specifically for the client. The additional features of service quality are:

a) **Quality of customer service**

Customer service is important in any organisation. The current challenge for the sector is to meet the needs of customers. In a service sector, satisfying customers and knowing their implicit requirements is more difficult. For example, Flipkart, Amazon and Snapdeal are online services that always meet the needs of their customers.

b) **Quality of service design**

The design of quality services consists, first of all, of formulating a plan to satisfy a specific need or problem. The services are usually made to order, so it is important that the service is designed according to the specific requirements of the client. For example, the software developed for an organisation requires the complete specific program for the unique design requirements.

c) **Quality of service delivery**

The quality of delivery is important in all sectors, but services are key criteria to success. There are so many organisations that work in delivery, such as Ekart Logistics, etc. So it is better for business growth.

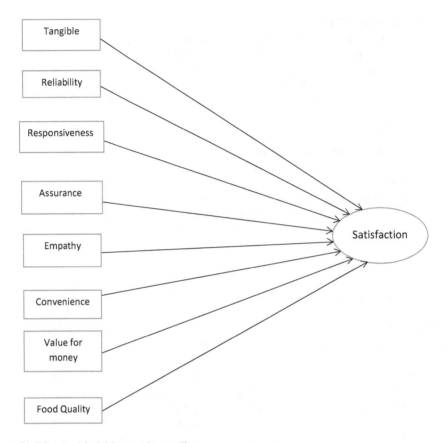

FIGURE 1.1   Model for service quality.

1.4   DEFINITION OF QUALITY

1. Quality is defined as degree of excellence.
2. A quality process or product is fit for its purpose.
   Evolution of this definition took place in quality circles. It is applicable to any process, product, or service. It thus makes this definition useful, but it is a bit difficult to measure quality according to this definition.
3. In manufacturing, a measure of excellence or a state of being free from defects and deficiencies is called 'quality.'
4. Garvin (1984) divides the definition of quality into five categories, including product-based, user-based, and value-based. Further, he gave eight attributes to define quality: Performance, features, reliability, conformance, durability, serviceability, aesthetics and perceived quality, etc.
5. According to Crosby (1979) 'Quality is conformance to requirements/specifications.'
   This is an ideal definition for quality control teams that need to validate processes, systems, services, and product quality. Depending on the requirements, they can easily validate compliance and identify nonconformities.

The problematic part of this definition is that it can offer a biased and subjective view of quality. In many cases, the requirements are little more than the ideas of the business stakeholders. Often there is no objective validation that these ideas give a quality result.

6. Deming stated that the definition of quality is 'meeting or exceeding customer expectations.'
7. According to Juran (1979) 'Quality is a measure of fitness for use.'
8. In the mathematical method, quality is defined as the ratio of performance to expectation.

$$\text{Quality}\,(Q) = \frac{\text{Performance}\,(P)}{\text{Expectation}\,(E)}$$

Case1. If, $P > E$ it means quality is best
Case2. If, $P = E$ it means quality is good
Case3. If, $P < E$ it means quality is worst

9. QUALITY also stands for
Q = Quest for excellence
U = Understanding customers' needs
A = Action to achieve customer appreciation
L = Leadership
I = Involving all people
T = Team spirit for common goal
Y = Yardstick to measure progress

10. Quality is cost.
Traditionally, the quality of the product was considered in terms of the cost of the materials. A gold watch is of better quality than a plastic watch. High-quality sheets have a number of threads of 180 or more. High-quality moisturiser for hands has a high shea butter content.

11. Quality is price.
It is the price that customers might be willing to pay for a product or a service. Quality is a crucial part of many business models. Different definitions of quality have been put forth by economists. According to some economists, quality is synonymous with the expensiveness of the product. In other words, the bigger the price of the product, the higher would be its quality.

12. The manufacturing industry was the first to seriously consider quality. Concerns regarding the quality of products are on the rise among the manufacturers due to the manufacturing process quality.
If they make a million cars a month, they cannot afford to manufacture inferior products that will be returned by their customers. They cannot bear liability problems for products derived from nonconforming products. Neither can they afford inefficient processes.

13. Quality is a satisfying experience.
As savings moved from one product to another, marketers looked for quality definitions that would explain why customers buy services.

1.5 HISTORICAL REVIEW OF QUALITY

Frederick Taylor conducted time and motion studies in the 1920s. The total quality movement had its roots in such studies. Taylor is popularly identified as the father of scientific management. He contributed his efforts to the growth of industrial management. After his contribution, many other quality experts followed his efforts on quality. Table 1.1 shows the history of quality management.

1.6 QUALITY GURUS

There are many gurus who work on quality and they define quality from different viewpoints.

1.6.1 Dr. W. Edwards Deming

Greater productivity leads to long-term competitiveness in the market which is a result of achieving higher quality in all the processes, as said by Dr Deming. The theory is that upgraded quality standards lead to decrease in costs and enhance productivity (number of acceptable products). This is evident from less work (mainly re-working) and fewer errors with fewer delays leading to better usage of time and other resources. Conquering a greater market share to stay in business is possible when a company provides better quality at lower price.

TABLE 1.1
History of Quality Management

Year	Author	Work	Contribution
Early 20th century	William Sealy Gosset (Student)	He worked for statistical quality control	Origins of the practical use of statistical quality control
1920s	Walter Andrew Shewhart	He was devoted to statistical quality control	Control mechanism and control chart
1930s	Nicolas Dreystadt	Quality philosophy at Cadillac	Salvage of the brand despite the Great Depression. Linking quality and marketing
1950	William Edwards Deming	Commenced operations in Japan	Ideas of quality control
1951	Armand Vallin Feigenbaum	Quality control	Concept of Total Quality Management
1954	Joseph Moses Juran	Work in Japan	Ideas on quality control, application of Pareto Principle in quality management
1962	Kaoru Ishikawa	Methods of implementation quality in company	Concept of quality circle
1982	Kaoru Ishikawa	Techniques of problem	Ishikawa Diagram

I. **Deming Philosophy**

A system of deep knowledge with grasp and admiration for the system's different aspects, with the theory of knowledge and the psychological aspects involved in different sections of society like individuals or groups was integral to Deming's theory. Deming provided the concept of quality control. Dr. Deming's best known 14-point theories were a part of his extensive knowledge system. Your knowledge and contribution to quality definitely improves the growth of an organisation. Deming's knowledge system consisted of four theories, namely, theory of optimisation, variation, knowledge, and psychology.

Explanations of these four knowledge-based interrelated parts are given below.

a) **Theory of optimisation**

Deming's optimisation theory suggests optimisation for the entire system. The objective of an organisation or company is the optimisation of the entire system, which includes all the parts and not the optimisation of individual subsystems. The complete system includes all components: Customers, employees, suppliers, distributors, manufacturers, shareholders, community, and environment. The long-term goal of a company is to create a win–win situation for all its partners.

The subsystem optimisation process works contrary to this objective and may lead to a suboptimal total system. Dr. Deming calls it poor management; as an example, purchase of materials at the lowest price regardless of the quality levels. It works at the expense of the system. Usage of materials that are available at cheaper costs may lead to very inferior quality. It might lead to excessive cost escalation during the rework at the manufacturing and assembly stage.

b) **Theory of variation**

Dr. Deming estimated that variation was a major cause of poor quality. This means a variation in a product belongs to poor built-in quality. In mechanical assemblies, for example, variations in the dimensional specifications of the parts can lead to more wear and tear and further result in premature failure and inconsistent performance. Frustrated customers can hamper the commercial reputation for any organisation which mainly arises with service lacking consistency. Dr. Deming emphasised and taught how to determine whether a process was in statistical control. Statistical process control with control charts was taught by Dr. Deming to observe the deviations in a process. His students also learned how to optimise the results of statistical process control.

c) **Theory of knowledge**

Deming believed that knowledge generation was possible only with theory and experience in conjunction. Thorough knowledge of the theory describes the system and provides experience after a long time. Its practice and subsequently its experience can describe that a theory can be validated with experience and on its own without experience cannot help in its administration. The theory on the other hand shows causality (Ishikawa diagram), is a beneficial tool for making predictions for the future. An important lesson to learn from the usual benchmarking for generalising is that its indiscriminate copying may mostly lead to erroneous outcomes unless the theory is understood in a contextually appropriate setting, which might lead to it affecting the overall performance causing a variety of problems.

d) **Theory of psychology**
    A scientific study of psychology aids in understanding people and their interactions among themselves and others under different circumstances or conditions, and interactions within the hierarchy of any management system. Psychology connects the people that make up the management system. Therefore, people management requires knowledge of psychology. It also requires knowledge of what motivates people. With due motivation, they can work more efficiently. Job satisfaction and motivation to excel are part of the need. Reward and recognition are extrinsic; it does not mean a need, but a motivation. Therefore, management must create the right combination of intrinsic and extrinsic factors to motivate employees.

e) **Deming's 14 points for Total Quality Management**
    Monitoring and preparing long-term action plans/business plans needs development of knowledge from the workplace. Hence, Dr. Deming addressed and created 14 points for the same. The interpretation has been extensive on both quality and on various management disciplines.

Deming's 14 points

1. First, create reliability of purpose toward enhancement of product and service, with the aim of becoming competitive, remaining in business, and providing jobs.
2. Adopt the new philosophy. Western management must be stimulated by the challenge, must learn their responsibilities, and take on leadership for change.
3. End dependence on mass inspection; build quality into the product from the beginning.
4. End the practice of granting business on the basis of price tag alone. Instead, minimise total cost. Select based on a long-term connection of loyalty and trust.
5. Improve continuously and forever the system of production and service to improve quality and reduce waste.
6. Introduce training and retraining.
7. Institute leadership. The aim of observation should be to lead and aid people in discharging their duties better.
8. Drive out fear so that everyone may work effectively for the company.
9. Remove the hurdles step-by-step between various departments like research, design, sales, and production to help them work cohesively, more as a group, to predict and solve problems in production.

10. Eliminate slogans, exhortations, and targets for the workforce, as they do not necessarily achieve their aims.
11. Eliminate numerical quotas in order to take account of quality and methods, rather than just numbers.
12. Remove barriers to pride of workmanship.
13. Introduce a dynamic programme of education and re-training for both the management and the workforce.
14. Management and workforce must work together.

f) **The Deming cycle**

Shewhart invented the concept of Plan-Do-Check-Act (PDCA cycle), which was later on propagated by Dr. Deming. Their cyclic approach for planning and testing purposes is to make a full-scale implementation of improvement and finally formalising it. This cycle provides the complete information of evaluation and basic ideas. An improvement idea needs testing on a smaller scale before it can be utilised for full-scale implementation. By doing small-scale testing, validation of its benefit is possible before large-scale implementation is undertaken. Furthermore, resistance from the employees is also reduced owing to more time being available for them to accept and adjust to the newer methods. This way it is more likely that employees will support such initiatives.

The Deming PDCA Cycle (Figure 1.2) provides opportunities for continuous evaluation and improvement.

The steps in the Deming PDCA or PDSA Cycle as shown here.

1. First step is to make a plan for an improvement causing change or test (P).
2. Second step is to do it (D). To conduct small-scale testing of the planned improvement change.
3. Third step is to check it (C). To check the effects arising from the conducted test. It is also called 'study' sometimes (S).
4. Next and last step is to act on learning from the first step (A).
5. Keep repeating Step 1, with knowledge generated from previous steps.

1.6.2 DR. JOSEPH JURAN

The trilogy of quality focuses on the roles of advanced quality planning, quality control, and quality improvement. Quality planning aspires to aid operators with

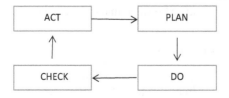

FIGURE 1.2 PDCA cycle.

proficiency to produce goods and services to meet the customer's expectations and needs. It also provides a method that will be implemented for customer satisfaction. In the stage of quality planning, it is important that customers and their needs are identified by the organisation. Based on in-depth knowledge of quality planning, develop the characteristics of the product or service that meet your needs, develop product and service processes, and transfer plans to operational forces.

1.6.3 PHILIP CROSBY

Philip Crosby suggested the meaning of quality in different aspects, and he taught the meaning of quality on the basis of defects, prevention, requirements, and the price of nonconformance etc.

1. Quality is conforming, not to goodness, but to the requirement.
2. Quality is defined as a system where prevention leads to quality, and not the appraisal.
3. The performance standard must be 'no defects at all,' instead of the standard being 'close enough.'

1.6.4 GENICHI TAGUCHI

Genichi Taguchi's contributions translate into a robust design in the area of product development and optimised product manufacturing. The Taguchi loss function, the Taguchi method (experiment design), and other methodologies have largely contributed to reducing variations and greatly improving the quality of engineering and productivity. This method optimises the results by taking different parameters. By careful and purposeful consideration of these factors, the reduction of failures in the field, and, ultimately, Taguchi's methodologies will help to ensure client satisfaction.

Taguchi product development includes three stages:

1. System design –
   In the system design, the non-statistical stage for engineering, marketing, customer, and other knowledge is determined.
2. Parameter stage –
   Determines how the product should be run against the defined parameters. For example, to optimise the material removal rate result, use different parameters such as cutting speed, feed rate, depth of cut, and so on.
3. Tolerance design –
   It determines the balance between manufacturing cost and loss.

1.6.5 ARMAND V. FEIGENBAUM

The American expert in quality control is the man behind the concept of Total Quality Control (TQC). Already in the 1950s, Feigenbaum had warned against the costly effects of not producing good quality for the first time, an idea shared by all subsequent quality concepts.

1.6.6   DR. KAORU ISHIKAWA

This is the Japanese professor best known for the Ishikawa cause-and-effect diagram (fishbone diagram). The professor suggested guidelines and establishment of quality circles. Dr. Ishikawa was also very concerned about the concept of quality across the organisation. His study also noted that quality does not just happen in the industry.

1.6.7   SHIGEO SHINGO

His contribution to Toyota's production system should not be underestimated. Poka Yoke (Intrinsic Security), Just-in-Time, and Single-Minute Exchange of Die (SMED) are due to this ingenious Japanese businessman. Today, one of the most prestigious corporate awards in the world bears his name: the Shingo Award for Manufacturing Excellence.

1.6.8   FREDERICK TAYLOR

Frederick Winslow Taylor (1856–1915) is called the father of scientific management. His experience at the lowest level of the organisation allowed him to first know the problems of the workers. Taylor's main concern was to increase production efficiency, not only to reduce costs and increase profits, but also to increase workers' wages through increased productivity.

The fundamental principles that Taylor saw underlying the scientific approach to management may be summarised as follows:

1. Replace the working methods of the golden rule with methods based on a scientific study of tasks.
2. Select and train each of the workers scientifically instead of promoting passive training.
3. Cooperation is required for ensuring the implementation of scientifically developed methods.
4. Dividing the work among workers and managers such that the managers are able to use the principles of scientific management for planning of the work, while workers execute the assigned tasks.

Taylor was a proponent of productivity and wages based on productivity achieved by the workers. He focused on the study of time and motion and other techniques for measuring work. His ideas were humanistic, with the thought of protecting the interests of every employee of the firm by ensuring harmony among the different stakeholders.

Lastly, Dr. H. James Harrington and Dr. Walter A. Shewhart have also made a significant impact on the field of quality in the world with their contributions to improving businesses along with a variety of governmental, military, hospitality, educational facilities, and a few other establishments like healthcare facilities.

1.7   DIMENSIONS OF QUALITY AND THEIR MEASURE

Garvin (1984) provides discussion of eight critical dimensions of product quality. The summarised key points concerning these dimensions of quality are provided below.

a) **Performance**

This is the fundamental dimension of product quality. Discuss the performance evaluation of the product/service based on specific features, characteristics, and learn how it works from the customer's viewpoint.

b) **Reliability**

This is about the quality of a product based on its reliability, the probability of not having faulty components in products such as cars or airplanes during their service in a given period. It must be reliable, because its reliability threshold is lower, plus there are the possibilities of repair or replacement. This is why it affects the quality of the product.

c) **Durability**

Durability is the effective life or longevity of the product before it is declared unusable. Repair is not possible after this phase of life. This means that when the product is not sustainable, it completes its useful life.

d) **Serviceability**

This is the ability to provide a service to customers. The customer's opinion of quality is also influenced by the speed and economic profitability of a routine maintenance activity. Show how much your company is serious about your product services. For example: a) time taken to rectify an error in a credit card statement issued by a bank? b) time to correct an error in your Aadhar card statement (UIP) by the service provider?

e) **Aesthetics**

This concerns the visual appearance or the appearance of the product, often taking into account factors such as model, colour, style, packaging, tactile characteristics, and other sensory characteristics. For example, when I want to buy a car, I take into account all aspects of aesthetics.

f) **Features**

The tendency of customers is usually to go for a product with more and more value-added features. This can go beyond the basic criteria to enter the market. Characteristics are also the fundamental dimension of product quality. A feature can also be defined as an additional or secondary attached feature, and complements the main function of a product. An example of a car provides clarity, where the stereo of the car can be considered as a feature and the main function of the car remains transport.

g) **Perceived quality**

This signifies the reaction of a customer after the use of the product and/or service. The product must have a perceived quality that enhances customer satisfaction. This dimension is directly affected by any product failure that is highly visible to the public or by the way the service is delivered to the customer when a product quality issue is resolved. Customer loyalty and brand loyalty are closely tied to perceived quality. For example, if an airline is usually late and often loses baggage in transit, then in such a scenario, a frequent flyer might not prefer that airline to travel and would rather take up another airline which provides better facilities in terms of punctuality and safe transit of the checked-in baggage. The reason here can be linked clearly to the perceived quality. The loyalty here is clearly linked to the quality provided by the airline and so perceived by the flyer. Therefore, it will qualify this very small dimension for the said operator, which also decreases its market in this area.

h) **Conformance to Standards**
Compliance with standards is also a fundamental dimension of quality. Conformance to quality provides the standard for value.

1.8   IMPROVING PRODUCTIVITY THROUGH QUALITY

Productivity and quality management are key factors in competitiveness and always preoccupied the productive sectors, especially in open economies. Quality is the fundamental factor by which improvisation intervenes in productivity. Targeted efforts improve productivity, and quality management of an organisation often results in greater internal and external satisfaction because costs and reliability are met. Here are some factors of quality through which productivity can improve:

a) **Analyse process**
The whole process needs to be analysed where the focus needs to be on the processes, and not on those who perform those processes. The policy to standardise procedures of the company helps in maximising the efficiency of the company. Follow the standard value for any type of product. When appropriate training is provided to all the staff, they can produce high-quality products in a short period of time.

b) **Align business processes with other companies in the sector**
Find out how other competing companies are organising and conducting business in a way that allows for the integration of the business process and, as a result, improvements. It needs to be well-organised and have alternatives planned for any type of operation. All information is important because it can save time and money. This exercise also provides good ideas for improvement.

c) **Develop performance measures**
To improve productivity, managers should appreciate the quality of developed performance parameters. Problem identification, prediction of outcomes of the future, and productivity gains measurement with key sectoral performance indicators should use current processes as the point of reference. For example, quality measurement and productivity of the customer call centre can be done by recording the average time required in closing

the problems pointed out by the customers, and ratings given by customers regarding the resolution of the problem.

d) **Build quality tests in processes**

In each organisation, to improve productivity through quality, quality testing must be integrated into the process. Experience is gained during the process and not just at the end, so it provides options and alternatives for better results. This does not create a situation when it is more expensive to repair. Automated tests can be performed which takes less time to provide results in processes that are easy to explain, modify, correct, approve, or reject.

e) **Use business strategies to improve productivity and quality management**

To improve productivity through quality, always develop business strategies and use them. It helps in identifying the root cause of problems and intervenes to improve or optimise processes. In quality management, production must be a control so that defects are corrected immediately before they affect their final product or result.

f) **Pay attention to feedback**

Feedback collection from all the stakeholders likes employees, customers, suppliers, vendors, and business partners for their opinion on products or services. Provides information on whether the selected route is correct or not. Organisations use customer feedback to improve current products and influence the design of new products.

1.9   CONCLUSION

Product quality and product services are an integral part of quality. The quality of the product means its level of excellence and its adaptation to the desired objective. 'The main objective of quality improvement is the goal of quality management; these are service industries and service jobs in the manufacturing industries. Many service industries such as information technology, agriculture, banking, communication, institutes, medical care, etc. have a well-developed quality assurance system and pass the ISO 9000 certification. Many people have made a significant contribution to quality and improvement. W. Edward Deming is the best-known quality specialist. The Japanese industry has adopted Deming's methods, which has led to a significant improvement in quality. Deming believed that quality was the responsibility of management. The dimension of quality and its principal is also a fundamental part of quality; Garvin offers a discussion on eight dimensions of product quality.

1.10   CASE STUDY ON THE MOTOROLA COMPANY

Robert W. Galvin, President of Motorola Inc. had proclaimed that 'quality is a way of life in a business, not an advertising term' in October 1962. Motorola grew to become a leader in military, space, and commercial communications along with becoming a leading consumer electronics manufacturer. This happened before *Quality Assurance*, a predecessor to the *Quality* magazine, reported Motorola's quality initiative a 'live and vibrant issue' in one of its published stories 40 years ago.

Quality has remained a lively, dynamic field of study as on today. At the same time evolution of quality has happened hand-in-hand with the Motorola business. In the last 40 years, the philosophy of quality in Motorola has grown from a primary goal of manufacturing products to excellence to all the areas of their business. Motorola's commitment to quality in every facet of product development was evident when quality assurance was introduced in the company. The company approach is three-pronged: Quality of forecasts, quality of the workforce, and quality of objective self-assessment which strengthens this notion about Motorola. Putting differently, the quality program considered the three production stages, namely, pre-production, production, and post-production. This way of dealing has indisputably allowed Motorola to be ranked first among US companies over the next few years. Motorola's expansion to the international markets began in the 1960s. They gradually turned away from the consumer electronics segment in the markets. The company pushed out itself of the colour television receiver business in some mid-1970s, allowing it to converge energies on budding hi-tech markets in sectors like government, industry, and commercial. An evolution of quality initiative was required to progress with the company given that the new approach in conducting businesses needed a focus on quality that could lead to growth of companies. This resulted in the creation of the first ever 'quality manager' position in Motorola in 1980. In 1981, the Motorola Training and Education Center (MTEC) was created. It provides employees with education and training in quality processes and participatory management skills. Motorola had become a global provider of cell phones by the end of the 1980s. Perceptions about the Japanese was still that they were undisputed as leaders of the electronics market. A comparative study in 1986 indicated that creation of products of same or superior quality only would let Motorola survive against Japanese quality, despite its significant progress. This led to the Six Sigma initiative on quality coming into existence in 1987. The returns on investments in Six Sigma initiative bore fruit in 1988, making Motorola the first big winner when the entire company received the 'Malcolm Baldrige National Quality Award', an award by the US Congress to recognise and inspire quality research in US companies.

Today, Motorola is leveraging the power of wireless, broadband, and internet technology to offer end-to-end network communications solutions and chip-level networks integrated into homes, work groups, vehicles, and consumers. The target here is to achieve an uncomplicated, smarter, harmonic, and innocuous business and life by creating products and executive services with the involvement of intelligence almost everywhere. This performance excellence program based on the Baldrige model is actually the evolution of the quality program to achieve the targeted goal in Motorola. This model demands steadfast adherence to quality at multiple levels: Leadership with vision, organisational learning, agility, employee commitment, intelligent management, and orientation toward results. Motorola considers quality from the customer's point of view. Going by the saying 'make the first impression count the most', meaning, there is a single opportunity with each product delivered to the customer to get a favourable response i.e., a positive impact on the customer. Non-delivery of the expectations puts the business at risk of losing the client. The idea of industry averages does not suffice here. Each product reaching its customer must have no deviations from the quality standards. From 1987 to 1999, the company achieved noteworthy results. These were the first 12 years of Six Sigma at Motorola. In 1999, Motorola was able to get rid of 99.7% of all the defects in the process. The cost associated with substandard quality was brought down by more than 84% per unit and the savings in accumulated manufacturing costs have reached more than $18 billion. Employee productivity also increased significantly, by 12% per year. To ensure a commitment to quality in all the internal processes, Six Sigma is cardinal. However, this is only the first step. Holistic integration of quality to the business fabric is essential for Motorola in order to continually improve customer satisfaction. In other words, it paves the way to shaping consumer perceptions in an environment of trust, commitment, and communication along with satisfying the customers' expectations of high-quality products at competitive prices. We thus describe this as total satisfaction of the customers. Because the quality depends on the external client's voice, we regularly measure the satisfaction of our clients and ask their opinion on the development of action plans and the implementation of the procedures that will provide a superior experience.

This approach of commitment has been rewarded well through the results of our studies showing higher customer satisfaction rates. Results have indicated that 79% of our customers intend to remain loyal to Motorola's products and its services in the future, while 75% had inclinations toward recommending Motorola to their colleagues. In addition, 63% appreciated and were very much satisfied with the ease of doing business with Motorola. Foreseeing the needs of the customers, Motorola has made a significant effort in establishing rapport with the customers by displaying innovation and nurturing loyalty which builds a solid base of trust for the organisations. With the evolution of technology and challenging economic circumstances, Motorola's efforts to make available the products to the customers making their lives uncomplicated, smarter, secure, and harmonic will continue. Motorola believes that the best way is to successfully implement the Performance Excellence business system. This case study has taught us important lessons that have enabled us to expand our commitment to quality which includes:

1. Commitment and participation down. Demonstration of fierce commitment with participation in the initiatives for quality from the business leaders. Playing an active role in the audit process sets first, an example to look for ways to develop and make progress in the businesses.
2. Proper systems in place to make accurate measurements to monitor progress. Motorola's perpetual commitment to research and tracking of measurable results at the macro- and micro-levels is much needed.
3. Set high goals. Motorola's regular evaluation for the best companies to evaluate products/services makes sure that the topmost standards are set for our organisation. Continuous improvement being the key for survival, Motorola must never be satisfied.

Meeting and exceeding the quality of competitors is the belief Motorola holds onto. Its primary use is to upgrade performance levels and maintain the competitive edge.

POINTS TO REMEMBER

- Quality is defined as a degree of excellence.
- Deming stated the definition of quality is 'meeting or exceeding customer expectations.'
- The features of product quality are functionality, reliability, usability, maintainability, efficiency, portability, etc.
- Internal satisfaction and external satisfaction help in cost reduction as well as reliability, which are possible with improvement in productivity and quality management.
- Dimensions of product quality are reliability, performance, durability, serviceability, aesthetics, features, perceived quality, conformance to standards.
- Quality of service delivery, quality of service design, and quality of customer service are some of the extra features of service quality.
- The quality of conformance provides standard to the value.

SELF-ASSESSMENT QUESTIONS

1. Explain the role of products and services in quality.
2. Define quality in a product.
3. Write down the definition of quality.
4. What is meant by Juran's fitness of quality?
5. Explain the definition of quality by Deming.
6. What are the dimensions of quality?
7. What do you understand by the theory of optimisation in quality by Deming?
8. Explain the Deming cycle.
9. How can you improve productivity through quality? Explain in detail.
10. Explain the terms 'reliability' and 'serviceability.'
11. Name quality gurus and state the quality definition given by them.
12. Explain the mathematical method of quality.

BIBLIOGRAPHY

Bendell, T., Penson, R., & Carr, S. (1995). The quality gurus–their approaches described and considered. *Managing Service Quality: An International Journal, 5*(6), 44–48.

Crosby, P. B. (1979). *Quality Is Free: The Art of Making Quality Certain* (Vol. 94). McGraw-Hill, New York.

Darling, J. R. (1992). Total quality management: The key role of leadership strategies. *Leadership & Organization Development Journal, 13*(4), 3–7.

Das, S., Roy, K., & Nampi, T. (2020). Total quality management and quality engineering. In: *Handbook of Research on Developments and Trends in Industrial and Materials Engineering* (pp. 451–468). IGI Global, Pennsylvania.

Deming, W. E. (1981). Improvement of quality and productivity through action by management. *National Productivity Review, 1*(1), 12–22.

Deming, W. E. (2018). *Out of the Crisis*. MIT Press, Cambridge.

Garvin, D. A. (1984). Product quality: An important strategic weapon. *Business Horizons*, *27*(3), 40–43.

Goolsby, J. R., & Hunt, S. D. (1992). Cognitive moral development and marketing. *Journal of Marketing*, *56*(1), 55–68.

Hamid, S. R., Isa, S., Chew, B. C., & Altun, A. (2019). Quality management evolution from the past to present: Challenges for tomorrow. *Organizacija*, *52*(3), 157–186.

Juran, J. M. (1979). *Quality Control Handbook*, 3rd edn. McGraw-Hill, New York, 5–12.

Kumar Kale, S. (2020). Enriching the field of quality management: Study of contribution by quality gurus. *Our Heritage*, *68*(1), 1788–1795.

Pattanayak, D., Koilakuntla, M., & Punyatoya, P. (2017). Investigating the influence of TQM, service quality and market orientation on customer satisfaction and loyalty in the Indian banking sector. *International Journal of Quality & Reliability Management*, *34*(3), 362–377.

Pryor, M. G., & Cullen, B. (1993). Learn to use TQM as part of everyday work. *Industrial Management*, *35*(3), 10–14.

Rattan, R. (2019). *Quality Matters* (Vol. 31). Quintessence Publishing Co. Ltd., London.

Stimson, W. A. (2005). A Deming inspired management code of ethics. *Quality Progress*, *38*(2), 67–75.

Zhang, C., Moreira, M. R., & Sousa, P. S. (2020). A bibliometric view on the use of total quality management in services. *Total Quality Management & Business Excellence*, *31*, 1–28.

2 Total Quality Management (TQM)

2.1 DEFINITION OF TOTAL QUALITY MANAGEMENT (TQM)

Total Quality Management (TQM) seeks to integrate all organisational functions, such as marketing, finance, design, engineering, production, customer service, etc. to focus on meeting customer needs and organisational objectives.

TQM is defined as:

Total = Made up of the whole.
Quality = Degree of excellence of product/service provider.
Management = Art of handling, controlling and directing.

TQM sees an organisation as a set of processes. It argues that organisations must strive to continually improve these processes by integrating the knowledge and experiences of workers. The simple goal of TQM is 'To do things right, the first time, always.' TQM is infinitely variable and adaptable. This management approach covers several areas, although it was originally applied to manufacturing operations. For several years, it has only been used in this field. From now on, TQM is identified as a generic management tool, which also applies to services (health and safety), industrial enterprises, and the public sector. There is a series of evolutionary units, with different sectors creating their own versions of the common predecessor.

Total Quality Management is also defined as a customer-driven process and goals for continuous improvement of business operations. It ensures that all related work (in particular the work of the employees) is directed towards the common objectives of improving the quality of the product or the quality of the service, as well as the production or execution process of the services. However, the focus is on evidence-based decision-making, with the use of performance measures to monitor progress (Deming).

2.1.1 THE KEY PRINCIPLES OF TQM

a) Commitment from the Management
   - Plan (drive, direct).
   - Do (deploy, support, and participate).
   - Check (review).
   - Act (recognise, communicate, revise).
b) Employee Empowerment
   - Training.
   - Excellence team.

- Measurement and recognition.
- Suggestion scheme.

c) Continuous Improvement
  - Systematic measurement.
  - Excellence teams.
  - Cross-functional process management.
  - Attain, maintain, improve standards.

  - Customer Focus
  - Partnership with suppliers.
  - Service relationship with internal customers.
  - Customer-driven standards.
  - Never compromise quality.

2.1.2 BENEFITS OF TQM

Total Quality Management implementation leads to benefits for an organisation:

- It increases knowledge and culture of maintaining quality within the organisation.
- Distinctive attention and importance will be given to teamwork.
- It will lead to a commitment to continuous improvement.

2.1.3 ESSENTIAL REQUIREMENTS FOR SUCCESSFUL IMPLEMENTATION OF TQM

a) Commitment
   Quality improvement (in all aspects) must be the work of all members of the organisation. A clear commitment on the part of management must be provided, removing barriers to continuous quality improvement and the steps necessary to create an environment conducive to attitudinal change. Training and support in this regard should be expanded.

b) Culture
   Culture is a step for successful implantation of TQM. Therefore, before changes take effect in the culture and attitude of the organisation, suitable training and awareness is necessary.

c) Continuous Improvement
   Improvement needs to be understood as not only a one-time affair. Rather, it is a process that is continuous in nature. It is basically a need of the customer, as well as of the service provider.

d) Customer Focus
   A customer-oriented approach ensures the intention of the organisation is to attain perfection with no defects and giving comprehensive satisfaction to the end-user. The users could be internal to the company or external.

e) Control
   A process control exercise through monitoring and regular checks ensures no deviation from the intended course of implementation.

2.1.4   PDCA CYCLE

Plan–Do–Check–Act is also known as the PDCA cycle.

2.1.4.1   Planning Phase

This is a very crucial phase for TQM where employees put forth their queries and problems which need to be addressed. A list made by employees of various daily challenges in activities helps in understanding and analysing the root causes for the problems. Proper research from the gathered data can help them find solutions for almost all these difficulties. So it is more reliable for achieving lasting solutions.

2.1.4.2   Doing Phase

A plausible solution is developed by the stakeholders (employees in this case) in the planning phase. Well thought out policies/tactics are formulated and then implemented to address the challenges presented to the employees. The efficiency and effectiveness of the employed strategies, as well as the solutions, are evaluated at this stage.

2.1.4.3   Checking Phase

During this phase, a comparative analysis is performed before and after to evaluate the effectiveness of the processes and measure the results. Therefore, it provides an efficient result for the process.

2.1.4.4   Acting Phase

During this phase, documentation of the results obtained is undertaken by the employees. They proceed to address further problems.

2.2   ELEMENTS OF TQM

TQM is a synergic application of a variety of activities. For the successful implementation of TQM, an organisation must concentrate on the eight key elements. These eight elements are based on four groups, according to their function,

- Foundation: Namely of ethics, integrity, and trust.
- Building bricks: It also includes three elements of TQM such as training, teamwork, and leadership, etc.
- Binding motors: Communication is only one included in this group.
- Roof: It includes recognition only.

Eight elements of TQM are shown in Figure 2.1.
   Here is an explanation of the eight elements of TQM:

a) Ethics
   Ethics is basically the principle of discipline, the discipline of good and evil in any situation. Multi-faceted issues represent the organisational level and the individual level of ethics. Organisational ethics is a blanket code of

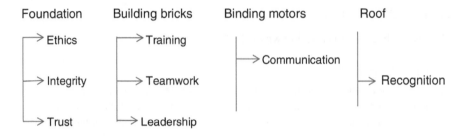

FIGURE 2.1   Eight elements of TQM.

professional ethics applicable to all the employees, and they are expected
to follow it closely in carrying out their work. Individual ethics includes
personal rights or errors.

b) Integrity

TQM has an element of integrity that implies honesty, morals, values,
impartiality, respect for facts, and sincerity. The integrity feature is what
clients (internal or external) expect and deserve to receive. Lack of integrity
is perceived as duplicity and it is believed that TQM would not survive in an
environment of duplicity.

c) Trust

After studying ethics and integrity, the role of trust is very important. Trust
is a by-product of integrity and ethical conduct. Without trust, the total
quality management framework cannot be built. Trust ensures complete
participation from different members. It allows for accountability that
encourages the pleasure of ownership and encourages commitment.

d) Training

Training has a strong relationship with the productivity of employees. The
better the training, the more productive workers become. Training employees periodically instils thoroughness in the implementation of total quality
management. The departmental level of implementation of TQM is undertaken by the supervisors. They also help in making sure their employees
gain better knowledge.

e) Teamwork

In order to use resources effectively, it is necessary to work as a team.
Teamwork is a crucial aspect of TQM, which is essential in making a business successful. Through the use of this tool, the company will receive faster
and more efficient solutions to problems. Teamwork helps in getting better
and more permanent solutions to improve various processes and operations.

f) Leadership

This is perhaps the most important element of total quality management.
Without leaders, the organisation cannot stand up. Leadership is omnipres-
ent in the organisation. A manager is expected to provide inspirational goals
and vision, and at the same time define strategic steps to move forward in
the business, which are comprehensible for all the employees, which are

some of the requirements of leadership in TQM. For TQM to succeed in the business, the supervisor must commit to directing its employees.

g) Recognition

Recognition should be provided for the suggestions made, as well as for the achievements of teams and individuals. This gives employees the morale boost to work more efficiently. Employees want to receive recognition for themselves and their teams. 'Detecting and recognising employees are the most important job of a supervisor.' As people are recognised, their self-esteem, productivity, quality, and the effort required can change significantly. Recognition is the most effective when given to employees immediately after their actions.

h) Communication

Communication unites everything. It means connectivity for every person in the organisation. From the foundation to the roof of the TQM house, everything is joined by the strong mortar of communication. It acts as a dynamic link between all the elements of TQM. To reinforce communication, it is important to maintain a strong relationship of ideas between the sender and the recipient. The success of TQM requires communication among all the stakeholders of the organisation, including suppliers which are external to the organisation.

2.3   QUALITY LEADERSHIP

The administration is responsible for the selection of the right people, the creation of teams, providing various resources, and configuring the system as required within the organisation. Senior management has complete responsibility for the problems of quality and maintenance. A few key points responsible for quality leadership are explained below.

a) Sincere Enthusiasm

Each team admires the members of the team and if the team wants to give them everything, the members will also have to be enthusiastic. The team is motivated through the efforts of their team-mates and their leader. The greater the efforts that are put in by the people, the harder the complete team works. In short, it improves the growth of the organisation.

b) Integrity

Integrity is an essential part of any organisation succeeding. Without this, no real success is possible, be it in a section team, a football field, an army, or an office. Honesty and integrity are two important requirements that make a good leader.

c) Great Communication Skills

Good communication skills are one of the most important traits of any leader. To reinforce communication, it is important to maintain a strong relationship of ideas between employees and managers. Words can make wonders and might inspire people to do the unthinkable and the extraordinary. If communication skills are used effectively, this can lead to better results.

d) Loyalty

Loyalty is the main factor for quality leadership. A good leader is a personality highly appreciated by employers and employees. All teams, as well as organisations, are kept together or dissolved by loyalty. Loyalty, trust, and commitment are really the glue that keeps relationships going for maximum benefit.

e) Decisiveness

A high-quality leader must have the ability to make decisions. In addition to having a revolutionary vision, a good leader takes the right decisions at the appropriate time. These decisions have a profound impact on people. A leader must be able to think for a long time before making a decision, but once the decision is made, stick with it so that the decision will improve the process.

f) Managerial Competence

This should be necessary for quality leadership. Management competence creates a healthy environment. It offers the possibility of quality leadership.

g) Empowerment

People might not always do the right thing. It could be the result of a lack of understanding of the difference between right and wrong at that point in time. It thus becomes very important for a leader to focus on primary responsibilities rather than others. It is usually prudent to leave the secondary issues to others. This delegation of tasks to the subordinate ranks in the hierarchy helps in embedding a feeling of empowerment in them. It is also important to see how they behave. This approach provides them with all the resources and support they need to reach the goal and gives them the opportunity to accept responsibility.

2.4 ROLE OF QUALITY LEADERS

Leaders of any organisation play an important role for maintaining quality. As we know, the leader in TQM is a person who inspires, by suitable means, having sufficient capability to affect a group of individuals to become willing followers in the achievement of the organisational goals. Research identifying the keys of successful leadership in quality management reports the following:

(a) Attention through vision.
(b) Meaning through communication.
(c) Trust through positioning.
(d) Confidence through respect.

Describing the characteristics of leaders in quality management, they have an unprecedented vision and concern with the results; are excellent in the area of communication; they are predictable and make their positions known; they must have positive self-esteem and a commitment to bring out the best in others. Here are the seven most identified qualities of great leaders and executives:

a) Vision

Good entrepreneurs have a very inspirational and farsighted vision which they share passionately with the employees. Their clarity of goals is of a sensational level. Also, they are experts in strategic planning. Quality is what makes them different from managers. They have a clear vision, which transforms the individual into a particular type of person. This quality of vision transforms a 'transactional administrator' into a 'transformational leader.'

b) Courage

'Value is, rightly, considered the main virtue, because everyone else depends on it,' according to Winston Churchill. One of the most important qualities of a good leader is value. It also depends on the ability of the leaders. Willingness to take risks in pursuit of achieving goals indicates the quality of courage, while following such thinking does not guarantee any success. Every commitment made by the leaders and every action they take carries any risk.

c) Integrity

According to Zig Ziglar, 'With integrity, you have nothing to fear because you have nothing to hide, with integrity, you will do the right thing and you will not be guilty.' In each strategic planning session for large and small companies, the first value that all leader groups agree on for their business is integrity. Everyone agrees on the importance of total honesty in everything they do, both internally and externally. The heart of integrity is the truth. Integrity always requires telling the truth to everyone.

d) Humility

According to Larry Bossidy, humility gives results. Humility is the quality of being humble. Humility is a leadership quality where strong and decisive leaders are humble at the same time. Humility does not mean that it makes leaders weak or uncertain. It means that they have the self-confidence and self-awareness necessary to recognise the value of others without feeling susceptible. One of the rarest traits of leadership is where a strong, decisive leader is humble which requires the leader to be a master of self-confidence.

e) Strategic Planning

'The strategy is not the consequence of planning, but quite the opposite: it is the starting point.' According to Henry Mintzberg, strategic planning is remarkable. Without strategic planning, leaders cannot imagine their success. They have the ability to look to the future, to anticipate with some precision the evolution of industry and markets. Leaders have the ability to foresee trends long before their competitors. They constantly ask: 'According to what is happening today, where is the market going? Where will it be in three months, six months, one year, and two years?' They do so through thoughtful strategic planning. Anticipating the market is the key which only a few leaders or organisations practise, but which eventually go on to outlast their competition in the market. It gives the advantage of moving first in the marketplace.

f) Focus

Successful people maintain a positive direction in life, no matter what happens around them, focus on past successes instead of past failures, and on the next steps to bring them closer to home rather than the other distractions that life presents to them.

Jack Canfield

Leaders always focus on the needs of society and the situation. The leaders focus on the results, what they must do themselves, the others, and the company. Great leaders focus on their strengths, on themselves, and on others. They focus on the strengths of any type of organisation, in what the company does best to satisfy demanding customers in a competitive market. Leaders must have the ability to take things on themselves when required, ensuring the complete focus of the employees, and making productive use of the time to perform well.

g) Cooperation

'If their imagination leads them to understand the speed with which people access their requests when they appeal to their own interests, they have virtually nothing to do' – Napoleon Hill. The ability to make everyone work and join together is essential for success. Leadership is the ability to make people work for them because they want to.

2.5   ADVANTAGES OF TQM

There are so many advantages to implementing TQM in an organisation. Here we explain some of the advantages of total quality management (TQM) which include:

1. *Cost reduction* – If applied consistently over time, total quality management can reduce costs throughout the company, especially in the areas of scrapping, recovery and on-site processing, and reduced warranty costs. Since these cost reductions directly impact net profits without incurring additional costs, this can result in a surprising increase in profitability.
2. *Customer satisfaction* – Because the company offers better products and services, and customer relations are relatively effective, there should be fewer customer complaints. Fewer complaints can also mean that resources dedicated to customer service can be reduced. Increased customer satisfaction can also lead to a bigger market share, as current customers will work on behalf of the company to attract more customers.
3. *Defect reduction* – TQM places great emphasis on improving quality within a process, rather than integrating quality into a process. The reduction of defects leads to an improvement in quality. This not only reduces the time required to repair errors, it also reduces the need for a team of quality control personnel.
4. *Morale* – These are the fundamental benefits of total quality management. The continued success of TQM, and, in particular, employee participation in this success, can significantly improve employee morale, which reduces employee turnover and, consequently, hiring and training costs for new employees.

2.6 IMPLEMENTATION STEPS OF TQM

The relevant prerequisites relate to the history of the organisation, its current needs, the events that led to the management of total quality, and the quality of working life of employees. If the current reality does not include important preconditions, the implementation of TQM should be delayed until the organisation is in a favourable state for its success.

If an organisation has a proven track record of environmental awareness and has been able to effectively change the way it operates when necessary, TQM will be easier to implement. If an organisation has always been unreceptive and lacks the capacity to improve its operating systems, employees will be unhappy and qualified change agents will be lacking. If this condition prevails, a comprehensive management and leadership development programme can be established. A management audit is a good evaluation tool to identify the current levels of operation of the organisation and the areas that require changes. An organisation must be fundamentally healthy before starting TQM. Implementation steps of TQM are shown in Figure 2.2.

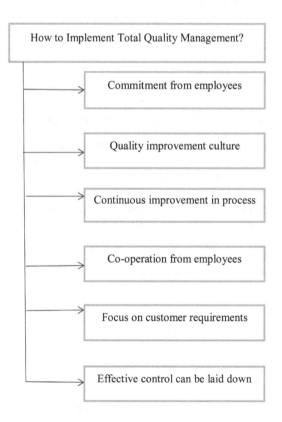

FIGURE 2.2 Implementation steps of TQM.

2.7   PILLARS OF TQM

TQM is basically dependent on five pillars, as shown in Figure 2.3.

These pillars provide strength to TQM. It is the base for the quality improvements. These pillars are:

1. Product.
2. Process.
3. System.
4. People.
5. Leadership.

TQM as a system helps in enabling integration of aspects like quality development, maintenance, and improvement of various groups in a company on a continuous basis. It enables different facets of businesses like marketing, engineering, production, and finally, the services to operate at a cost which is at optimum level and allows for full customer satisfaction.

On the basis of all the logical conclusions and a review of the literature, it seems that for the implementation of TQM to be successful, it must be based on some pillars to strengthen the base of the strategic measures. The researchers propose that the implementation of TQM is effective if it is based on eight pillars. The pillars work well by linking together cohesively, rather than in silos. On successful implementation, the goal of utmost importance, i.e. the goal of TQM can be achieved. Here is an explanation of the eight pillars of TQM.

2.7.1   PILLAR ONE (P1): CREATION OF QUALITY MANAGEMENT ENVIRONMENT

A philosophy of integral quality management must begin with a process where the atmosphere of quality management is created and furthermore, it gives a free hand to the employees for investigating and correcting problems associated with quality. It requires an organisation to have a clear vision and mission with respect to the implementation of TQM. The mission and vision statement need widespread circulation within the organisation so that all the employees align themselves with it. TQM is a challenge that affects the entire organisation. TQM transformation has a prerequisite of knowledge of the fact that a product/service quality needs improvement. Therefore, an awareness programme is needed to implement TQM to create a positive environment throughout the organisation.

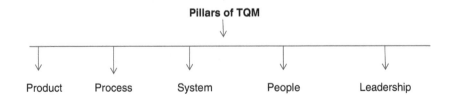

FIGURE 2.3   Pillars of TQM.

2.7.2 Pillar Two (P2): Development of Teamwork

Unless the requirements of a customer are measured accurately, it is difficult for a company to look for the goal of continuous improvement. A business must be organised to obtain the necessary feedback on quality levels of products/services and also to obtain reliable information on the identification of the actual needs of customers. Customer satisfaction must be taken into account by all employees who automatically mandate a workplace to involve the front-line employees in the decision-making process. Establishing and valuing the contributions of the team is an essential component of TQM.

2.7.3 Pillar Three (P3): Practice of Quality Control Tools and Techniques

Primary responsibility in TQM lies with the employees. Only the application of the correct tools and techniques can enable the employees to identify the right problems with the quality. Statistical Process Control (SPC) is by far the best tool to improve the quality of the products/services. It includes seven basic techniques, namely, Pareto diagram, process flow diagram, cause-and-effect diagram, sheet paper, histogram, control charts, and scatter chart. This technical tool can be used to improve its capacity.

2.7.4 Pillar Four (P4): Focus on Customer

TQM recognises the futility of efforts involved in manufacturing a seemingly perfect product that no client wants. Needless to say, thus, that quality has to be customer oriented. Being customer oriented leads to more attention towards the goal of customer satisfaction which needs to be integrated in the planning processes and their maintenance on a day to day basis. For continuous improvement, the customers' requirements must be systematically measured and met. The company must organise itself to obtain the necessary information to identify the needs of the clients and obtain reliable and timely comments on the quality levels of the products/services currently available.

2.7.5 Pillar Five (P5): Focus on Supplier Relationship

It is important that the administration allows the purchasing department adequate time to identify several qualified low-cost providers and analyse the information provided. Poor selection of suppliers is possible if an unrealistic deadline is given to the department due to lack of sufficient information from the providers. Better coordination is necessary among different departments such as procurement, engineering, and quality control to evaluate the qualifications for the manufacturing processes of the services. Close working relationships need trust and credibility among the stakeholders which is practically difficult. Companies need to apply the right tools and techniques with systems to establish a favourable and satisfactory relationship with the suppliers. Some of these systems include 'supply systems'; 'advanced planning and planning'; and 'transport planning systems.'

2.7.6 PILLAR SIX (P6): BENCHMARKING

One of the best tools in understanding and implementing the practice of continuous improvement is benchmarking. It helps in understanding the level of the organisation in terms of its performance as against the best practices in the industry. It borrows the best of the ideas and adapts them to give it a competitive edge in the market. The need for benchmarking begins with the identification of gaps in established process objectives and existing practices and achieves the desired improvements defined in accordance with best practices. Since benchmarking is not a strategy or a business philosophy, it must be used correctly to achieve the expected benefits. Comparative analysis is fast and economical, as the process is imitation- and adaptation-based. It is not a pure invention.

2.7.7 PILLAR SEVEN (P7): IMPROVEMENT OF PROCESSES

Training of employees and adapting for newer technologies can lead to process improvement. Process improvement can be the beginning of a quality programme. Most authors favour an attitude of zero defects and a 'just in time' attitude for the quality agenda, which implies a zero faults mentality. Refinement involves activities that continuously improve a process that is not interrupted. This improves efficiency and effectiveness. It is easier for all to adopt this policy to undertake doing things faster and better with little waste. Innovation and technological advances are key factors in the renewal strategy which lead to important improvements.

2.7.8 PILLAR EIGHT (P8): INVOLVEMENT OF EMPLOYEE

Continuous improvement in a process is achieved when employees are involved in decision-making. This happens when they are trained to make decisions. This is one of the objectives of the TQM implementation. It aids in improving quality and a rise in productivity. It is clear that employees must participate in any process of change, including quality management practices. Employee participation in the implementation and planning phase of reward and recognition activity is essential. Rewards for efforts that are appreciated by the administration should be one of the strategies in rewarding people in the organisation. An important reward system based on the achievements of the team can be considered. An effective reward and recognition system must be based on the evaluation of the performance of the employees. This shall serve as a basis for their career advancement in the company in terms of promotions or salary hikes. It also helps in aligning the employee with the organisation's goals.

2.8 OBSTACLES TO IMPLEMENTING TQM

Organisations have a number of difficulties in implementing TQM. A few common obstacles are:

a) Lack of Management Commitment
   When management talks about TQM, but its actions fail, it will eventually not be able to meet expectations. The result is distrust and the difficulty of

launching another attempt. For the implementation to be successful, the administration must clearly communicate the reason for adopting TQM.

b) Inability to Change Organisational Culture

Changing the culture of an organisation is very difficult and takes time. The fear of change must be addressed, conflicts between the social partners and companies must be resolved, and the focus of the organisations must no longer be maintained. Without this, no-one will have confidence in the organisation.

c) Improper Planning

All parts of the organisation must participate in the development of the implementation plan and the changes as the plan evolves.

d) Lack of Continuous Training and Education

TQM raises the problem of adequate education and training. Training and education are most effective when senior management leads the training on the principles of TQM.

e) Ineffective Measurement Techniques and Lack of Access to Data and Results

TQM depends on data-driven decision-making. Access to data and rapid recovery are necessary for an efficient process. A process to create and maintain a TQM environment must be accurate, fast, and reliable.

f) Paying Inadequate Attention to Internal and External Customers

TQM does not pay enough attention to internal and external customers. It must understand the changing needs and expectations of customers. To avoid this obstacle, it is necessary to find the right way to get directly to the client.

2.9   QUALITY COUNCIL: CORE VALUES AND VISION

(1) Quality Council: The Quality Council is made up of CEOs and senior managers of research, manufacturing, finance, sales, marketing, etc. as well as a coordinator and a union representative.

(2) Coordinator: The coordinator position must be a brilliant junior person with executive potential. This person will report to the CEO. Responsibilities:

a)   Establish mutual trust, propose the needs of the team to the board, share the expectations of the board with the team, and inform the board about the progress of the team.

b)   Ensure that the teams are trained and know their responsibilities.

(3) Activities:

a)   To assist the team leaders.

b)   To share lessons learned among teams.

c)   To have regular leaders' meetings – in smaller organisations where managers may be responsible for more than one functional area, the number of members will be smaller.

(4) The Quality Council develops, with the participation of all the manpower, the fundamental values, the vision statement, the mission statement, and the declaration of the quality policy. It develops a long-term strategic plan

with objectives and an annual quality improvement plan with objectives. It creates the total education and training plan.

(5) The Council determines and keeps a continuous track of the cost of having poor quality.

(6) The Council must continuously identify projects that improve processes, especially those that affect the satisfaction of internal and external clients. It must set up a multi-functional project and department/task teams and track their progress.

(7) Once the TQM programme is well-established, a typical meeting programme may include the following: Team progress report; Customer satisfaction report; Status of team meetings; Recognition Dinner; Benchmarking report.

'Quality statements are part of the strategic planning and development process. Once developed, reviewed, and updated, time and strategy are key elements of quality consulting.'

There are three types of quality statements:

- Vision statement.
- Mission statement.
- Quality policy statement.

Many organisations use different quality statements specific to their organisational appropriateness.

2.9.1 VISION STATEMENT

The mission statement is a short declaration of an organisation; it's about what they expect from tomorrow. A vision statement is the description of the future expected in the mission statement of an organisation. Successful visions are timeless, inspirational, and highly motivational, and become deeply shared within the organisation. For example:

a) Ford Motor Company.
b) Apple (computing).
c) Polaroid (instant photography).
d) IITS, NITS, and government institutes.
e) Disney (theme parks).

In other words, it is what an organisation desires to be tomorrow.

2.9.2 MISSION STATEMENT

A mission statement sets the short-term goal for the organisation. It's about what an organisation is. Mission statements answer many types of questions, such as 'who we are, who our customers are, what we do and how we do it.' The statement usually comprises a paragraph or less, is easy to understand, and describes the function of the company or organisation. It provides a clear indication of goals for employees, suppliers, and customers.

Here is an example of a mission statement:

Honda Motor Company is a global leader in automotive and automotive products and services, as well as in all types of new industries such as aerospace, communications and financial services..

2.9.3   QUALITY POLICY STATEMENT

The Quality Policy is a guide for all members of the organisation on how they should provide products and services to customers. It should be drafted by the general manager with comments from employees and approved by the board. A quality policy is a requirement of ISO 9000.

A simple quality policy is: 'Xerox is a quality company, quality is the cornerstone of Xerox, and quality is about providing our internal and external customers with innovative products and services that meet their requirements.'

A quality policy is a short document published by the executive management of an organisation that establishes what quality means to the firm. It is published to all employees and is often made public so that it can be accessed by investors, customers, suppliers, and regulators. It's a cornerstone document of several quality standards. A quality policy typically describes your business and your commitment to quality. The core information offered is a small set of quality principles.

The following are common examples.

2.9.3.1   Customer Needs

Indicate that the products will satisfy the needs of the clients. This is often formulated in terms of marketing; for example, the principle that products will please consumers in a safe and reliable way.

2.9.3.2   Customer Preferences

This indicates that products will be designed to customer requirements, be customisable, or be offered in varieties designed to suit customer preferences.

2.9.3.3   Service and Experience

A customer service and/or customer experience principle.

2.9.3.4   Listening

A commitment to listen to the customer and use their input to improve quality.

2.9.3.5   Compliance

This is the basic need for compliance with regulations and standards.

2.9.3.6   Health and Safety

Quality policy statements involve committing to a safe product. It always works towards a healthy and safe environment.

2.9.3.7   Defects

A commitment to work towards zero defects in products and services. A zero defects policy makes productivity high.

2.9.3.8   Accuracy

A commitment to accuracy beyond zero defects, such as accurate product descriptions, for example; a principle of honesty and directness.

2.9.3.9   Testing

Specifically mentioning how they will test products. For example, mentioning that every item is tested before it goes out the door.

2.9.3.10   Waste

A commitment to work towards zero waste. This also improves the productivity of the organisation.

2.9.3.11   Improvement

The principle that they will continually improve.

2.9.3.12   Industry Specific

Stating your value proposition. In other words, promising to be good at something.

2.9.3.13   People

A commitment to have a positive impact on the communities in which they operate.

2.9.3.14   Privacy

If your firm handles a good deal of customer data, a promise to secure it and keep it private.

2.9.3.15   Environment

A commitment to environmentally responsible products, services, and operations.

2.9.3.16   Sourcing

The principle that parts, materials, and services will be responsibly sourced.

2.10   CONCLUSION

TQM is a general concept that encompasses many good management techniques. TQM is the management focus of a quality-driven organisation that is built on the participation of all employees and aims for long-term success. This will result in customer satisfaction and benefits for all employees and the company.

TQM in summary:

- The focus of the management of an organisation.
- Quality is the core.

- The participation of each employee is essential.
- It aims for long-term success.
- Its goal is customer satisfaction and benefits for both employees and society.
- A philosophy of management and organisational practices.
- Understood to take advantage of the human and material resources of the organisation.

In this chapter, we discuss eight basic elements and five pillars of TQM that explore TQM in the industry. Next, we discuss the benefits of TQM in industry and why it is necessary in an organisation.

We then analyse how TQM is implemented in industry and discuss in more detail six basic barriers to TQM associated with industry. Finally, we analyse TQM's quality advice and core values, and TQM's vision, mission, and quality policy that influences an organisation.

2.11   CASE STUDY: TQM – A CASE STUDY OF SUNDARAM CLAYTON

Sundaram Clayton, based in Chennai, India, has been hailed and internationally recognised for setting global quality standards. Sundaram Clayton, the world-class flag bearer. A pneumatic brake systems and foundries manufacturer, it became the first Asian company to win the Deming Prize for foreign companies. The Deming Prize is the last word in the world of quality. Japan created this award 40 years ago to pay tribute to W. Edwards Deming, the man who gave quality to the world.

The Deming Prize defines quality as 'a system of activities designed to ensure the quality of products and services, in which the products and services required by customers are produced and delivered economically.'

Policies, People, Processes, and Products: the four pillars of Sundaram Clayton's TQM model integrated Deming's ten metrics to guarantee full employee participation, policy deployment, standardisation, kaizen, and training, as well as the promotion of employer–employee relations. All members of the company are turned into quality guardians.

Sundaram Clayton, led by its CEO, Venu Srinivasan, 45, has surpassed the national level in terms of total quality, to become part of a small group of global elites, who have integrated the ten parameters of Deming in their flow of practices. This small elite group consists of Florida Power and Light ($6.51 billion) (Deming Award winner of 1989); AT&T power systems division ($53.26 billion); and the Phillips Taiwan Unit ($8.05 billion).

On November 14, 1998, Venu Srinivasan became one of the 163 executive directors/leaders to whom the coveted prize has been awarded since its inception. Sundaram Clayton executives were successively exposed to the best quality practices of world leaders, trained in modern manufacturing techniques, and learned Total Quality Control (TQC), first from Yoshio Kondo at a workshop held at the Institute.

The results of the Sundaram Clayton Total Quality Movement are reflected in the company's books and its financial indicators over the five years from 1992–1993 to 1997–1998 show high-level performance of an average of 35% per year, between 1992–1998 and 1996–1997, although it was reduced by 25% in 1997–1998 due to the slowdown in the auto industry. The average growth of 83% per year in four years was a brilliant tribute to quality that led cost management, although it declined by 35% in 1997–1998. Its performance steadily improved despite the recession, with an increase of 18% in turnover per employee on average per year and an increase in gross value added by 12% on average.

POINTS TO REMEMBER

- TQM is a management philosophy that seeks to integrate all organisational functions (marketing, finance, design, engineering, production, and customer service, etc.) to focus on meeting customer needs and organisational objectives.
- The eight elements of TQM are Ethics, Integrity, Trust, Training, Teamwork, Leadership, Recognition, and Communication.
- Management has an important role to play in quality leadership. They are responsible for selecting people, forming teams, providing resources, and establishing the system in the organisation.
- According to Jack Welch, *good business leaders create a vision, articulate the vision, passionately own the vision, and relentlessly drive it to completion.*
- Loyalty, trust, and commitment are truly the glue that holds relationships together to get the maximum benefit.
- Integrity is the core part making any organisation successful. Without it, no real success is possible.
- TQM has a strong emphasis on improving quality within a process, rather than integrating quality into a process.

SELF-ASSESSMENT QUESTIONS

1. Define the term Total Quality Management.
2. Explain the elements of TQM.
3. What are the effects of quality leadership?
4. What is the role of quality leaders in TQM?
5. What are the advantages of TQM?
6. Write down all the pillars of TQM.
7. Explain the obstacles to TQM.
8. What are the vision statement, mission statement, and quality policy statement in TQM?
9. How does customer satisfaction affect TQM?
10. How do product and process pillars affect TQM?
11. Can we imagine without vision and mission of quality in Industry?
12. Strategic planning is the main role of quality leaders. Explain.

BIBLIOGRAPHY

Bendell, T., Penson, R., & Carr, S. (1995). The quality gurus–their approaches described and considered. *Managing Service Quality: An International Journal*, *5*(6), 44–48.

Bendermacher, G. W. G., oude Egbrink, M. G. A., Wolfhagen, H. A. P., Leppink, J., & Dolmans, D. H. J. M. (2019). Reinforcing pillars for quality culture development: A path analytic model. *Studies in Higher Education*, *44*(4), 643–662.

Bounds, G. M. (1994). *Beyond Total Quality Management: Toward the Emerging Paradigm.* McGraw-Hill College, New York.

Bouranta, N., Psomas, E. L., & Pantouvakis, A. (2017). Identifying the critical determinants of TQM and their impact on company performance. *The TQM Journal*, *29*(1), 147–166.

Darling, J. R. (1992). Total quality management: The key role of leadership strategies. *Leadership & Organisation Development Journal*, *13*(4), 3–7.

Deming, W. E. (1981). Improvement of quality and productivity through action by management. *National Productivity Review*, *1*(1), 12–22.

Deming, W. E. (2018). *Out of the Crisis.* MIT Press, New York.

Galli, B. J. (2019). The true pillars of quality management: How to, view them. In: *R&D Management in the Knowledge Era*, Daim, T., Dabić, M., Başoğlu, N., Lavoie, J. R., & Galli, B. J. (eds.) (pp. 589–603). Springer, Cham.

Joseph, J . C. Jr., & Steven, A. (1992). Measuring service quality: A re-examination and extension. *Journal of Marketing*, *56*(3), 55–68.

Juran, J. M. (1979). *Quality Control Handbook*, 3rd edn. McGraw-Hill, New York, 5–12.

Kim, D. Y., Kumar, V., & Kumar, U. (2012). Relationship between quality management practices and innovation. *Journal of Operations Management*, *30*(4), 295–315.

Pryor, M. G., & Cullen, B. (1993). Learn to use TQM as part of everyday work. *Industrial Management*, *35*(3), 10–14.

Stimson, W. A. (2005). A Deming inspired management code of ethics. *Quality Progress*, *38*(2), 67–75.

3 Quality Management Practices

3.1 QUALITY MANAGEMENT PRACTICES

Quality management practices were originally developed after World War II for restructuring the economy of different countries. The main focus in these practices is continuous improvement in the field of product or services. These practices were also focused on improving the quality of products or services as per customer requirements. The ultimate objective is pleasing the customer, which can only occur through providing the best quality of products or services at the right time, in the right place, and at minimum cost. This requires a huge effort by all the employees of the organisation. A prerequisite of quality management practices is support from the top management who make the quality policy and the quality management system, and make the team of members and assign them the responsibility of completing the task. These practices improve the employer and employee relationship by simply making a synchronisation between the needs of the employees and the organisation. These practices focus on improving the quality of the products and services from the design stage to the distribution stage, i.e. from beginning to end, so as to ensure a defect-free operation. It shows the culture and mindset of a company that is always trying to provide the best quality of product or service as per customer requirements. Quality management practices are a powerful tool which require the overall involvement of people in the organisation. These practices are used in all industries, whether that is a manufacturing or a service industry. It focuses on eliminating those wasteful practices which create loss.

3.2 VARIOUS APPROACHES TO CONTROL AND MANAGEMENT OF QUALITY

All organisations nowadays use quality control tools to monitor and manage their quality initiatives for better customer satisfaction. In general, there are seven basic types of quality control tools that are mostly used in organisations. These tools are the different problem-solving techniques and can be used in all the different scenarios required in industries. These tools can be used in all types of industry, whether in the service sector or in the manufacturing sector. They are as follows:

1. Check sheet.
2. Histograms.
3. Pareto diagram.
4. Scatter diagram.

5. Process flow diagram.
6. Cause-and-effect diagram.
7. Run charts.

Descriptions of all these tools are as follows:

3.2.1 Check Sheet

A check sheet is a simple and useful tool of quality control. A check sheet is a planned document that is used to record all the activities that happen during a specific period of time on the shop floor. It collects real-time data at the location where the process has occurred. It provides the required information in a quick, easy, and efficient manner. A check sheet is a quality control tool that allows the collection and compilation of data in an efficient manner. It is a simple form in which all the information has been recorded in an organised manner by simply putting a tick mark in the column. A check sheet contains all the information regarding the process, including the location. A check sheet is a fundamental quality control tool that collects information in the required format. The check sheet shows how frequently an event occurs during a defined period of time. A check sheet, in short, can be defined as a structured form for collecting and analysing real-time data. It is used for the collection and organisation of the real-time data in a systematic process. It can collect and analyse both qualitative and quantitative data.

Data collection plays a significant role in decision-making, as it is the starting point of any analysis. In all organisations, data collection can be considered a difficult and hectic task as it generally occurs in an unstructured manner and is a cumbersome exercise. Data collection is the prerequisite for all statistical analysis. Data collected through check sheets can be used in brainstorming which is one of the best techniques for idea generation. A check sheet is used for investigating how many times a certain incident happens in the organisation. By just putting a tick mark on a check sheet, data can be collected easily which can then be used for obtaining the essential information.

A check list sometimes works as an input for other processes. It helps managers to ensure that all assigned tasks in a process have been completed. It is used as a guide to control risks. Managers use the check sheet to collect the data and then take corrective measures for resolving the different issues. It helps a manager to take corrective action so that the problems will not occur in future. Records in a check sheet can be collected on daily, weekly, monthly, or yearly basis as per the requirement of the organisation. The person using the check sheet collects the required information by performing an inspection. The check sheet also eliminates the possibility of skipping any necessary information. A check sheet is also a very powerful technique of performing stratification. A check sheet is a simple way of maintaining the records and facts of all incidents that have frequently occurred on the shop floor. It provides the basis for identification of problems that have occurred on the shop floor.

The check sheet is typically designed in such a manner that it can point out possible sources of errors. Because of the development of the computers and software which are capable of maintaining and keeping the high volume of data in the required format, check sheets are not in fashion nowadays. Still, they are a basic and necessary tool used in quality control and are used in the manufacturing sector, like automobile and steel industries, to obtain data. The purpose of the check sheet is to collect the data in raw form, which can then be easily processed for making decisions.

3.2.1.1 Steps Involved in Making a Check Sheet

1. Identify the problem or event for which the check sheet should be prepared by a critical analysis of the processes.
2. Decide the time and duration of the data collection.
3. Design the check sheet form carefully so that important information will be collected.
4. Test the check sheet properly for a small interval of time to ensure the appropriate data collection occurs in an effective and efficient manner.

3.2.1.2 Advantages of Using a Check Sheet

1. Data collection through a check sheet is an effective and efficient way of collecting and displaying data.
2. After making a check sheet, it is easy to analyse the data in a process.
3. A check sheet is an effective method of identification of the root cause of a problem occurring in a process/operation.
4. It is the very first step of preparing the other graphical tools.
5. It is a structured and uniform method of data collection.

3.2.1.3 Examples of a Check Sheet

(1) A plant XYZ makes water bottles in three different sizes: 300 ml, 500 ml and 1000 ml. The inspector inspects these bottles and observes its defects, recording those defects for noting the trends of problems occurring (Table 3.1).

   The inspector observes that in the 300 ml bottle, the problem of a scratch occurs, so he makes a tick mark for 'loose cap,' and notes more water bottle leakage, and it is observed that during a day shift, a total of 6 bottles have the problem or are defective. Similarly, 11 bottles of 500 ml are defective, and 11 bottles of 1000 ml also have the defects. Therefore, the inspectors observe overall that 28 bottles are defective by marking the check sheet. By doing so, the inspector can easily identify the most prominent problem in making water bottles.

(2) ABC is a production plant manufacturing a product. The supervisors observe that making a check sheet shows the defects and occurrence of defects during a shift of 5 days per week, 8 h per shift (Table 3.2).

   The supervisor observes that on Monday, there are 4 pieces which have defects of loose screws, 5 pieces have defects of dust in the sensor, 4 pieces have a bonding defect, and 3 pieces have lost part defects. Therefore, he summed up that on Monday, overall, 16 defective pieces have been manufactured. Similarly, at the end of the week, he concluded that on Tuesday, there were 20 defective pieces, Wednesday, 21 defective pieces, Thursday, 17 defective pieces, and on Friday, 16 defective pieces had been made (Table 3.2).

TABLE 3.1
An Example of a Check Sheet

Defects/Capacity	Scratch	Loose cap	Volume	Leakage	Frequency
300 ml	1	2	2	1	6
500 ml	2	3	3	3	11
1000 ml	3	4	0	4	11
Total	5	9	5	8	28

TABLE 3.2
Check Sheet Example Showing the Defects and the Occurrence of Defects

Day/Defects	Monday	Tuesday	Wednesday	Thursday	Friday	Total
Loose screws	4	9	7	5	2	27
Dust in sensor	5	3	5	4	3	20
Bonding defect	4	3	5	3	2	17
Operating defect	0	4	3	3	5	15
Part lost defect	3	2	1	2	4	12
Total	16	20	21	17	16	

3.2.2 Histogram

A histogram is one of the basic tools of statistical process control. It is one of simplest ways of understanding the distributed data. It is represented as a vertical rectangular bar showing the frequency of data in a graphical format. The bars of histograms start from the horizontal axis. The histogram is used to represent a large amount of data in a graphical format. It shows the maximum value and minimum value of data, and the spread of data so that it is easy to understand, if data is represented in a tabular format. Histogram is the visual/pictorial representation of data by using varying heights. The varying heights of the bars represents the variation of data.

A histogram is the graphical representation of the data in which the parameters like defect, height, etc. are on the x axis and the frequency/occurrence of data is on the y axis. The range of data is divided into equal numbers of smaller sections and the frequency of this data is counted to prepare the frequency distribution table. With the help of this frequency distribution table, the vertical bars formed originated from the horizontal axis. The height of the vertical bars is directly proportional to the frequency of that smaller section. It is generally used to show the graphical representation of frequency of a sample, number of defects, population, etc. The histogram represents how frequently each value in a group of data occurs. It is used for analysis of a process just by reading the average value and degree of variation of graph. It provides the improvement area in a process. The objective of a histogram is to represent the distribution characteristics of the different parameter. It also represents the skewness of data as it can be symmetrical data, right-oriented skewness, or left-oriented skewness. Therefore, it can conclude that the histogram is very useful to understand the properties of data. It is useful to understand the required parameters.

3.2.2.1 Advantages of Histogram

1. A histogram is used only for numerical data; it is unable to process qualitative data.
2. It represents the dispersion and the central tendency of data, to analyse the process and provide the basis for corrective actions as per customers' expectations.
3. It is useful to analyse the output from the supplier point of view.
4. It shows the process variation during a specified period of time.
5. It can also be used to compare more than one different process.

3.2.2.2 Example of Histogram

Table 3.3 shows the price range of pencils (in Rupees) and the number of the pencils a person sold.

Step 1: Draw the x and y axis and make an equal interval of each axis.
Step 2: Put the price of the pencils on the x axis and the number of pencils sold on the y axis and then level the axes.
Step 3: Choose a suitable scale for the y axis. The number of pencils sold ranges between 5 and 25. So say the scale 1 cm = 5 pencils on y axis.
Step 4: On the x axis, write the price range of the pencils.
Step 5: Draw the appropriate bars for each class interval. As for the price range of 5 to 10, the frequency is 10, so draw the bar of an appropriate length. Similarly, other bars of different length can be drawn and the histogram shown in Figure 3.1.

3.2.3 Pareto Diagram

Analysis of numerical data plays an important role in decision-making. This data can be analysed in different ways, like a bar diagram, a histogram, a Pareto diagram, and a pie chart. A Pareto diagram is special type of statistical chart. The creator of the Pareto chart was an Italian economist, Vilfredo Pareto. It is problem-solving tool which decides the direction of efforts to satisfy the customer's requirements. It is also known as even Pareto distribution or a Pareto graph. A Pareto chart is the combination of two graphs, namely, a bar chart and a line graph. A Pareto chart contains a vertical bar chart in descending order of relative frequency which starts from extreme left to right. The horizontal axis or x axis contains the independent variable.

TABLE 3.3
An Example of a Histogram

Price range of pencils (in Rupees)	5–10	10–15	15–20	20–25
Number of pencils sold	10	15	25	20

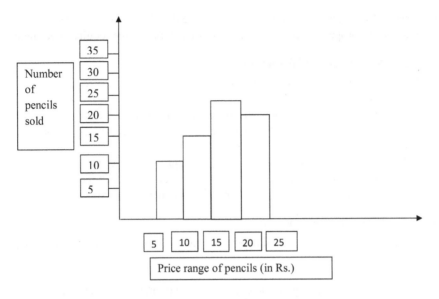

FIGURE 3.1 Histogram.

The length of the bars in the Pareto chart represents the frequency. It is a prerequisite of graphical analysis. It is based on unequal distribution. In a Pareto chart, the most frequent data is at the extreme left and the least frequent data is on the other side. The basic principle of Pareto analysis is that in almost every process, 80% of the problems are incurred due to only 20% of the causes/reasons. Therefore, by focusing on the major causes, which are fewer in number, you can sort out the maximum number of problems. The purpose of the Pareto analysis is to know the most important and serious issue to focus on.

A Pareto chart is a special type of quality control chart that can be used in different situations. It is generally used to decide the priority of causes. It mainly has two objectives: the first one is to arrange the data in descending order, and the second one is to identify the improvement areas by prioritising the efforts. In a large database, it is very important to understand the most significant data on which to focus, which can generate the fruitful results.

3.2.3.1 Utilisation of Pareto Diagram

1. Identification of the most significant problem.
2. Identification of the reason for the problem.
3. To prioritise actions.
4. To review the corrective measure that has been taken.
5. Allows explaining of important tasks.

3.2.3.2 Advantages of Pareto Analysis

1. It is an easy and efficient tool of quality control.
2. The Pareto chart provide the basis for the segregation of a problem and its root cause.

3. It helps to identify the minimum number of problems that creates the maximum number of problems.

It represents the most important problem easily.

It is one of the best visualisation tools.

3.2.3.3   Limitations of Pareto Analysis

1. The Pareto principle is not a universal rule; it cannot be applicable in all cases.
2. It is unable to provide root cause of problem; it only shows the major problems.
3. For large volumes of data, it is sometime difficult to draw the Pareto chart effectively.
4. A Pareto chart is only focused on past value or data. It is not useful for future or present/current scenario.

3.2.3.4   How to a Construct Pareto Diagram

Step 1: Select the items for which the Pareto analysis is required.

Step 2: Draw the horizontal and vertical lines showing the x axis and the y axis.

Step 3: Divide the x axis and the y axis on a suitable scale as per the requirement.

Step 4: Draw the bars from the extreme left side of highest frequency and move to the right side with decreasing frequency.

Step 5: Labels the bars. On the horizontal axis below each bar, label the bars so as to know which cause each bar represents, as shown in the graph below.

Step 6: Continue in this way to make all the bars.

Step 7: Make the dot for each and every item, corresponding to the frequency for each item. For every item, plot a dot on the graph. For this dot, start from the left, point on the bar or above it, corresponding to the value of frequencies for each of them.

Step8: Join all the dots by using a scale.

Step 9: Mention the title of the chart.

3.2.4   SCATTER DIAGRAM

A scatter plot or scatter diagram is a mathematical diagram. It is also called as a scatter chart or scatter graph. It is one of the best tools for quality control. It uses Cartesian coordinates to represent a set of data. The data is shown as a compilation of points. In this, the point is located on the horizontal axis, and its value is on the vertical axis. It represents the relationship between the points. It shows the correlation between variables; if the point lies near the line or curve, the better will be the correlation. A scatter diagram is used to observe the connection between the two paired, interconnected data types. It gives a fair idea of how closely two data points are related. It clearly identifies the critical point to focus on through which the problem can be controlled and sorted out. In a scatter plot, the controlled parameter is plotted on the x axis, and the measure of the dependent parameter is plotted on the y axis. If the collected data did not contain independent and dependent variables, then any data points can be plotted on any axis, and in this case the scatter plot will suggest the degree of correlation.

The scatter diagram is used to examine the relationship between the different data points. The scatter diagram can only be used for paired quantitative data. It is generally used with regression, modelling, and correlation techniques. It is used to identify the fundamental problems occurring in a process. It is used after the brainstorming technique and the fishbone diagram to determine the basic cause-and-effect diagram. Each and every point on a scatter diagram shows a relationship between dependent and independent variables. By the use of a scatter diagram, various types of correlation can be obtained between data points, like rising, falling, or null correlations. In a positive or rising correlation, the pattern of dot points is moving from lower left to upper right, and in negative or falling correlation it is from upper right to lower left direction. The best fit line, usually known as the trend line, is used to study the correlation between variables. Linear regression is used for linear correlation and it is able to generate the correct solution in a definite interval of time. A scatter plot is also able to show the nonlinear relationship between variables. Scatter diagrams are used to observe and identify the best possible inter-relationship between the changes occurring in different group of variables, which is helpful in decision-making.

3.2.4.1   Steps of Scatter Diagram
1. Collect the data in the process for which scatter diagram is to be plotted.
2. Put thet independent variable on the x axis and the dependent variable on the y axis. For each pair of data values, make a dot/point or a symbol.
3. Closely observe the pattern of points to understand the pattern and inter-relationship between the points. This may be a curve or line. Then use a regression or correlation technique to find the best possible solution.

3.2.5   PROCESS FLOW CHART

A flow chart is a chart that shows how a number of essential processes interact with each other for completion of the process. It is the pictorial representation of all the steps required to complete a process in a sequential manner. This is known as one of the best techniques of quality control and is widely used in industries. It contains the sequence of operation or flow of material in a process, i.e. the input and output of the machines. It includes the time required for completion of the process. This is a fundamental quality control tool that can be used in a wide variety of purposes in manufacturing or in service sectors. It is used to understand the basic knowledge of process and can be used as a process improvement technique. It is used in the planning phase of the product development process, for better understanding of processes and communicating the process to other department of the company. To draw the flow chart, it is required to identify key persons and key processes involved in the process. Nowadays, a flow chart is drawn by computer software.

3.2.5.1   How to Construct the Flow Chart

Step 1: The very first step to draw the flow chart is to understand the process. This requires the identification of all the sub-processes of the flow of material involved in a process. It includes the supplier and customers also.

Step 2: Arrange the processes involved in a sequential manner for completion of the process.

Step 3: Review the flow chart with some experienced person who has expertise in the field.

A flow chart can be classified as per the sequence of operations performed by a person or as per the movement/flow of material to complete a process. It is generally obtained by thoroughly inspecting the process and sequence of its operations. The following are the symbols used to draw the flow chart in quality control (Table 3.4).

3.2.6   Cause-and-Effect Diagram

A cause-and-effect diagram is also known as a fishbone diagram. In the year 1950, Ishikawa and associates first developed this tool in Japan, to explain the causes that affected the production of steel. It identifies all the probable reasons/causes of an effect or problem. It provides a basis for a brainstorming session and has a power to categorise ideas in to useful solutions. It gives a systematic representation of the causes and their effect on a problem. To solve the problem scientifically, there must be a clear understanding of the reasons that creates the problems and the consequences of those problems. In a plant, people, machines, materials, money facilities, the conditions of the machines, the operators' skill in performing the process, etc. are the main reasons that create problems and a decrease in production, low productivity of workers, and low turnover are the major effects that occur due to

---

TABLE 3.4

Flow Process Chart for Material

Activates	Operations				Distance moved (Meters)	Time (Minutes)	Remarks (if any)
	O	□	D	⇨			
Casting laying in foundry store							
Moved to gas cutting machine					8	3	By trolley
Wait, cutting machine being set						5	
Risers cut						20	
Wait for trolley						10	
Move to inspection dept.					6	2	
Inspection before machining						15	By trolley
Moved to machine shop					0	3	

Job – Material casting ready for machining.
Chart begins – Casting lying in foundry.
Chart ends – Casting ready for machining.

these problems. The cause-and-effect diagram shows the interrelations among these different causes with their possible consequences. To obtain better results in a process, it is required to identify the various causes and try to develop results so that corrective measures can be put in place. This is basically a problem-solving tool and it can be applied in various fields, like manufacturing or services. This diagram is able to provide all causes that affect a certain event. This diagram is widely used in product design and to identify all the possible causes/factors that affect the process (Figure 3.2 and Table 3.5).

3.2.6.1   How to Construct a Fishbone Diagram

Step 1: Define the problem statement, also known as the effect of a process.

Step 2: Conduct a brainstorming session to identify all the possible causes of a problem. The focus here is people, machines, materials, inspection and testing, maintenance, safety, services, or the after-sales service.

Step 3: Try to categorise all the possible causes.

Step 4: Again, try to identify all the sub-causes of the main cause by using the question 'Why?' and developing a high level of understanding of all causes.

Step 5: Draw the causes and all possible sub-causes in a diagram.

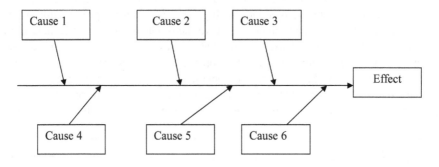

FIGURE 3.2   General layout of cause-and-effect diagram.

TABLE 3.5

The Important Possible Causes That Affect the Process

S. NO.	Manufacturing Sector	Service Sector
1	Machines	Product=Service ■ Price
2	Method	Place
3	Material	People Skills
4	Manpower	Productivity
5	Inspection and Testing	Quality
6	Money – power	Surroundings
7	Maintenance	Systems
8	Environment	Suppliers
9	Management support	Top Management Commitment

3.2.7 RUN CHART

A run chart is one basic tool of quality control. A run chart is a simple and useful process improvement tool. A process can be defined as a sequence of operations that transforms input into output, and to change from input to output requires some time called 'processing time,' or the actual operation time. If a change happens in a process during its operation, its output affected. A run chart is used to understand the effect of this change in a process. It does not require huge calculations; it simply plots the observed value on the vertical axis. With respect to what quantities this change affects, this is plotted on the horizontal axis. It is a graphical tool to capture the important process variables in a definite interval of time. These charts are used to identify the trends, patterns, and cycles of the process during a certain period of time. They are used to supervise significant process variables over a period of time. These charts show the quality and workload of a process. In this chart, on the horizontal axis are independent variables like time and duration, and on vertical axis, the required parameter is used. It is most suitable for the analysis of trends of the product or process. It is used to observe the changes in the process. It is drawn during a shift in a production plant to check the performance of the plant over a period of time. The difference between a run chart and a control chart is that a run chart does not show the control limits, while this is necessary in a control chart. It can easily observe the causes of variation in a process. In general, the patterns observed in a process are as follows:

    a. Ideal pattern or state of the product.
    b. Threshold pattern or state of the product.
    c. Brink of chaos pattern or state of the product.
    d. State of chaos pattern or state of the product.

If a process operates during an ideal state, it shows stability and target performance over a period of time. This type of process produces the output that will be as per the customer's requirement. In the threshold state of the product, the process did not consistently fulfil the customer's expectation, but still the process is in a predictable state. The occurrence of a chaos state shows the pattern just opposite to the threshold state, as it is unpredictable, but still able to fulfil the customer's expectations. In the fourth state of pattern, the process is unpredictable as well as not performing as per the customer's requirement.

3.3 CONTROL CHART

A control chart is one of the powerful techniques of quality control that is used to examine the behaviour of the process. It is a statistical process control technique. It identifies the stability of the process to see whether the process is under control or not. A control chart consists of three horizontal lines known as the centre line, the upper control limit line, known as UCL, and the lower control limit line, known as LCL. The control chart is a graph that represents the nature of the process during a certain interval of time.

By using previous or historical data, the central tendency and dispersal or range of the process is determined and if the process lies within these limits, known as control limits, only then is the process said to be under control, otherwise some corrective measures are required. It is impossible to make identical products in a process. There must be some variation in the final output of the process. These process variations are due to chance causes, also known as random causes and assignable causes. Process variations due to chance causes are minor factors such as air friction and atmospheric temperature variation that will affect the process. It is very difficult to remove the chance causes in a process and due to this, the specifications/dimensions of the product vary. Process variation due to assignable causes are due to major factors that can be controlled, like the quality of the raw material, the skills of the labourer, and the use of good quality manufacturing processes or tools. The objective of drawing the control chart is to check if the process is under control or not, and if it is not, then to take the fundamental corrective measures and make them as per the customer's requirement. The control chart is used to identify if a process is under control or not, and if the process is out of control, to find the solution immediately and bring the process back under control. Its ultimate objective is to ensure the quality of the process. It also gives the process variation that has been very helpful in setting the tolerance limits.

3.3.1   CLASSIFICATION OF CONTROL CHARTS

Control charts can be classified as follows:

3.3.1.1   Variables Control Charts

These are the characteristics of product that can be measured that are called variables. These variables are length of shaft, diameter, temperature, height, voltage, etc. The variable charts are drawn by X bar and R chart. An X bar and R Control Chart is one that shows both the mean value (X), and the range (R). The X bar portion of the chart mainly shows any changes in the mean value of the process, while the R portion shows any changes in the dispersion of the process. This chart is particularly useful, in that it shows changes in mean value and dispersion of the process at the same time, making it a very effective method for checking abnormalities within the process; and if charted while in progress, also points out a problem in the production flow in real-time mode.

3.3.1.1.1   Steps to Plot X and R Chart

The size of the sample is represented by the letter 'n,' and the number of subgroups is represented by the letter 'N.'

Step 1 – Find the mean value (X bar). Use the following formula for each subgroup:

$$\overline{X} = \frac{X_1 + X_2 + X_3 + X_4 + X_5}{n}$$

Step 2 – Find the range:

$$R = X(\text{maximum value}) - X(\text{minimum value})$$

Step 3 – Find the overall mean, or $\overline{\overline{X}}$.

$$\overline{\overline{X}} = \frac{\Sigma X}{N}$$

Step 4 – Compute the average value of the range $(\overline{R})$.

$$\overline{R} = \frac{\Sigma R}{N}$$

Step 5 – Compute the Control Limit Lines.

$\overline{X}$ Control Chart:

Central Limit (CL) = $\overline{\overline{X}}$

Upper Control Limit (UCL) = $\overline{\overline{X}} + 3\sigma / \sqrt{n}$

As we know that $\overline{R} = \sigma d_2$ therefore, $\sigma = \overline{R} / d_2$

Upper Control Limit (UCL) = $\overline{\overline{X}} + 3\overline{R} / (d_2 \sqrt{n})$

Upper Control Limit (UCL) = $\overline{\overline{X}} + A2 * \overline{R}$

Lower Control Limit (UCL) = $\overline{\overline{X}} - 3\sigma / \sqrt{n}$

Again, we know that $\overline{R} = \sigma d_2$ therefore, $\sigma = \overline{R} / d_2$

Lower Control Limit (LCL) = $\overline{\overline{X}} - 3\overline{R} / (d_2 \sqrt{n})$

Lower Control Limit (LCL) = $\overline{\overline{X}} - A2 * \overline{R}$

Where $A_2 = 3/ (d_2\sqrt{n})$ and d_2 and A_2 are the constant factor whose values depend upon the sample size n.

R Control Chart:

Central Line (CL) = $\overline{R} = \sigma d_2$

Upper Control Limit (UCL) = $\sigma d_2 + 3\ \sigma d_3$

Upper Control Limit (UCL) = $\overline{R} + 3\ \sigma d_3$

Upper Control Limit (UCL) = $\overline{R}\ (1 + 3\ (d_3/ d_2))$

Upper Control Limit (UCL) = $D4 * \overline{R}$

Lower Control Limit (UCL) = $\sigma d_2 - 3\ \sigma d_3$

Lower Control Limit (UCL) = $\overline{R} - 3\ \sigma d_3$

Lower Control Limit (UCL) = $\overline{R}\ (1 - 3\ (d_3/ d_2))$

Lower Control Limit (LCL) = $D3 * \overline{R}$

Step 6 – Draw in the Control lines CL, UCL, and LCL, and label them with their appropriate numerical values.

Step 7 – Plot the X bar and R values as for each subgroup. Mark any points that lie outside the control limit lines.

3.3.1.1.2 *Examples on Variable Control Chart*

(1) The following data gives reading for 10 samples, size 8 each in the productions of a certain components. Draw the control chart for the mean and range and point out which sample is out of range. **Table 3.6:**

TABLE 3.6

Data for 10 Samples

Samples	1	2	3	4	5	6	7	8	9	10
Mean	5.4	5.1	5.4	4.9	5.2	4.7	5.1	5.0	5.0	5.2
Range	0.4	0.7	0.7	0.8	0.9	0.6	0.5	0.6	0.7	0.6

For n = 8, d_2 = 2.847, D3 = 0.136, D4 = 1.864

Solution:

$\overline{X}$ **Chart:**

$\overline{\overline{X}} = \overline{X} / n = (5.4 + 5.1 + 5.4 + 4.9 + 5.2 + 4.7 + 5.1 + 5.0 + 5.0 + 5.2)/10 = 5.1$

$\overline{R} = (0.4+0.7+0.7+0.8+0.9+0.6+0.5+0.6+0.7+0.6)/10 = 0.65$

Since, we know that $\overline{R} = \sigma d_2$ therefore, $\sigma = \overline{R} / d_2 = 0.65 / 2.847 = 0.2283$

Central Limit CL = $\overline{X}$ = 5.1

Upper Control Limit (UCL) = $\overline{X} + 3\sigma / \sqrt{n}$

$\qquad\qquad = 5.1 + (3* 0.2283/\sqrt{8}) = 5.342$

Lower Control Limit (LCL) = $\overline{X} - 3\sigma / \sqrt{n}$

$\qquad\qquad = 5.1 - (3* 0.2283/\sqrt{8}) = 4.857$ (Figure 3.3)

Since in $\overline{X}$ bar chart, sample no. 1 and sample no. 3 cross the upper control limit due to some assignable cause, the process is out of control.

R Control Chart:

Central Line (CL) = $\overline{R}$ = σd_2 = 0.65

Upper Control Limit (UCL) = $\sigma d_2 + 3 \sigma d_3 = D_4 * \overline{R}$ = 1.864*0.65 = 1.2116

Lower Control Limit (UCL) = $\sigma d_2 - 3 \sigma d_3 = D3 * \overline{R}$ = 0.136*0.65 = 0.884
(Figure 3.4).

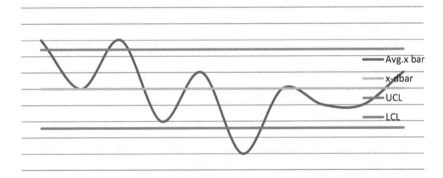

FIGURE 3.3 $\overline{X}$ bar chart.

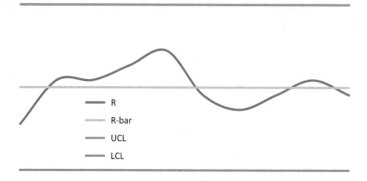

FIGURE 3.4 R chart.

As all the samples in range chart are within the control limits, so the process is under control.

3.3.2 Attributes Control Charts

Attributes control charts are those control charts in which the quality characteristics of the product cannot be measured quantitatively. They are a discrete type. These are the special types of quality control charts which deals with attribute quality characteristics. These quality characteristics are like the number of defects which are intangible in nature and countable but cannot be measured continuously (Figure 3.5).

3.3.2.1 Control Charts for Number of Defects per Unit (C Chart)

These charts are called the 'Counts of Defects.' These charts are used where there is no idea about sample size. C charts are made for a condition where we can compute only the number of defects, but it is very difficult to compute the proportion that is defective. These types of charts are used for the number of defects per piece or unit. It is the control chart in which the number of defects in a piece or sample is plotted. A defective piece may contain more than one defect, for example, a casting may have blowholes and surface cracks. It controls the number of defects observed per unit or per sample (sample size is constant) and is used for number of defects per sample. C charts are always used when the sample size is constant. Some other conditions where we look for C charts are customer complaints for mosquitoes in a room. Due

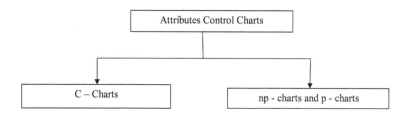

FIGURE 3.5 Classification of attribute control charts.

to randomness, C charts always follows Poisson distribution, and we know that in C charts, variance is equal to the mean of the sample.

Therefore,

Variance $= \sigma^2 = $ mean $= \bar{c}$ or $\sigma = \sqrt{\bar{c}}$
Central Tendency (CT) $= \bar{c} = (\sum c) / $ (Number of Samples)
Upper Control Limits UCL $= \bar{c} + 3\sqrt{\bar{c}}$
Lower Control Limits LCL $= \bar{c} - 3\sqrt{\bar{c}}$

3.3.2.1.1 Examples of C Charts

10 samples (constant sample size) of a product were inspected in during a surprise visit of supervisors. The results of the inspection are given below (Table 3.7).

Draw C chart and state your conclusion.

Solution:

Central Tendency (CT) $= \bar{c} = (\sum c) / $ (Number of Samples) $= 75/10 = 7.5$
Upper Control Limits UCL $= \bar{c} + 3\sqrt{\bar{c}} = 7.5 + 3\sqrt{7.5} = 15.7$
Lower Control Limits LCL $= \bar{c} - 3\sqrt{\bar{c}} = 7.5 - 3\sqrt{7.5} = -0.7 = 0$ (Figure 3.6).
Since all the samples lay within the spread, the process is under control.

3.3.1.3.2 Np Charts

These are used for those attribute quality control charts which deal with a number of defects in percentages. An np chart is easy to draw, as the number of defective per

TABLE 3.7
Data for 10 Samples

Sample No.	1	2	3	4	5	6	7	8	9	10
Number of Defects	7	6	6	7	4	7	8	12	9	9

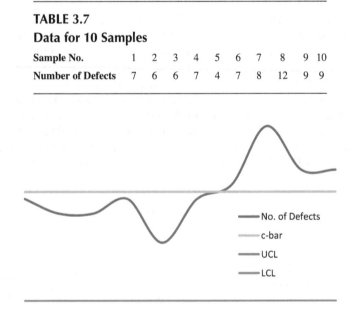

— No. of Defects
--- c-bar
— UCL
— LCL

FIGURE 3.6 C chart.

unit can be directly obtained from the inspection report. If the sample size varies, then we will use p charts.

Central Tendency (CT) = n $\bar{p}$ = ($\sum$ np) / (Number of Samples)
Upper Control Limits UCL = $n\,\bar{p} + 3\sqrt{n\bar{p}}\ (1-\bar{p})$
Lower Control Limits LCL = $n\,\bar{p} + 3\sqrt{n\bar{p}}\ (1-\bar{p})$
$\bar{p}$ = (1 / sample size)

3.3.1.3.2.1 Example of Np Chart

(1) A manufacturer finds from his experience that on average one out of ten items that are produced by a machine are defective on a particular day. The manufacturer selects a lot of 100 items randomly and finds that 16 of them are defective. Is the process under control?

Solution:

P = 1/10 = 0.1
Central limit CL = n $\bar{p}$ = 0.1 * 100 = 10
Upper Control Limits UCL = $n\,\bar{p} + 3\sqrt{n\bar{p}}\ (1-\bar{p})$
$\qquad\qquad = (100* 0.1) + 3\ \sqrt{(0.1 * 0.9 * 100)} = 19$
Lower Control Limits LCL = $n\,\bar{p} - 3\sqrt{n\bar{p}}\ (1-\bar{p})$
$\qquad\qquad = (100* 0.1) - 3\ \sqrt{(0.1 * 0.9 * 100)} = 1$

Since the number of defectives given in the problem, that is, 16, lies between the upper control limit and the lower control limit, that is, 1 and 19, that means 1<16>19. Therefore, the process is under control.

3.3.1.2.3 P Charts

These are called the control charts for the fraction of defective or population defected items. P charts are used when the products produced on the shop floor are inspected and can be classified as good or bad, accepted or rejected. It is used for the fraction of defective total products. P charts are used when both the total sample size and number of defects can be computed, but the sample size is variable.

The fraction defective (P) is defined as the ratio of the number of defectives produced (d) in a sample divided by the total number of products (n) in that sample.

$$P = \frac{d}{n} = \frac{\text{Number of defective produced in a sample}}{\text{Total number of products in a sample}}$$

Average Sample Population defective,

$$\bar{p} = \left(p_1 + p_2 + \text{--------} - p_N\right)/N$$

Average Sample Size, $\bar{n} = \left(n_1 + n_2 + \text{---------} - n_N\right)/N$
Central Limit (CL) = $\bar{p}$

Upper Control Limit, UCL $= \bar{p} + 3\sqrt{\bar{p}(1-\bar{p})/n}$

Upper Control Limit, LCL $= \bar{p} - 3\sqrt{\bar{p}(1-\bar{p})/n}$

Where $\sqrt{\bar{p}(1-\bar{p})/n} = \sigma\bar{p}$ is the standard deviation of the average proportion defective and it follows binomial distribution.

3.3.1.2.3.1 Example of P Chart 10 samples each of size 50 of a pipe were inspected in a pressure testing. The results of the inspection are given below (Table 3.8).

Draw a p chart and state your conclusion.

Solution:

Sample No.	Number of Defectives	p = fraction Defective = (number of defective/ Sample Size)
1	2	2/50 = 0.04
2	3	3/50 = 0.06
3	2	2/50 = 0.04
4	0	0/50 = 0
5	2	2/50 = 0.04
6	3	3/50 = 0.06
7	2	2/50 = 0.04
8	1	1/50 = 0.02
9	2	2/50 = 0.04
10	3	3/50 = 0.06

$$\bar{p} = \Sigma p / n = 0.40 / 10 = 0.040$$

$\sigma\bar{p}$ is the standard deviation $= \sqrt{\bar{p}(1-\bar{p})/n} = = \sqrt{((0.040(1-0.040)/50))} = 0.0277$

Central Limit CL $= \bar{p} = 0.040$

Upper Control Limit (UCL) $= \bar{p} + 3\sigma = 0.040 + 3\ 0.0277 = 0.1231$

Lower Control Limit (LCL) $= \bar{p} + 3\sigma = 0.040 - 3\ 0.0277 = -0.0431 = 0$

(Figure 3.7).

Since all the points are within the control limits, the process is under control.

TABLE 3.8

P Chart Data

Sample No.	1	2	3	4	5	6	7	8	9	10
Number of Defectives	2	3	2	0	2	3	2	1	2	3

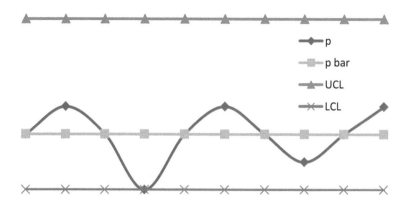

FIGURE 3.7   P chart.

3.4   PROCESS CAPABILITY

Process capability is used to compare the output of an in-control process to the targeted limits by using capability indices. The comparison is possible by forming the ratio of the specification 'width' to the spread of the process values. The process capability is defined as the capability of a process to constantly make a product that meets a customer-specified requirement tolerance.

The main purpose of process management is to avoid defects and to bring consistency to the manufacturing process. To reduce inconsistencies, it needs to create a relationship between the process variable and product specification. If a product meets the specification limits and the process is under control, the corrective actions may be initiated to compute and try to reduce the process variability to obtain productive results. Process capability analysis is used to know the process variability. Process capability is the inherent variation of the product in a process. It provides the prediction of the process sufficiency and shows the consistency of the process. It is a measurement with respect to the accuracy of a process. Capability information helps designers to set reasonable specification limits and plan the sequence of a process; it also helps designers to select good suppliers and hence reduces the chances of variability in a process.

$$\text{Process capability ratio (pcr)} = Cp = (USL - LSL)/6M$$

Where
    USL = upper specification limit.
    LSL = lower specification limit.
    M = process standard deviation (Figure 3.8).

It has been observed that approximately 99.7% of the data from a normal distribution is contained between $\pm 3\sigma$.

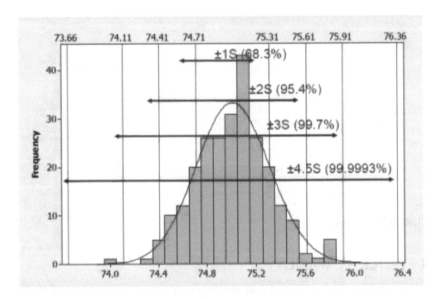

FIGURE 3.8   Process capability of a manufacturing process.

3.5   FAILURE MODE AND EFFECTS ANALYSIS (FMEA)

There are several product recalls in a plant because of faulty design, inferior quality of raw material used, substandard processes or technology used, or due to quality issues. All these products put a question mark on the reputation of company and show the inability of the company to make good quality products. Failure mode and effect analysis is a scientific methodology, and its prime objective is to identify all the possible causes of failure of a product from the very first stage, that is, the design or manufacturing process itself. Nowadays, it is known as one of best reliability improvement techniques.

Failure mode and effect analysis is also known as Failure Modes, Effects, and Criticality Analysis (FMECA). It originated in the year 1940. It is a systematic approach of identification of all probable failures during the product development process, starting from design through to services after sale. Failure modes are all the different methods by which a system can fail. Effects are errors or threats, defects that directly or indirectly affect the customer's expectation. Effect analysis means analysing the results of all those failures. Failures are grouped as per the seriousness of their consequences and how regularly they occur in a process. The objective of FMEA analysis is to take corrective actions to eliminate or reduce such failures. FMEA is not an alternative for high-quality engineering. It is the addition of superior engineering by applying the knowledge and understanding of a team (CFT) to evaluate the design progress of a product or process by analysing its threat of failure. Failure mode and effect analysis can be mainly classified in the following ways:

1. Design Failure Mode and Effect Analysis.
2. Process Failure Mode and Effect Analysis.

3.5.1 Design Failure Mode and Effect Analysis

Design FMEA (DFMEA) covers the possibility of product failure and a decrease in its useful life. These are due to the following reasons:

- Quality and properties of raw materials, components, and subcomponents.
- Geometry/design and shape of the product.
- Limits and tolerances given in the product.
- Alignment with other components/subcomponents, assembly, systems, or subsystems.
- Environmental causes.

3.5.2 Process Failure Mode and Effect Analysis

Process Failure Mode and Effect Analysis identifies all those causes of failure that impacts the quality of the product and reliability of the product's safety, and decrease the customer's satisfaction level. These are due to following reasons:

- Skills and experience of operators/supervisor.
- Manufacturing processes followed while processing.
- Quality of raw materials used.
- Quality of machineries used to process the material.
- Inspection and testing procedures.
- The effect of environmental factors that affect the performance of the process.

FMEA used for continuous improvement in a process. It is a document which has the description of all the possibility of failures of a system. In the early days it was used in the design process to prevent the different modes of failures, but now it is extended to all the processes from design to inspection and to the testing processes. It is also used after the quality function deployment process where the voice of the customer has become part of the attributes or characteristics of the product. Due to competition in the market and advances of technology, it is sometimes required to modify the existing product or services as per the changes in customers' requirements, and then FMEA is required accordingly. This tool is used continuously for the whole span of the product or services to reduce the chances of its failure.

3.5.3 Need to Perform Failure Mode and Effect Analysis

If a product fails after its launch or in the later stages of the product development process, it causes a huge loss in terms of the company's customer retention policy and reputation, and therefore it is better to find out the problem with a process during its early stages of life. FMEA is a technique to identify the failure of the product during the starting point of the product development process and hence provides the following possible advantages:

1. Finding the problem during early stage of its development process allows a lot of alternatives to reduce its adverse effects.

2. It allows higher potential for confirmation and justification of changes.
3. It can provide the solution for the problem with a lower cost.
4. It can eliminate or reduce waste or defects.
5. It can avoid the horrible consequences of reduced performance.

3.5.4 The Right Time to Perform Failure Mode and Effects Analysis (FMEA)

There are numerous times during the product development process when it is better to perform FMEA. It is good to apply FMEA during the planning phase, at the time of designing the product, and also at the time of selecting the quality raw material and adoption/selection of manufacturing process. It is also the right time to apply FMEA when it is required or desired to increase the quality-related issues of the product. It can also be used to increase the reliability of the product by relatively reducing the chances of product failure. In addition, it is possible to execute an FMEA infrequently all through the life-span of a process. Quality-related aspects and the reliability of the product must be constantly examined so that it will be a superior product with the most favourable results.

3.5.5 Advantages of FMEA

FMEA offers several advantages by identifying problems/errors very near to the beginning stages of design, production, or during the process. Some advantages of FMEA are as follows:

1. Better, more consistent, and reliable products.
2. Increased level of customer satisfaction.
3. Improved reputation of the product in the market.
4. Reduction in breakdown maintenance cost.
5. Reducing the cost of poor quality products.

3.6 QUALITY FUNCTION DEPLOYMENT

Quality Function Deployment (QFD) is the process of allocating or assigning the quality-related responsibility to the entire relevant department from design to service. In other words, QFD is the technique of allocating the specific responsibility of specific departments. It is the process of sharing the quality responsibility with all the department right from design, production inspection, quality, and after-sales service in any organisation. The QFD process can be applied in all organisations, whether that is a manufacturing industry or a service industry.

3.6.1 Mechanism of Quality Function Deployment

The basic mechanism of quality function deployment is to convert the customer requirements that arise from the voice of customer to a technical requirement via

QFD. The voice of customer arises from surveys, research, or analysis. QFD converts customer requirements into the product's attributes (Figure 3.9).

3.6.2   PHASES OF QUALITY FUNCTION DEPLOYMENT

Quality function deployment is a four-phase process which is the sequence of operation during the development of product as per the customer's expectation. The phases of quality function deployment are as follows:

3.6.2.1   Product Definition

Product definition is the first phase of quality function deployment. It starts with the voice of the customer and finishes with the product specifications. It also provides a comparative analysis of the rival company's product. This step is prerequisite of the initial design phase of the product.

3.6.2.2   Product Development

Product development is the second phase of the QFD process. The objective of this phase is to identify the critical components, assembly, or subsystem and then determine the critical product attributes. Its functional specifications are also required to be defined during this stage.

3.6.2.3   Process Development

The objective of this phase is the identification of critical process characteristics and development of the process flow. All the assemblies and subsystems must be designed as per the given specifications.

3.6.2.4   Process Quality Control

The last, but very important step is to ensure the quality of the product by performing the appropriate inspections or any quality control techniques. This step guarantees the success of the product after its launch.

3.7   HOUSE OF QUALITY

House of quality is a systematic approach which shows the interrelationship between the voice of the customer and the product characteristics. It is a planning matrix that represents how the voice of the customer has been translated into the product specification so that it is able to meet the customer's requirements.

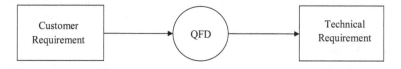

FIGURE 3.9   Mechanism of quality function deployment.

3.7.1 Procedure to Develop 'House of Quality'

Step 1: To Identify the 'Voice of the Customer'

The very first step is to identify correct the market segment and the targeted customers. The QFD team then collects the information about the product and what are the features that the customers are looking for in the product. This is not an easy task, therefore, the team uses various practices of management to carefully collect the customers' requirements. These requirements will have been noted carefully, as if they are not understood correctly, then the whole process will generate defects, and that will cause a huge loss for the organisation.

Step 2: Regulatory Requirements

It has been observed that sometimes customers are also unable to give all their expected characteristics for the product, so it is up to the QFD team to provide all the documents that will contain all the regulatory standards of the product.

Step 3: Rating of Customer Importance

After collecting all the requirements of the customer, the next step is to give the importance of the requirements on a scale that may be from 1 to 5. This exercise will be helpful at the time of making the relationship matrix.

Step 4: Customer Rating of the Competition

The objective of this step of the house of quality is to understand the customer's knowledge about the competing product. In doing so, there will be the possibility of restructuring of the house of quality and it can further add objectives for continuous improvement of the product, and identification of sales opportunities for the product.

Step 5: Voice of the Engineer

After understanding the voice of the customer, the next step is to identify the technical descriptors. These are those attributes of the product that can be measured and standardised as per the market/competition. This will generate the product specification as per the customer's requirement.

Step 6: Track of Development

After knowing the technical descriptor of the product, the next step is to add a track for the improvement of each descriptor of the product if possible. This step will ensure that customer's need has been understand clearly and the product is able to fulfil the customer's expectation in a better way.

Step 7: Relationship Matrix

The next step is to prepare the matrix that represents the correlation between the customer's expectation and organisation's ability to fulfil those expectations. The QFD team tries to find the relationship between the voice of the engineers (also known as technical descriptors) and customer's wants on a scale from 1 to 9. These relationships can be weak, average, or strong and can be converted into quantitative terms.

Step 8: Managerial Complexity

After preparing the relationship matrix, the next step is to synchronise the customer's wants and organisational capability. It is possible that some characteristics of the product are not a match with the company's ability.

Step 9: Analysis of Competitor Products Technically

The next step is to understand the rival company's product's technical descriptors so that the original product descriptors will be better match with customer's requirements. This process requires the reverse engineering of the rival company's product.

Step 10: Target Values for Technical Descriptors

At this stage, the team is trying to establish the standard target values for every technical descriptor. This is very important to analyse to what level of its own standard values the product is strong enough to meet customer's wants.

Step 11: Formation of the Correlation Matrix

The next step is the formation of a correlation matrix which shows how different technical descriptors affect each other. The objective is to determine which descriptor shows a strong negative effect. The QFD team members should have a close look at these descriptors and try to eliminate these physical conflicts.

Step 12: Determination of the Absolute Importance of Each Technical Descriptor

The last step is the determination of the absolute importance of each technical descriptor. This can be calculated with the help of the customer's importance rating. In doing so, the preference of each technical descriptor can be easily understood. This will help the product development team a lot, and the customer's requirement can be fulfilled in a much better way.

In short, it can be concluded that the prime objective of the house of quality is to determine whether the customer's wants are being properly converted into the suitable technical requirements or not. In doing so, the performance of the product can also be improved in the future.

The QFD process has been illustrated in Figure 3.9. In Figure 3.10, the input has been shown as a flow chart from design stage to inspection and testing stage, and it converts into the output. As per the feedback from the customer, which has been collected from various other means, the customer's requirement has been converted into a Technical Requirement (TR) through the process known as quality responsibility.

These will actually become the product characteristics and it is the prime responsibility of each and every individual department to make suitable changes to achieve these product characteristics. If there is any problem in the design of the product, for example, then the design department will take corrective action and sort out the problem and make their product suitable as per the customer's expectation. Similarly, if any requirement arises in the production process and the quality department, then they must ensure they respond quickly and satisfy the customer's requirement. QFD is practically applicable in various fields of manufacturing and services such as consumers' daily routine products and services.

3.8 CONCLUSION

In today's competitive scenario, every organisation wants to provide high-quality products at reasonable cost. Therefore, quality is the prime concern of all types of industries, whether they are manufacturing or service industries. By focusing on

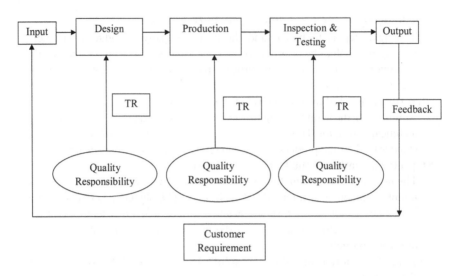

FIGURE 3.10 Quality function deployment in a manufacturing process.

different quality management practices, the industries ensure that the customers' expectations can be fulfilled in better ways, and remain competitive in the market by focusing on continuous improvement in all departments of the organisation. The managers in the organisation agree that poor quality products result in loss of market share and consumer belief in the product. This ultimately results in heavy loss to the organisation. It is essential to implement all the quality-related tools within the production process in a manufacturing organisation. All the above-mentioned practices are used in the organisation to reduce the problems associated with the products and services. Therefore, it can be stated that the characteristics of the product have been largely improved by the application of quality management practices and these practices of management are also helpful to enhance the productivity of the organisation. It is also essential for top management to start educating their team to use these quality management practices because these practices are used in every sphere of the organisation. Different programmes related to quality management practices have to be organised by the management to ensure the achievement of the best practices of quality management, and this will reduce the chances of failure of the product, as well as minimising the cost of poor quality. This allows organisations to deliver quality goods at minimum cost.

3.9   CASE STUDY: APPLICATION OF QUALITY MANAGEMENT PRACTICES TO IMPROVE QUALITY IN A CEILING FAN MANUFACTURING COMPANY

XYZ is a manufacturing company which manufactures different types of ceiling fan. The company's turnover is Rs.2700 million, with an export component of 20%. In the manufacturing plant, the following four types of defects has been observed:

1) Upper and lower ribbon size variation.
2) Varying length of down rod of fan.
3) Canopy size variation.
4) Oversized ribbon.
5) Inaccuracy in size of blade flange.

Now, the objective is to eliminate all these troubles and to ensure a defect-free manufacturing process. To achieve this objective, the management has decided to implement quality practices. Top management has decided on the following general layout of quality management practices to improve the quality of the product and fulfil the customer's expectations. These techniques are helpful in identifying the problems associated with the product and providing the solution in order to correct them.

3.9.1 FLOW CHART

The flow chart is one of those techniques of quality management that is used to study the whole process, and to identify the various problems in the process. It systematically analyses the whole process. The flow chart covers the whole process from the arrival of the raw material to the completion of the end product, and after conducting the study it has been concluded that all the problems have occurred in the manufacturing section. Therefore, it has been decided that that all the other techniques will be implemented one by one (Figure 3.11)

3.9.2 CHECK SHEET

The check sheet is the tool that is used to collect and record real-time data and provide the occurrence of the data during a specific period of time. This collected data is the prerequisite for the Pareto chart and histogram. Data has been collected through the check sheet for a period of 15 days and results are as given in Table 3.9.

3.9.3 PARETO CHART

The Pareto chart shows that 80% of the problems in a process are due to only 20% of the reasons. The data in Pareto chart is arranged in decreasing order of their severity (Figure 3.12).

After preparing the Pareto chart, it can be concluded that two major problems in the process are the 'Upper and lower ribbon size variation' and 'Varying length of down rod of fan.' These two problems contribute 80% of the defects in the process. Therefore, if we are able to sort out these problems, the majority of defects can be avoided.

3.9.4 HISTOGRAM

A histogram as shown below shows the size variation of ribbon. The following observation has been made for preparing the histogram (Table 3.10) Figure 3.13.

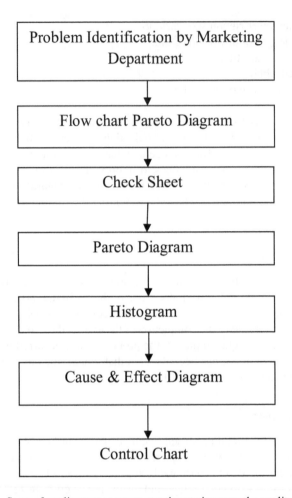

FIGURE 3.11 Steps of quality management practices to improve the quality of ceiling fans.

3.9.5 CAUSE-AND-EFFECT DIAGRAM

By constructing the cause-and-effect diagram of two major issues, it has been concluded that various causes are related to people, machines, and improper use of methods to perform the operation (Figure 3.14).

The various identified causes are as follows:

1) Lack of skills of labourer/operator.
2) Less motivation for employees.
3) Poor storage conditions.
4) Poor quality control and inspection techniques.
5) Problem in machine components, like leakage and problems in the compressor.
6) Delay in the moulding process.

TABLE 3.9
Data Collected from the Case Study Company

S.N.	Defects	Total produced items	Rejected items	Percentage rejected items	Cum. Items	Percentage cumulative items
1	Upper and lower ribbon size variation (ULRV)	1200	355	53.5%	355	53.5
2	Varying length of down rod of fan (VLDR)		118	17.8%	473	71.30
3	Canopy size variation (CSV)		82	12.42%	555	83.72
4	Oversize of ribbon (OR)		91	13.75%	646	97.47
5	Inaccuracy in size of blade flange (ISBF)		16	2.53%	662	100
	Total	1200	662	100%	662	100

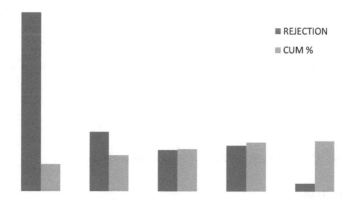

FIGURE 3.12   Pareto chart of case study company.

TABLE 3.10
The Size Variation of Ribbon

S.N.	Cell boundaries (in cm)		Frequency
1	16	16.5	4
2	16.5	17	3
3	17	17.5	2
4	17.5	18	0
5	18	18.5	7

After the identification of the main defects and the root causes, the top management decided to remove the defects from the process by taking some corrective measures, like conducting various training programmes. Now, to check if the process is under control or not, the control chart has been developed to know the spread and mean of the process, and to check the stability of the process.

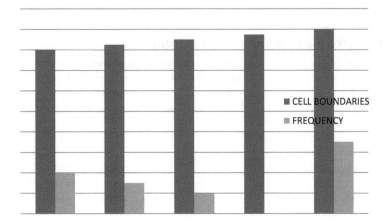

FIGURE 3.13 Histogram of case study company.

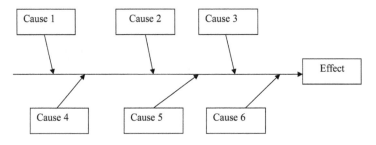

FIGURE 3.14 Cause-and-effect diagram of case study company.

3.9.6 CONTROL CHART

The following dataset (Table 3.11) has been gathered to prepare the control chart (Figures 3.15 and 3.16).

Range Chart

TABLE 3.11
Individual Measurement Data

Sample No.	Individual Measurement					
	1	2	3	4	5	6
1	15	0.25	0.35	0.46	0.65	0.52
2	28	0.82	0.55	0.44	0.35	0.67
3	88	0.88	0.66	0.24	0.84	0.53
4	0.47	21	0.29	0.88	0.35	0.54
5	0.18	0.43	0.67	0.28	0.44	0.44
6	0.66	0.58	0.22	0.68	0.54	0.56

Note: $\overline{X}$ chart

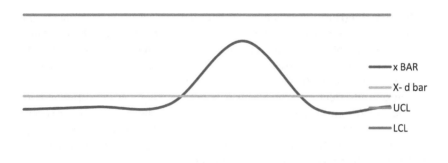

FIGURE 3.15   X̄ chart of case study company.

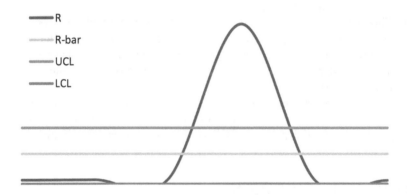

FIGURE 3.16   R chart of case study company.

3.9.7   CONCLUSION OF THE CASE STUDY

From the above case study, it can be concluded that the use of management practices is essential for identification and removal of defects in the manufacturing process. These practices can be applied at any stage for defect-free production and they
ensure a high-quality product which can fulfil the customer's requirement.

POINTS TO REMEMBER

- **Check sheet:** The check sheet is the data recording sheet used to collect
  data in a systematic manner for recording and analysing the situation during a real-time scenario. It is used to record and interpret collected data.
- **Histogram:** A histogram is a combination of vertical bars which shows the
  frequency distribution.
- **Pareto diagram:** This is a graph that shows the different possible problems
  occurring in a process in descending order of their frequently occurrence.
  It helps management to decide the priorities and to set the target of which
  task should be focused on first. This chart shows the information in an
  organised and systematic manner.

- **Scatter diagram:** This is a graph between two variables to identify the relationship between them. On the horizontal axis, there will be the independent variable and on the vertical axis, the dependent variable is used. It is a prerequisite of the trend analysis which can be further used to analyse and plan the production of the component in the future.
- **Cause-and-effect diagram:** This is a tool that identifies the different reasons for problems in a process and their possible consequences. The reasons are people, machines, material, money, or method-related, but it ultimately is a loss for the industry as it is unable to fulfil the customer's expectations.
- **Control chart:** The control chart shows the real performance of the product and compares the desired limits with the customer's requirements. It shows the process variation of a product and ensures that the process is under control and if at any period of time it is not under control, then corrective measures are taken.
- **Flow chart**: This is a chart that shows the sequence of the process to develop the product. This is essential for planning the material and manufacturing resources for developing the product. It also shows what resources are required at what time, and in what quantity to produce a product within a specific period of time.
- **Quality function deployment:** This is the systematic approach to assign the quality-related responsibilities to all the employees in the organisation in their respected departments. QFD converts customers' requirements into technical requirements.

SELF-ASSESSMENT QUESTIONS

1. What are the various approaches to control and management of quality in a manufacturing firm?
2. What do you mean by check sheet? Write down the various steps involved in making a check sheet in the automobile industry.
3. Describe the importance of a histogram. Also mention its advantages.
4. What is a Pareto diagram used for in decision-making? Enumerate its advantages and limitations.
5. What do you mean by a scatter diagram? Discuss in detail its importance.
6. What do you understand by a process flow chart? List various steps to draw the process flow diagram of any manufacturing firm.
7. What is the use of a cause-and-effect diagram? How it is helpful for managers?
8. What do you mean by control chart? State its importance.
9. Classify the control chart.
10. Write down the various steps involved in drawing the control chart of a variable.
11. Differentiate the use of a p chart and an np chart.
12. Write a short note on process capability.
13. What is the importance of failure mode and effect analysis?

14. What is the need to perform the failure mode and effect analysis? Also mention its key advantages.

15. With the help of an example, explain quality function deployment.

16. A certain quality of characteristics is measured and the $\bar{X}$ and R values are computed for each subgroup. After 20 groups, $\sum \bar{X} = 347.5$ and $\sum = 8.5$. Compute control chart limits. All point in both charts fall within these limits. If the specification limits are 14.40 ± 0.40, what conclusions can you draw about the ability of the existing process to produce the products within these specifications? Suggest some of the best possible ways by which the situation can be improved, given that $A_2 = 0.58$, $D_3 = 0$, $D_4 = 2.11$, $d_2 = 2.326$.

BIBLIOGRAPHY

Ahire, S. L. (1997). Total quality management interfaces: An integrative framework. *Management Science, 27*(6), 91–105.

Anderson, S. W. (1995). A framework for assessing cost management system changes: The case of activity-based costing implementation at General Motors, 1986–1993. *Journal of Management Accounting Research, Fall*, 1–51.

Anderson, S. W., & Sedatole, K. (1998). Designing quality into products: The use of accounting data in new product development. *Accounting Horizons, 12*(3), 213–233.

Chong, V. K., & Rundus, M. J. (2004). Total quality management, market competition and organisational performance. *The British Accounting Review, 36*(2), 155–172.

Chowdhury, S. (2005). *The Ice Cream Maker: An Inspiring Tale About Making Quality the Key Ingredient in Everything You Do.* Crown Business. Doubleday, Random House, New York.

Crosby, P. B. (1979). *Quality Is Free: The Art of Making Quality Certain* (Vol. 94). McGraw-Hill, New York.

Crozier, M. L. (1995). QFD: The customer-driven approach to quality planning and development. *Quality Progress, 28*(5), 172.

Cua, K. O., McKone, K. E., & Schroeder, R. G. (2001). Relationships between implementation of TQM, JIT, and TPM and manufacturing performance. *Journal of Operations Management, 19*(6), 675–694.

Damnjanovic, I., & Reinschmidt, K. (2020). Statistical project control. In: *Data Analytics for Engineering and Construction Project Risk Management* (pp. 277–303). Springer, Cham.

Das, S. C. (2019). *Management Control Systems: Principles and Practices.* PHI Learning Pvt. Ltd, India.

Deming, W. E. (1996). *Out of the Crisis.* Center for Advanced Engineering Study, Massachusetts Institute of Technology (MIT) Press, Cambridge.

Domański, P. D. (2020). Does control quality matter? In: *Control Performance Assessment: Theoretical Analyses and Industrial Practice* (pp. 3–25). Springer International Publisher, Springer Nature Switzerland AG.

Drucker, P. (2014). *Innovation and Entrepreneurship.* Routledge, California.

Feigenbaum, A. V. (1956). Total quality control. *Harvard Business Review, 34*(6), 93–101.

Feigenbaum, A. V. (1991). *Total Quality Control,* 3rd ed. McGraw- Hill, New York, 130–131.

GOAL/QPC Research Report No. 90-12-02. (1990). 12B Manor Parkway Salem, New Hampshire.

Hauser, J. R., & Clausing, D. (1988). The house of quality. *Harvard Business Review, May–June*(3), 63–73.

Kaplan, R. S., Cooper, R., Maisel, L., Morrissey, E., & Oehm, R. M. (1992). *Implementing Activity-Based Cost Management: Moving from Analysis to Action*. Institute of Management Accountants, New Jersey.

Kaynak, H. (2003). The relationship between total quality management practices and their effects on firm performance. *Journal of Operations Management, 21*(4), 405–435.

Kim-Soon, N., & Jantan, M. (2010). Quality management practices in Malaysia: Perceived advancement in quality management system and business performance. In: *IEEE ICMIT Conference*, Singapore.

Lau, R. S. M., Zhao, X., & Xiao, M. (2004). Assessing quality and management in China with MBNQA criteria. *The International Journal of Quality & Reliability Management, 21*(7), 699–709.

Lewis, W. G., Pun, K. F., & Lalla, T. R. M. (2006). Exploring soft versus hard factors for TQM implementation in small and medium-sized enterprises. *International Journal of Productivity & Performance Management, 55*(7), 539–554.

Miller, W. J., Duesing, R. J., Lowery, C. M., & Sumner, A. T. (2018). The quality movement from six perspectives. *The TQM Journal, 30*(3), 182–196.

Reilly, N. B. (1999). *The Team Based Product Development Guidebook*. ASQ Quality Press, Milwaukee, WI.

Rosenthal, S. R. (1992). *Effective product design and development: How to cut lead time and increase customer satisfaction*. Business One Irwin, Homewood, IL.

Sullivan, L. P. (1986). Quality function deployment. *Quality Progress (ASQC), 19*, 39–50.

4 Customer Involvement

4.1 CUSTOMER PERCEPTION

The customer can be defined as the person or group availing of services provided by a company at a reasonable cost. The customer can be categorised into two groups: the internal and the external customer. The internal customers are those who inter-link with the organisation, like the marketing department is the internal customer for production department, etc., whereas external customers are those customer who utilise the end-product or services provided by company. Both types of customer are required to sustain long term relationship of the farm. Long-term sustainability of the process depends on customer satisfaction, and customer will be satisfied by the fulfilment of their requirements. In the market, there is a kind of customer with a different perception of quality. According to the TQM philosophy, the customer perception of quality is continuous improvement. This concept emphasises that there is no definite quality level, because the customer's needs and expectations continuously change with time. We can say that if a company wants to satisfy its customers, it needs to change or update according to customer perception. After completing this chapter, the reader will able to understand customer needs and requirements, the customer satisfaction model, the quality of perception, customer feedback, service quality, and customer retention.

4.2 CUSTOMER NEEDS AND REQUIREMENTS

The question arises of what are the customer's needs and requirements? The needs of the customer are considered to be the problems resolved by the purchase of goods or services. According to CEO of Apple Inc., Steve Jobs, 'Get closer than to ever to your customer.' This means the customer should be close to you, so you tell them what they require whether or not they realise it themselves. For successful business, it's important to know about customers, their needs, quality perception, etc. More knowledge of the customer helps in marketing and sales. Customer information is a powerful tool for planning and implementing. For long-term sustainability development of a company, it needs to know about the customers, e.g., 'who is the customer,' 'the needs of the customer,' why they want to buy, etc. Here is some brief information to know about customer, such as:

1. Who is the customer?: A person or group of persons that avail of the services provided by the company at some cost is considered a customer. The company should know who is the customer, the customer's age, their occupation, and gender, and the customer's perception about your company. All these things help to improve performance of the company and helps marketing and sale.

2. Customer occupation: It is important to know the occupation of the customer so that it is easy for production planning, etc. The customer's occupation is an important factor that influences sale. The customer's occupation helps to categorise the customer into different categories on the basis of their budget, because these are the main factors that drive production planning.

3. Why they want to buy product: If you know the reason for their need of the product, you can easily fulfil the customer's requirements. That is helpful to business growth.

4. When they want to purchase: If the company forecasts when the customer will want to purchase, it helps with scheduling of production. The production schedule can reduce the inventory cost and it's helpful for just-in-time (JIT).

5. Method of purchase: Nowadays customers have more options for methods of purchase, like online, where a customer can purchase through a website. Another is offline, where a customer visits a shop and makes a purchase.

6. Budget of customer: A business can grow by matching the product cost offer by the company with the customer budget.

7. What gives a customer delight: If you know what can delight a customer, you can serve them what they prefer.

8. Expectations of customer: You can stand to gain repeat business if you provide the expected reliable delivery as per customer demand.

9. Customer perception toward company: Customers are likely to buy with you if they enjoy dealing with you and get the proper satisfaction. In the case of proper satisfaction, the customer will purchase more items, as well as promoting the products. Customer perception towards the company may be positive or negative, but positive perception helps the business succeed.

10. Customer perception of your competitor: It's important to know the customer perception of your competitors. There are three different categories of this requirement:

    (i)   Normal requirements – Requirement that is fulfilled by companies just asking the needs of customers.

    (ii) Expected requirements – This deals with the compulsory requirements. For example, in a coffee shop, if they serve coffee hot, then they have satisfied the customer and if it is served cold, then he is dissatisfied.

    (iii) Exciting requirements – Exciting requirements are beyond the customer's expectations. If provided, the customer would be delighted. If not provided, they will not be happy with the service.

Customer information: Customer information can be gathered in the following ways:

a. By interviews.
b. By survey.
c. Focus groups.

a) By interview: this process implies some of the following steps:
   • First, make a team which has at least two members. One member focuses on questioning and the other one is listening carefully and taking notes.

- Prepare notes of everything whether you want to hear it or not.
- Interviews can be conducted by personal meeting or by telephone.

b) By survey: these processes include some of the following steps:
  - Prepare a good questionnaire.
  - Mail questionnaire or distribute personally and collect it after response by customer.
  - Analyse all data and draw conclusions.

c) Focus groups:
  - Prepare group for discussion.
  - Resolve conflicting views.
  - Include a skilled member of the group.

4.3 CUSTOMER SATISFACTION MODEL

Customer satisfaction can be defined as the product supplied by the company performed the intended function or that it met the measure of customer expectation. J. Willard Marriott (founder of the Marriott Corporation) stated that the needs of the customer may vary, but their bias for quality never does. It is considered an important tool to improve business in any organisation. There are some reasons which are important to customer satisfaction.

1. Retaining old customers is cheaper than obtaining new ones: Retaining old customers is most important for a successful business. Retaining old customers is cheaper than obtaining a new customer.
2. Customer satisfaction leads to a re-purchase intention: If the customer is satisfied with a given product or service, they have an increased re-purchase intention. It depends on the product features.
3. It helps brand recognition: Nowadays, customers help to spread the brand value of the product with the help of the internet and other ways like social media chatting, etc. People respect and like those businesses which provide better customer service.
4. It reduces negative impacts in business: It's directly related to customers' satisfaction; if customers are satisfied, it will increase the chance of re-purchase, as well as new customers. Word of mouth directly affects the business growth. Whether it is bad word of mouth or good word of mouth will depend on customer satisfaction. If the customer is happy with your product and service, then he will give good word of mouth, and otherwise it will be bad word of mouth which increases the negative impact on the business.

4.3.1 HOW TO INCREASE CUSTOMER SATISFACTION

Customer satisfaction is most important tool for business growth. To increase customer satisfaction, small- and medium-size businesses must be concentrating on building a customer experience. Some of the methods for doing this are listed below:

4.3.1.1   Treat Your Customers as Important to You

- Thank customers for being with you.
- Know about any help needed by the customer.
- Sort out any customer problems without delay.
- Keep promises to the customer about any help.
- Try to impress your customer as a good service provider.

4.3.1.2   Create Customer Loyalty to Increase Customer Satisfaction

As per American author and business trainer Jeffrey Gitomer, "Customer satisfaction is worthless whereas customer loyalty is priceless' (Gitomer, 1998). The primary aim of the company should be to create loyal customers who are not easily influenced by the other companies.

4.3.1.3   Set Customer Expectations Early

High expectations and ridiculous promises that are made by the companies are the most common mistakes and hence may lower the satisfaction level of the customer.

4.3.1.4   Survey Your Customers to Find the Right Direction

A customer feedback survey is an important way to know how you are going to satisfy the customers. Personal interview and online questionnaires are some common tools that are used for the survey and it will vary from customer to customer.

4.3.1.5   Track and Monitor Social Media to Help Find Out How to Make Customers Happy

In the present scenario, social media plays an important role in getting information about customer satisfaction and how it can be improved. The use of social media to monitor the feedback is most commonly used. Customer feedback on social media also helps to know about exactly what customers want and you can make a plan to resolve them.

4.4   KANO'S MODEL FOR CUSTOMER SATISFACTION OR CUSTOMER DELIGHT

The aim is to connect customer satisfaction with the products and being fulfilled by the products. There are several types of requirements that influence ultimate customer satisfaction. The model describes customer satisfaction by classifying product attributes based on their perception by customers and their effect on customer satisfaction. The classifications are used for guiding design decisions.

4.4.1   Project Activities in Which the Kano Model Is Useful

- Getting information about the needs of customers.
- Getting information about functional requirements.
- Developing concepts.
- Studying the competitive products.

4.4.2   Other Tools That Are Useful in Conjunction with the Kano Model

- Elicited customer input.
- Prioritisation matrices.
- Development of quality function.
- Value analysis.

4.4.3   Introduction

The product attributes are divided into three categories:

1) Must be or threshold.
2) Performance or one dimension.
3) And excitement or attractive.
   At a given cost that the market can bear, a competitive product meets the basic attributes like maximised performance and much excitement.
   Kano's model of customer satisfication is shown in Figure 4.1.

4.4.3.1   Must Be or Threshold
Threshold attributes are referred to as the prime requirement that deals with the minimum criteria needed to be met by the services and products. In the case of unfulfilled demand, the product loses their utility for the customer.

4.4.3.2   Performance Attributes
Performance attributes is another attribute that might be helpful in improving customer satisfaction. Poor performance of products reduces customer satisfaction. A number of needs asked for by the customer fall into the category of performance.

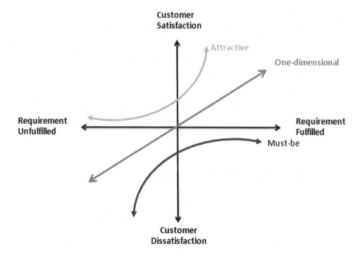

FIGURE 4.1   Kano's model.

78 Total Quality Management

The price that a customer will pay is closely linked to the performance of the product/service. For example, a customer will pay more for a four-wheeler that has better fuel economy.

4.4.3.3 Excitement Attributes or Attractive Attributes

These are unexpected and unexplained by customers, but provide a high level of satisfaction to the customer. Sometimes it provides for the unspoken needs of which customers are unaware.

4.4.3.4 Other Attributes

There are some other attributes that are not covered by the Kano Model. For example, a list of parts which are used by a repair mechanic.

4.4.4 APPLICATION OF THE KANO MODEL ANALYSIS

- A simplest approach to the Kano Model is to ask two simple questions of consumers for each attribute:
  1. If the product has this attribute, then rate your satisfaction.
  2. If not, then rate your satisfaction.

Customers should be asked to rate it on the following scale:

A) Satisfied.
B) Neutral (as usual).
C) Dissatisfied.
D) Don't care.
   - In most of the cases a neutral response is obtained for first question and the dissatisfied for the other one because the customer has no idea about that attribute.
   - But performance/excitement attributes are closely related to customer satisfaction or dissatisfaction. A trade-off analysis is also needed against the cost. 'How much extra would you be willing to pay for this attribute or more of this attribute?' will aid in trade-off decisions, especially performance attributes.
   - Consideration should be given to attributes that receive the response 'Don't care,' because they are not going to affect customer satisfaction nor motivate the customer to pay higher price.

4.5 CUSTOMER PERCEPTION OF QUALITY

Quality is a relative term that is generally used with reference to the end application of the product. For example, if we are going to use equipment in sugar cane then we cannot demand a surface finish, tolerance, and accuracy compared to equipment used in the headstock of the lathe. Hence, quality deals with the fitness of the product for a particular application at an economic level.

The quality depends on the perception of a person in a given situation. The situation can be user-oriented, cost-oriented, or supplier-oriented.

The quality has a variety of meanings such as:

- Fitness for purpose or fitness for use.
- Conformance to requirement.
- Compliance to specification.
- Degree of excellence.
- Customer satisfaction.
- The ability of a product or service to perform the intended function satisfactorily.
- Quality is the totality of the product characteristics which enable it to satisfy customer requirements.
- A quantitative definition of quality is the ratio of performance of the product to the expectation of the user.

4.6   FACTORS AFFECTING THE QUALITY OF THE PRODUCT

The prime factors affecting quality are:

1. Product design.
2. Material used.
3. Manufacturing technology used.
4. Human factor.
5. Machine tools used.
6. Inspection and testing procedure.
7. Service after the sale.
8. Costumer feedback.

4.7   QUALITY CHARACTERISTIC OF A PRODUCT

There are ten product characteristics which will completely define the quality of product. These characteristics are:

1. Performance.
2. Conformance.
3. Reliability.
4. Feature.
5. Durability.
6. Response.
7. Service.
8. Safety.
9. Aesthetics.
10. Reputation.

4.8   CUSTOMER FEEDBACK

Customer feedback is the collection of data from various resources like website, email, personal interviews, etc. from a customer about the product provided by manufacturers, for a given use in a given intended function. With the help of customer feedback, any manufacturer can find out about customer loyalty to their product. Customer loyalty is important for any business to mature.

For any organisation to survive in a competitive marketplace, it's necessary to know about the customer, their thinking about the product, their thinking about your competitor, their thinking about your service, etc. Customer opinion also helps the growth of the business. There are various ways to profit by customer feedback. There are several reasons, why feedback is important for business.

1. Customer feedback can improve the quality of products and services: In starting off in business, there is no idea about what customer needs, but if you introduce your product after feedback, it helps to know your customers' requirements. After feedback, any organisation improves and modifies their product according to customer requirements.

2. Through customer feedback you can measure the satisfaction level of customer: Through customer feedback, you can easily analyse and measure the satisfaction level of the customer about your product. Customer satisfaction is the prime element of TQM. And the fourth dimension of TQM is always directed towards the accomplishment of the prime objective of any TQM programmes, and hence it yields better performance and quality of the process. For example, industries, institutes, services, and manufacturing.

3. Through customer feedback, you can measure the value of manufacturers from the customer's point of view: Through customer feedback and their loyalty to the firm, you see the value of manufacturers, or you can say what their place is in the competitive market. If manufacturers judge their own position in the market, then they improve by taking corrective action towards the improvement. Through customer feedback, any company can analyse their flaws. Any organisation when asking the customer if they are happy with service provided by an organisation shows that the organisation is always with the customer, and makes the customer feel good and they will spread positive views of the organisation.

4. Customer feedback, you generate the best customer experiences: Today, the sustainability of any organisation heavily depends on the experiences people have with products, brands, and services. They do not buy Nike products just because they are good, but they buy them because they know their status and affiliation to a particular brand or group. They do not buy Levi's clothes because their durability is high; they buy because of customer experience and their group status. Therefore, if you concentrate on providing the best customer experience to satisfy the customer, they will stay loyal to your brand.

5. Customer feedback helps to improve customer retention: If the customer is satisfied with your service, then they will stay with you, otherwise they

leave. Customer feedback helps to know if a customer is satisfied or dissatisfied. If the customer is satisfied, that means they will stay with you. A dissatisfied customer can leave, so this is the right time to be sorry about your service and take corrective action towards sorting out their problem in every way. This is the right time to show your reliability and customer backing; it can also improve the loyalty of the customer.

6. Customer feedback is a reliable source for information about the product or service to another customer: Nowadays, consumers believe customer feedback, rather than commercial advertisement and expert opinion. Any customer, if going to purchase anything, will first visit Facebook and other trustworthy blogs and take feedback from them. After that, they decide to choose a product or service provider. So, customer feedback is important to your business, as well as a reliable source of information for another customer.

7. Customer feedback gives you information that helps make decisions toward business growth: Any organisation's growth depends on customer satisfaction and customer loyalty which is updated and developed by customer feedback. To sustain a business in a competitive marketplace, it's important to make a business decision on the base of true feedback. There is no place for business decisions in the competitive marketplace based on false information. Nowadays, any company can get reliable information from customer feedback. Any organisation's growth depends on customer satisfaction, which is why the customer should be at the centre of your business. For business growth, the customer's voice should not be avoided. The customer's voice can be converted into technical requirements with the help of QFD and the allocation of quality responsibility to the department concerned. In other words, QFD is an assignment of specific quality responsibility to a specific department. Therefore it is a process of sharing quality responsibility by all the departments right from design, production inspection, testing, and after-sales service in any organisation. QFD is basically a mechanism which converts customer requirements into technical requirements. QFD is an important tool to improve customer requirements towards customer satisfaction. The customer's voice is important for any business, so never stop listening to the customer's voice.

4.9   SERVICE QUALITY

Customer satisfaction depends directly on the service quality, which is a basic opportunity to help to run a business smoothly. The growth of the business and the profit of the business are especially based on the reliability of the customer. For any organisation, it is crucial to know the customer's perceptions about a service regarding its satisfaction levels. As a result, customers' interest would increase, and the company will grow, as well as the number of clients increasing.

Customer dissatisfaction is mainly dependent on the customer's perceptions about the service. What is the customer's view about the service, and the service gap? The service gap can be found out by the analysis of customer views and feedback. The following are few important service gaps:

1. Understanding: The understanding gap arises due to a lack of knowledge of customer needs. In other words, we can say there is a communication gap between customers and manufacturers. It can be reduced by spending time taking feedback from the customer about their requirements.
2. Promotional: This type of gap arises due to the improper advertising of products or services, and the customer being unaware of your service quality and various promotional schemes.
3. Performance gap: This is the gap between what was said and what was provided. It is the difference between the given specification and the actual services provided.
4. The gap between promise and delivery: This type of gap arises due to the difference between promises and delivery.
5. Management perception about consumer: This is the difference between management perceptions about consumers and vice versa.

A few important service gaps have been shown in Figure 4.2.

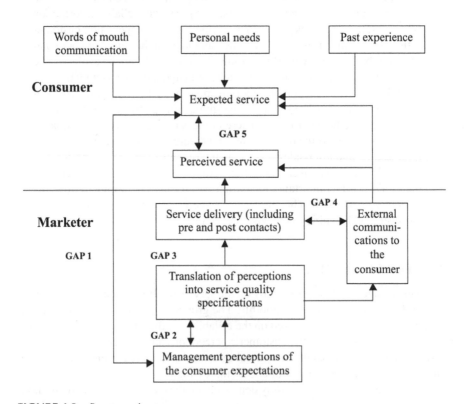

FIGURE 4.2   Some service gaps.

4.10   CUSTOMER RETENTION

Early on, a company was focused on making new customers rather than thinking about retention of the customer, but now retention of the customer is most important. There may be different questions, e.g., what is customer retention, why are they needed, and what is the benefit of customer retention.

As mentioned earlier, if a customer is satisfied with your service, then they will stay with you, otherwise they leave. Customer feedback helps to know if the customer is satisfied or dissatisfied. If the customer is satisfied, that means they will stay with you. A dissatisfied customer can leave, so customer retention is important to any business if they want to stay in business.

Customer retention can be explained as how any organisation or company are able to maintain their existing customer base by providing good products, after-sale service, and good relationships with the customer, helped by your good Customer Relationship Management (CRM) strategy. It is important these days to retain customers. Firstly, it is cost-effective, and secondly, it is a profitable strategy. Customer retention provides an ability to survive in a business world in the long-terms. There are several benefits of customer retention:

- Increasing the re-purchasing behaviour of the customer.
- Increasing the number of customers.
- Increasing the loyalty of the customer.
- Increasing the reputation of companies.
- Decreasing negative customers.
- Converting a negative customer to a positive customer.
- Spreading positive word-of-mouth recommendations.

Consumer behaviour drives customer relationship marketing which is tactical in nature. Johnson (1998) has given some philosophies toward customer retention; these are:

1. It requires allocating market resources. According to Johnson, to generate higher profits, the company has to use some marketing activities for consumers. Decisions regarding keeping company budgets flat or otherwise depends on increasing sales/profits.
2. Actively based on customers retained. Customers like to feel in control and they like to feel good about their decision-making and choices. Marketers profit from this behaviour through promotional marketing by engaging the potential customers and making them feel awesome about it.
3. Keeping the relationship between the company and consumer alive in order to retain them. They might slip away if the company doesn't keep in touch with the customer. There is a great chance that customers might slip away from the company due to the uninterested approach of the company towards them.
4. Customer data collection is a dynamic process, and thus marketing becomes highly evolved and dynamic. The marketers have to go back and forth, because they must listen to what their customers require.

4.11   CONCLUSION

Customers' and employees' involvement are the most important for every organisation towards quality production, control of quality, etc. In the market, you have a kind of customer with a different perception of quality. According to TQM philosophy, customer perception of quality leads to continuous improvement. This concept emphasises that there is no definite quality level, because the customer's needs and expectations are continuously changing with time. Various researchers and authors have given some methods for customer satisfaction. The Kano model is one of them. Customer perception of quality varies with the customer. The quality of the product depends on the purpose of use or its fitness for use. Overall, quality can be improved by customer feedback. Customer feedback can show the company's status. Customer feedback can be said to be the data provided by the customer toward quality production.

Retention of a customer of any organisation depends on the customer's satisfaction level. There are three types of satisfaction level. The first is satisfied, then dissatisfied, then the delight level. If a customer is delighted, they will always be with the organisation; another one is satisfied, and they are searching for alternatives which then could lead to them quitting the existing organisation. The last one is the dissatisfied customer; they cannot be retained again in the existing organisation.

4.12   CASE STUDIES

4.12.1   CASE STUDY 1: CUSTOMER SATISFACTION SURVEY OF ETDC CHENNAI, INDIA

Electronics Test and Development Center (ETDC) Chennai is generally engaged in testing and calibrating of electronics items. In the year 1996, before implementing the TQM programme, the company decided to do a survey on the customer satisfaction index, for the company had done many steps like brainstorming with senior executives. For the survey, they used four parameters to measure the Customer Satisfaction Index (CSI).

1. Promptness of service (P1).
2. Quality of customer service (P2).
3. Quality of testing and calibration (P3).
4. Quality of test and calibration reports (P4).

At the end of the financial year, the CEO sent a letter to 150 clients and requested and motivate them to give feedback. In the feedback form, they were given the four parameters of CSI. They asked to clients to rate the above parameters against the scale from 5 to 1: 5 for excellence, while 1 was for poor. About 35% of the clients gave feedback, then the customer satisfaction of each parameter were determined by the weighted average method. The weighted average method is explained as follows:

For example, assuming that 12 clients has given feedback for CSI.

S. No.	Rank	No. of respondent
1.	5 = Excellent	8
2	4	2
3	3	1
4	2	1
5	1 = Poor	0

Then, CSI for Promptness = $5\times8+4\times2+3\times1+2\times1/12 = 44/12 = 3.67$.

In this example, the CSI was expressed in terms of the above four parameters. This exercise was repeated continuously over three years, and the results obtained were as follows.

S. No.	Year/Parametrers	P1	P2	P3	P4
1	2000–2001	3.55	3.76	3.96	3.83
2	2001–2002	4.27	4.11	4.11	4.04
3	2002–2003	4.36	4.2	4.33	4.3

4.12.2   CASE STUDY 2: CAR OWNER SATISFACTION (MERCEDES-BENZ)

Jeff S. Bartlett shared his experience and gave feedback by the client. Under the survey results, the average price for new cars continues to rise, according to the National Automobile Dealers Association.

The Consumer Reports members shared the experiences they'd had with more than 500,000 vehicles in our 2018 auto surveys. Primarily, they were asked whether they would buy the same car again. That decision is the basis of CR's owner satisfaction score.

This year's data is on how owners rated their cars on satisfaction in five categories: driving experience, comfort, value, styling, and audio controls, showing where a car shines and where it comes up short.

The survey results showed that in every vehicle type, there is a significant spread between the models that met expectations and those that were disappointing.

POINTS TO REMEMBER

- **Customer Needs and Requirements:** Customer needs can be defined as the problems that customers sort out by the purchase of products, goods, or services. According to CEO of Apple Inc., Steve Jobs, you should 'Get closer than to ever to your customer.'
- **Customer Satisfaction Model:** Customer satisfaction can be defined as the product supplied by the company performed the intended function, or you

can say that it is a measure of customer expectation. Customer satisfaction is the most important tool to improve business in any organisation. There are some reasons which are important to customer satisfaction.

- **Customer Perception of Quality:** The quality depends on the perception of a person in a given situation. The situation can be user-oriented, cost-oriented, or supplier-oriented. Quality has a variety of meanings such as:
  1. Fitness for purpose or fitness for use.
  2. Conforming to requirements.
  3. Compliance with specifications.
  4. Degree of excellence.
  5. Customer satisfaction.
- **Customer Feedback:** Customer feedback is the collection of data from various resources like a website, by mail, personal interview, etc. about a customer that they are pleased with the product provide by manufactures, and it is working in its given intended function. With the help of customer feedback, any manufacturer can find out customer loyalty about their product. Customer loyalty is important for any business to go ahead.
- **Service Quality:** Customer satisfaction directly depends on service quality which gives one the basic opportunity to help to run a business smoothly, and to grow the business and the profit of the business, especially depending on the reliability of the customer.
- **Customer Retention:** Early on, any company was focused on making new customer rather than thinking about retention of the customer, but nowadays retention of the customer is most important. There are different questions: what is customer retention, why is it needed, and what is the benefit of customer retention.

SELF-ASSESSMENT QUESTIONS

1. Discuss in brief the customer's needs and requirements.
2. Explain the customer satisfaction model.
3. Write about the customer satisfaction level.
4. What do you mean by customer perception of quality?
5. What do you understand by customer feedback and how it helps organisational growth?
6. What do you mean by service quality?
7. What is customer retention and how do you retain a customer?

BIBLIOGRAPHY

Agyekum, C. K., Haifeng, H., & Agyeiwaa, A. (2015). Consumer perception of product quality. *Microeconomics and Macroeconomics*, *3*(2), 25–29.
Al-Azzam, A. F. M. (2015). The impact of service quality dimensions on customer satisfaction: A field study of Arab Bank in Irbid city, Jordan. *European Journal of Business and Management*, *7*(15), 45–53.
American Customer Satisfaction the Index. (2014). Online Available at: http://www.theacsi.org/customersatisfactionbenchmarks/benchmarks-by-industry.

Amin, M., & Isa, Z. (2008). An examination of the relationship between service quality perception and customer satisfaction. *International Journal of Islamic and Middle Eastern Finance and Management, 1*(3), 191–209.

Andersson, E. (2014). *Transforming Customer Needs to Technical Requirements-Study of a New Product Development Case at Volvo Car Group* (Master's thesis).

Angur, M. G., Nataraajan, R., & Jahera, J. S. (1999). Service quality in the banking industry: An assessment in a developing economy. *International Journal of Bank Marketing, 17*(3), 116–125.

García-Alcaraz, J. L., Montalvo, F. J. F., Sánchez-Ramírez, C., Avelar-Sosa, L., Saucedo, J. A. M., & Alor-Hernández, G. (2019). Importance of organizational structure for TQM success and customer satisfaction. *Wireless Networks, 25*, 1–14.

Gitomer, J. (1998). *Customer Satisfaction Is Worthless, Customer Loyalty Is Priceless: How to Make Customers Love You, Keep Them Coming Back, and Tell Everyone They Know.* Bard Press, Austin, TX.

Gomes, C. F., Small, M. H., & Yasin, M. M. (2019). Towards excellence in managing the public-sector project cycle: A TQM context. *International Journal of Public Sector Management, 30*(3), 182–196.

Huang, C. C., & Guan, S. S. (2012). Application of Kano model in study of satisfaction with quality of website browsing environment. *Bulletin of Japanese Society for the Science of Design, 59*(1), 49–58.

Johnson, M. D. (1998). *Customer Orientation and Market Action.* Prentice Hall, Michigan.

Matzler, K., Fuchs, M., & Schubert, A. (2004). Employee satisfaction: Does Kano's model apply? *Total Quality Management and Business Excellence, 15*(9–10), 1179–1198.

Mihelis, G., Grigoroudis, E., Siskos, Y., Politis, Y., & Malandrakis, Y. (2001). Customer satisfaction measurement in the private bank sector. *European Journal of Operational Research, 130*(2), 347–360.

Mmutle, T. (2017). Customers' perception of service quality and its impact on reputation in the hospitality industry. *African Journal of Hospitality, Tourism and Leisure, 6*(3), 1–25.

Satisfaction, C. A. Field study of Arab Bank in Irbid City, Jordan. *European Journal of Business and Management, 7*(15), 2822–2839.

Sauerwein, E., Bailom, F., Matzler, K., & Hinterhuber, H. H. (1996). The Kano model: How to delight your customers. *International Working Seminar on Production Economics, 1*(4), 313–327.

Seth, N., Deshmukh, S. G., & Vrat, P. (2005). Service quality models: A review. *International Journal of Quality and Reliability Management, 28*(2), 73–82.

Singh, H. (2006). The importance of customer satisfaction in relation to customer loyalty and retention. *Academy of Marketing Science, 60*, 193–225.

Singh, S., & Chaudhary, N. J. S. M. K. (2014). A study of customer perception towards service quality of life insurance companies in Delhi NCR Region. *Global Journal of Management and Business Research, 14*(7), 1542–1563.

Tung, W. C. (2003). A customer perception and satisfaction survey for a Chinese buffet. *The Graduate School University of Wisconsin-Stout*, May 2003 (PhD Thesis).

5 Employer Involvement and Supplier Participation

5.1 EMPLOYER INVOLVEMENT AND SUPPLIER PARTNERSHIP

Employee involvement and supplier partnership can both help towards organisational development. Total Employee Involvement (TEI) pertains to teamwork in any organisation. TEI simply promotes a participative culture within the organisation, meaning 100% participation of all. So TEI is not merely confined to the involvement of all team players (workers) toward the quality objective, continuous quality improvement, etc. TEI is the first dimension of the TQM model. Supplier partnership is important for any organisational growth. Supplier performance depends on the bilateral efforts of the supplier as well as the buyer. Supplier support is needed whenever applying just-in-time (JIT) in an organisation. The organisation and the supplier are both dependent on each other, so we can say that it is a bilateral effort. A joint effort can improve areas such as quality, services, environmental and social responsibility, managerial capability, and the area of cost optimisation.

The question arises of who is a supplier. A supplier is a party or any organisation that supplies goods or services to another firm. Suppliers can be categorised in terms of a long-term supplier and a short-term supplier. If I hope that the supplier will supply in the long-term, the supplier should be chosen as a partner. If you are choosing a long-term supplier or supplier partner, there should be some joint efforts, like:

1. Similar goals: Every company has some goal, whether a long-term or short-term goal. The company sets the goal and does work to achieve it. So it's important that the goal should be similar for the supplier as well as for a buyer, for the organisation's growth and fulfilment of environmental and social responsibility.
2. Transparent communication: The concept of transparent communication is important for a sustainable business. Transparent communication is not easy because some suppliers do not support it. Supply partners should surely support these ideas to update on what is happening with your product and service. The supply partner is always with you whether the news is good or bad. The supply partner should be honest and work with you in all conditions.
3. Sharing cost optimisation: In the present scenario, the main target of companies is to optimise the cost over time. A supply partner continuously works on cost optimisation and shares cost saving with suppliers. A supply partner always shares ideas about changes in design, improved processes, etc.

After completing this chapter, the reader will able to understand: improving quality through employee involvement; teamwork; the suggestion system; quality circles; the effective recognition and reward system; benefits of employee involvement; principles of customer–supplier relations; supplier selection; and supplier rating.

5.2   IMPROVING QUALITY THROUGH EMPLOYEE INVOLVEMENT

The quality of a product includes fulfilling the demand of customers and it should not be restricted to the product's functional characteristics. As per ISO 9000:2015 'Quality is the degree to which a set of inherent characteristics fulfills requirements.' Philip B. Crosby stated that 'quality is conformance to requirement' (1979). The quality concept starts with identification of the quality demand of the customer and finishes after placement of the final order in the hands of a customer that remains satisfied through different stages of the relationship with the seller. Quality also deals with the intended function of the product while satisfying customer expectations.

The employee's involvement is important for any successes in full business. We can say that employees are the strength of a company. TEI means involving employees, empowering them, and including them in the decision-making process. It gives an opportunity for continuous improvement. The Quality Circle (QC) is a group of employees which aims to analyse and solve work-related problems. The objective of the QC is the continuous improvement of the organisation.

Employee involvement improves quality, because:

- Employees make things better because they are experts in their own field.
- They make better decisions using expert knowledge of the process.
- They suggest good ideas to improve quality.
- Employees are better able to analyse the problem and solve them.
- Immediate corrective actions are also possible by the employees toward performance improvement.
- Involvement of employees helps to overcome faulty decisions.
- Employee involvement increases the morale of employees by including them in making decisions.
- Employees have the capability to accept change because they are experts in their field.
- Employees' involvement increased commitment to unit goals because they are involved.

Employee involvement is the second dimension of the TQM model, contributing to continuous improvement of the performance of the organisation.

5.3   TEAMWORK

A team is defined as a group of members with a common goal. Teamwork throughout any organisation is an important component of TQM implementation. In any organisation, the Quality Improvement Team (QIT) is a group of people with specific knowledge, skills, and experience in a particular area who are brought together to analyse the problems and solve them. Teamwork is the concept of effective utilisation of knowledge, skill, and experience of team members, because every member has specific knowledge, skill, and experience in the particular field. The characteristics of teams are:

- The ability of a team is more than the sum of the ability of an individual member.
- Teams satisfy human social needs.
- Teams increase the potential of the individual members.
- Teams increase productivity.
- Teams helps better utilisation of skills.
- Teams promote group work culture.

5.3.1 MAKING TEAMS AND ASSIGN WORK

The purpose is to make a team for the specific task and assign the task to them. The steps involved in that are the selection of team members, their naming, mission statement, and developing mutual relationships among them.

5.3.1.1 To Decide the Size of the Members

The team members should be able to satisfy the goal of the team efficiently and effectively. The team makeup mainly depends on the task that assigned to the team and it may be project oriented, departmental, or process improvement. Employees of the department come together to implement initiatives like QCs. Otherwise, in process improvement, the team is usually cross-functional.

5.3.1.2 Choosing Team Members

The main step of teamwork is to identify the potential team members for the task before putting them together. Sometimes there will be more potential members than members actually needed for the task. The next step is to compile the list.

5.4 SUGGESTION SYSTEM

Another important task that is needed for teamwork and deals is to collect good ideas from employees. It provides a good opportunity to individuals to contribute to the organisation. It is management's responsibility to make the system easy for the employees for making suggestions and improvements. It may be helpful in developing the creative process.

Suggestion systems and programmes are based upon the reasonable assumption that employee can contribute thoughts for the purposes of the organisation's operations and/or decreasing costs. A relation is developed between employees and the organisation and employees are rewarded for their worthy ideas.

There are some rules for a stimulating and encouraging suggestion system:

- Regularly asking employees for their suggestions.
- Welcome all suggestions from employees.
- Focus on problems instead of employees, helping to remove fear in them.
- Quickly respond to suggestions whether they are effective or not.
- Reward the employees for their good ideas.

The processes for the employee suggestion system are:

1. Collect ideas from employees.
2. Determine the department for implementing it.
3. Analyse the ideas – are they feasible or not?
4. If it is feasible to implement, send it to review.
5. Analyse and nominate employees for rewards.

An employee suggestion system process is shown in Figure 5.1.

5.5   QUALITY CIRCLES

A Quality Circle (QC) is also known as a quality control cycle. A QC can be defined as a group of employees in the workplace who perform the same work or function in their job. These groups of employees will normally number 3–10 and be led by a supervisor. Members of the group meet regularly and discuss problems and discover the solutions related to their role at work.

QC motivates the employees to share their problem related to work and get solution for improving the performance of the organisation. Normally, the QC focuses on the areas of manufacturing processes, ergonomics, and working environment, etc.

The Japanese professor Kaoru Ishikawa has first used the term 'QCs' in 1985. After that, various Japanese and American companies implemented the QC for improving performance of their organisations. First, the Toyota Company successfully implemented a QC. The main objectives of the QC are:

- QC formed to improve the performance of an organisation.
- QC contributes towards the development of an organisation.
- To improve the working environment such that employees can perform effectively in work.
- To utilise the hidden potential of the individual employees to do specific work.
- To improve the productivity of the organisation.
- To improve the quality of the product.
- To create a participative culture in the organisation.
- To motivate employees to share their hidden skills at a particular task.

Generally, the QC has three to ten people. These people are trained for problem-solving tools, statistical process, etc. The QC process is shown in Figure 5.2.

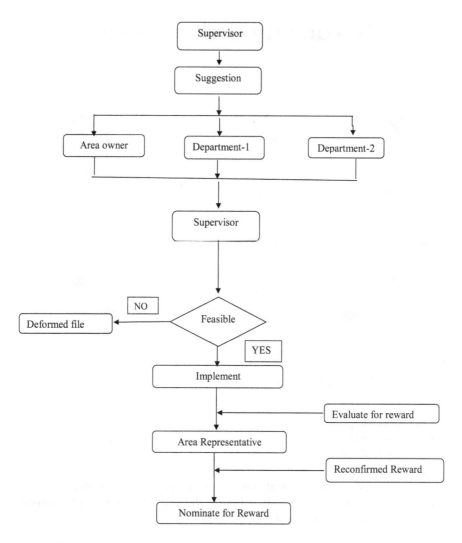

FIGURE 5.1 Employee suggestion system process.

5.6 QUALITY CIRCLE TOOLS

It uses different types of tools depends upon the role of their job. Some of the QCs deal only with problems and their solutions, and for that purpose a simple notepad is sufficient. However, some quality tools dealing with the main issues and trying to fix them are listed below:

- Scatter plots.
- Graphical tools.
- Flow chart.
- Run chart.

The quality circle process

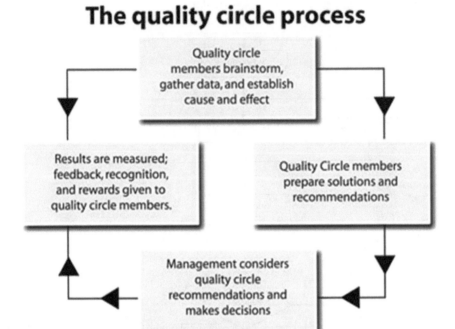

FIGURE 5.2   Quality circle process.

- Process mapping tools.
- Pareto charts.
- Fishbone diagrams.

Depending on the specific problem, a number of potential tools are used. A quality control circle works more efficiently at finding the issue and proposing the solution when it is equipped with the right tools.

5.7   EFFECTIVE RECOGNITION AND REWARD SYSTEM

To take competitive advantage, a recognition and reward system should be placed in the organisation. The main focus of the organisation is improvement in quality with reduction in cost. The reward and recognition award system may be more effective at motivating the employee and changing their work habits to the organisation's benefit.

5.7.1   REWARD

This is a small appreciation given by the organisation head to employees for doing exceptional work. The token of appreciation could be monetary or in some other form. The idea is to motivate employees to continue achieving. There are two types of rewards:

- *Extrinsic rewards*: Concrete rewards that an employee receives in the form of bonuses, salary raise, gifts, promotion, etc.
- *Intrinsic rewards*: Personal satisfaction to the individual. For example, information/feedback, recognition, trust/empowerment, etc.

5.7.2 RECOGNITION

This is the acknowledgment given to an individual or team's behaviour, effort, and accomplishments that support the organisation's goals and values.

5.7.3 DESIGN A REWARD PROGRAMME

Reward programmes help to motivate employee toward sustainable development. Some key points in developing reward programmes are:

- Identification of the organisation goal.
- Make sure the developed reward programme supports the company goal.
- Identification of employee strength and skills that will apply the company's goal.
- Determine the employee's performance based upon the previous achievements.
- Find out appropriate rewards.
- Communicate with employees.

5.7.4 TYPES OF REWARD PROGRAMMES

There are different types of reward programmes for individuals and groups.

1. **Variable pay:** This type of reward programme depends on the company performance, revenue in business, etc. Variable pay can be a reward to employees or teams, and it could be on an individual or a group basis. Some companies pay their employees less compared to a competitor, but the company may try to motivate and reward employees through various reward programmes. The reward programme is a powerful tool to retain skilled employees in the organisation.
2. **Bonuses:** The bonus is one of the reward programmes in which the company pays extra, other than salary, based on individual performance. Generally, this type of programme is implemented in a marketing company like insurance, real estate, etc. It could encourage a salesperson to generate extra business or higher revenue. The bonus is provided to an employee based on individual accomplishment.
3. **Profit Sharing:** In this type of reward system, the company gives a profit share based on salary structure rather than the cash. Profit-sharing is a good concept to tie the employee to the organisation. Profit-sharing motivates the employee to give 100% towards company growth.
4. **Stock Options:** In recent years, a stock option was a very popular method of rewarding employees. This method was employed in mature companies,

as well as the start-up companies. This programme gives the employee a right to buy a specified number of shares at a fixed price for a specified period of time. Most of the companies award some shares to an employee based on their contribution or accomplishments.

5.8   BENEFITS OF EMPLOYEE INVOLVEMENT

Employee involvement means the participation of all employees in creating a positive working environment and development of the organisation. There are various benefits of employee involvement given as follows:

1. Employee involvement motivates the employee to align their goal with a company goal.
2. Employee involvement creates a positive work environment.
3. Employee involvement develops collaborative work and creates problem-solving.
4. Employee involvement creates a feeling of responsiveness within employees.
5. Employee involvement helps to meet an organisational goal.
6. They are more committed to helping their organisation to achieve success.
7. They are more likely to suggest improvements in current methods and processes.
8. They are more likely to recommend their organisation to others.
9. Employee involvement increases productivity.
10. Increased product quality.
11. Increased quick response to customer services.
12. Decreased delay in the delivery of goods and services.
13. Employee involvement creates new innovation.
14. Employee involvement increases team cohesion.

5.9   PRINCIPLES OF CUSTOMER–SUPPLIER RELATIONS

An organisation spends approximately 60% of the product cost on purchasing raw materials. For the production of good quality products, it's important to purchase good quality raw materials at optimum cost, and this depends upon the customer–supplier relationship. The customer–supplier relationship is the business relationship between them in terms of material quality, reworking services, customer complaint handling, and delivery performance. The customer and supplier should have the same goal – to satisfy the end-user – hence, having a healthy customer–supplier relationship is important for any business.

Here are some basic principles of the customer–supplier relationship:

- Both the customer and the supplier are responsible for the production of best quality.
- Both the customer and supplier are responsible for quality control.
- Both are responsible for healthy relationships.

- Both are responsible for exchanging information. It helps with quality production.
- Both make their decisions independently.
- Both the customer and the supplier goal should be the same – towards the end result of customer satisfaction.
- Both the supplier and customer enter into a contract with respect to quality, service, on-time delivery, availability, reliability, reversibility, etc.
- Both the customer and supplier learn the method of quality development.
- Both the customer and supplier should be supportive of each other respect of technology, planning, and exchanging information
- The customer should make sure they provide sufficient information, funds, and data to the supplier, so the supplier can produce a quality product on time.

From the suppliers' end, the relationship is based on the following factors:

1. Reliable at meeting customers' needs.
2. Conformance to standards.
3. Creativity or innovation.

From the customers' end, the relationship is based on the following factors:

1. Provide sufficient funds on time.
2. Personalisation of the relationship.
3. Provide flexibility to supplier.
4. Share adequate information.

5.10   SUPPLIER SELECTION

The supplier selection process is the most important for manufacturing industries, because a large percentage of costs are the raw materials and services. It will help to reduce the direct cost to the bottom line. It is also important in green supply chain management. Nowadays, most manufacturing industries have a lot of pressure from environmental legislation and from society for cleaner production, and it is only possible when suppliers provide non-hazardous raw materials.

Most of the revenue is generated by the product spend on raw materials, so the company's success heavily depends on the supplier; that's why supplier selection is important for the organisation. Supplier selection also helps to implement quality programmes in organisations like just-in-time (JIT), and TQM, etc. The success of JIT implementation in any organisation depends on various factors like delivery time after order placed, reliability of supplier, capacity of supplier, quick response by supplier, etc. The bottom line of the supply chain cost depends on the suppliers.

A reliable supplier enables reducing the inventory cost of manufacturing and improving quality, which is why supplier selection for manufacture is a prime concern. It is observed that the selection of supplier and the supplier relationship are the key factors for manufacturers to take competitive advantages.

For reliable supplier selection, the purchasing department should observe all critical selection criteria and performance. In the literature, authors discuss different selection criteria for selection of the best supplier. Supplier selection is important for any organisation for long-term business and sustainable development in a competitive marketplace.

5.10.1 SUPPLIER SELECTION CRITERIA AND STRATEGIES

Supplier selection criteria and strategies will vary with purchased raw material, products, and component, for supplier selection, choosing a team which collects data by survey, or personal interview. Then analyse the data and find out the appropriate selection criteria. Common vendor and supplier selection criteria include:

1. Previous experience and performance of the raw material/product or services to be purchased.
   - The supplier should meet the customer requirements with the required quality.
   - The supplier should follow the quality system.
   - The supplier should have a quality system registration (e.g., ISO 9001).
   - The supplier should have the ability to meet the current and potential capacity requirements on the desired delivery schedule.
   - Flexibility in design change.
   - The supplier should have sufficient technical support.
   - Product or component cost should be optimum.
   - The supplier track record in business should be acceptable.
2. Methods for determining how well a potential supplier fits the selected criteria:
   - Get a financial report on the supplier.
   - Obtain performance history over different criteria.
   - Request the supplier provide their financial as well as technical capability and testing methods.
   - Visit to the supplier firm by the selection team.
   - Determine supplier quality status – whether they are registered or not in quality system, or if they have a certificate which is provided by the quality system.
   - Confirm quality with another customer which is served by the supplier.
   - Analyse all the information collected by survey, personal meetings, and based on data or certificate obtained from the quality system.

5.11 SUPPLIER CERTIFICATION

This is a process by which a company manages supplier relationships in order to act as one entity to create value for all the stakeholders. Supplier certification is a specified minimum requirement expected from the supplier so that they are eligible to work with an organisation or customer. The main aim of this process is continuous improvement. Supplier certification is important due to the following reasons:

- Supplier certification enables the process of identifying suppliers which fulfil the requirements of the organisation.
- It helps to show the real potential of the suppliers.
- Through supplier certification, the company avoids some processes, like inspections
- It makes the supplier capable of continuous improvement.
- It helps to establish an open and strong relationship.
- Customer certification helps the organisation to better serve the end-users.
- It helps to improve communication and sharing of information.

Generally, the factors to be considered for certification varies with the companies. However, some of the most important factors are as follows:

- Cost.
- Quality.
- Design.
- Transportation costs.
- Delivery time.
- Financial status.
- Environmental standards.

There are three major types of certification:

- ISO 9000, ISO 14000, and self-designed certifications of an organisation.

5.12   SUPPLIER RATING

Supplier rating is the process in which supplier has been rated according to their performance. This is a necessary part of the organisation to minimise downstream supply chain costs. A supplier rating is treated as feedback for the supplier – it is important for both suppliers, as well as the organisation. With a supplier rating, a supplier can know their strengths and weaknesses. It is a powerful tool for the supplier to improve them, and it helps the organisation to choose better suppliers according to their work. The supplier rating depends on various factors like:

1. Design.
2. Quality.
3. Delivery capability.
4. Supplier performance history.
5. Return policy.
6. Inventory or component cost.
7. Production technique.
8. Technology used.
9. Information system.
10. Reputation.
11. Training system for employees with technology.

12. Repair policy.
13. Financial capability.
14. Attitude.
15. Technical capability.
16. Cleaner production.
17. Green product.
18. Environmental certification, etc.

The selection criteria may change according to the organisation, the place, and the government's laws. In the literature, the authors invented various methods to rate suppliers, like the linear averaging method, the cost ratio method, the categorical method, etc.

5.13 CONCLUSION

Employee involvement and supplier partnership is a powerful tool for any organisation to take competitive advantages. TEI is simply promoting the participative culture within the organisation, meaning 100% participation of all. So TEI is not merely confined to the involvement of all team players (workers) toward the quality objective, continuous quality improvement, etc. For organisational growth, the teamwork culture is an important tool. Teamwork is the concept of effective utilisation of knowledge, skill, and experience of a team member. Every member should have a specific knowledge, skill, and experience in the particular field. The other tools like QC help to improve quality production. The main objective behind the formation of a QC is to motivate the employees to share their problem related to work and get the solution toward improving the performance of the organisation. In this chapter, we focus on the employee involvement and supplier partnership and their competitive advantages, and ways to improve various quality programmes like a reward system, vendor selection, supplier certification, etc.

5.14 CASE STUDY: A CASE STUDY AT TECUMSEH PRODUCTS COMPANY

This case study was carried out at the Tecumseh Product Company. This case study was made by Kalva and Srinivasu (2017) and carried out in the compressor manufacturing division. The following steps were involved in the QC programme.

1. Identification of problem.
2. Selection of problem.
3. Define the problem.
4. Analysis of the problem.
5. Identification of causes.
6. Data analysis.
7. Developing a solution.
8. Probable resistance.

9. Trial implementation.
10. Follow-up/review.

Step 1 – Identification of problem: The problem can be in the concerned department, identified by the departmental quality control circle. Suppose 50 problems were identified.

Step 2 – Selection of the problem: In this section, the identified problem is categorised into three groups:

Group A: In this group, they kept the problem which gets sorted out by itself (Team). Suppose this is an 'X' problem.

Group B: In this group, they kept that problem which is solved by the help of others (Experts). This is a 'Y' problem.

Group C: In this group, they kept the problem which was solved by the involvement of management. This is a 'Z' problem.

The QC team has selected some problems from group A and rated them on the basis of importance, urgency, and feasibility.

Step 3 – Define the problem: In this section, the team has selected the most rated problem. Let's say 'tapping' defects are selected.

Step 4 – Analysis of the problem: The team has identified where the tapping defect is occurring in the manufacturing process.

Step 5 – Identification of causes: The QC team has identified some causes after brainstorming.

Step 6 – Data analysis: After an investigation of causes, the team has verified causes through '3W' and '1 H.'

Step 7 – Developing a solution: In these steps, develop an appropriate solution with the team.

Step 8 – Probable resistance: An awareness programme is conducted for all the operators, who were working in the line, the solution is explained to them, and they are asked to express their views for its trial implementation.

Step 9 – Trial implementation: With help from team and approval from local management, the trial implementation of the solution occurs.

Step 10 – Follow-up/Review: In the last step, do a follow-up or review of the results.

POINTS TO REMEMBER

- **Improving quality through employee involvement:** Employees' involvement is important for any successes in full business. We can say that employees are the strength of a firm. TEI means involving employees, empowering them, and involving them in the decision-making process. It gives an opportunity for continuous improvement. The QC is a group of employees which aims to analyse and solve work-related problems. The objective of the QC is the continuous improvement of the organisation.
- **Teamwork:** A team is defined as a group of members with a common goal. Teamwork throughout any organisation is an important component of TQM

implementation. In any organisation, the QIT finds a group of people with specific knowledge, skills, and experience in a particular area and brings them together to analyse the problems and solve them. Teamwork is the concept of effective utilisation of knowledge, skills, and experiences of team members.

- **Suggestion System:** The suggestion system may be defined as welcoming good ideas from employees. Suggestion systems are designed to provide the individual with the opportunity to be involved by contributing to the organisation. It is the responsibility of management to make it easy for employees to suggest improvements. Encouraging employee participation starts the creative process.

  Suggestion systems and programmes are based upon the reasonable assumption that employees can contribute their thoughts for the purposes of the organisation's operations and/or decreasing costs. Essentially, a contract is set up between employees and the organisation in which the employees are offered rewards for worthy ideas.

- **Quality Circles**: QC is also known as the quality control cycle. A QC can be defined as a group of employees in the workplace who perform the same work or function in their job. This group of employees will normally number 3–10 and be led by a supervisor. Members of the group meet regularly and discuss problems and discover the solutions related to their role at work.

- **Effective Recognition and Reward System:** For taking competitive advantages, an organisation should have a recognition and reward system. In a competitive business environment, the organisation will be looking at improvements in quality while reducing costs. Effective reward and recognition programmes are powerful tools to motivate the employees to change work habits towards the organisation's benefit.

- **Benefits of Employee Involvement:** Employee involvement means the participation of all employees in creating a positive working environment and development of the organisation.

- **Principles of Customer–Supplier Relations**: An organisation spends approximately 60% of the product cost to purchase raw materials. For the production of a good quality product, it's important to purchase good quality raw material at optimum cost, and this depends upon the customer–supplier relationship. The customer–supplier relationship is the business relationship between them in terms of material quality, re-working services, handling customers' complaints, delivery performance, etc. Customer and supplier should have the same goal – to satisfy the end-user – hence, having a healthy customer–supplier relationship is important for any business.

- **Supplier Selection:** The supplier selection process is most important for manufacturing industries, because a large percentage of their costs are the raw materials and services. It will help to reduce the direct cost to the bottom line. It is also important in green supply chain management. Nowadays, most of the manufacturing industries have a lot of pressure from environmental legislation and from society for cleaner production, and it is only possible when supplier provide non-hazardous raw materials.

- **Supplier Certification**: This shows the quality management skill of the supplier. It is a specified minimum requirement expected from the supplier, and it makes it eligible to work with a customer or organisation.
- **Supplier Rating:** Supplier rating is the process in which the supplier is rated according to their performance. This is the necessary part of the organisation to minimise the downstream supply chain cost. The supplier rating is treated as feedback for the supplier – it is important both for suppliers as well as an organisation. With a supplier rating, the supplier can know their strengths and weaknesses. It is a powerful tool for suppliers to improve their performance.

SELF-ASSESSMENT QUESTIONS

1. Explain how to improve quality through employee involvement.
2. Explain teamwork and how it helps in organisational growth.
3. Write about the suggestion system.
4. Explain the process of the employee suggestion system.
5. What do you mean by the quality circle?
6. What do you understand by the recognition and reward system? Explain some reward programmes.
7. Write down the benefits of employee involvement.
8. Explain the principle of the customer–supplier relationship.
9. Why is supplier selection important for the organisation?
10. What do you mean by supplier rating?

BIBLIOGRAPHY

Abdul Rahim, S. (2013). *Supplier Selection in the Malaysian Telecommunications Industry* (Doctoral dissertation, Brunel University Brunel Business School PhD Theses).

Bakotić, D., & Rogošić, A. (2017). Employee involvement as a key determinant of core quality management practices. *Total Quality Management & Business Excellence, 28*(11–12), 1209–1226.

Barbarosoglu, G., & Yazgac, T. (1997). An application of the analytic hierarchy process to the supplier selection problem. *Production & Inventory Management Journal, 38*(1), 14–21.

Benson, G. S., & Lawler, E. E. III. (2016). Employee involvement: Research foundations. In: *The Psychologically Healthy Workplace: Building a Win-Win Environment for Organizations and Employees*, M. J. Grawitch & D. W. Ballard (Eds.) (pp. 13–33). American Psychological Association.

Braglia, M., & Petroni, A. (2000). A quality assurance-oriented methodology for handling trade-offs in supplier selection. *International Journal of Physical Distribution & Logistics Management, 38*(1), 14–21.

Chan, F. S. (2003). Interactive selection model for supplier selection process: An analytical hierarchy process approach. *International Journal of Production Research, 41*(15), 3549–3579.

Chen, Y. M., & Huang, P. N. (2007). Bi-negotiation integrated AHP in suppliers' selection. *Benchmarking: An International Journal, 14*(5), 575–593.

Crosby, P. B. (1979). *Quality Is Free: The Art of Making Quality Certain* (Vol. 94). McGraw-Hill, New York.

Dixon, G. W. (1966). An analysis of supplier selection systems and decisions. *Journal of Purchasing, 2*(1), 28–41.

Gözükara, İ., Çolakoğlu, N., & Şimşek, Ö. F. (2019). Development culture and TQM in Turkish healthcare: Importance of employee empowerment and top management leadership. *Total Quality Management & Business Excellence, 30*(11–12), 1302–1318.

Haffar, M., Al-Karaghouli, W., Djebarni, R., & Gbadamosi, G. (2019). Organisational culture and TQM implementation: Investigating the mediating influences of multidimensional employee readiness for change. *Total Quality Management & Business Excellence, 30*(11–12), 1367–1388.

Ishikawa, K. (1984). Quality control in Japan. In: *The Japanese Approach to Product Quality,* Sasaki, N. and Hutchins, D. (Eds.) (pp. 1–5). Pergamon Press, Oxford.

Jaeger, M., & Adair, D. (2016). Perception of TQM benefits, practices and obstacles. *The TQM Journal, 28*(2), 317–336.

Kalva, R. S., & Srinivasu, V. (2017). Quality circle in practice: A case study at Tecumseh products company. *International Journal of Engineering Development & Research, 5*(4), 1402–1411.

Ramesh, N., & Ravi, A. (2017). Determinants of total employee involvement: A case study of a cutting tool company. *International Journal of Business Excellence, 11*(2), 221–240.

van Assen, M. F. (2020). Training, employee involvement and continuous improvement–the moderating effect of a common improvement method. *Production Planning & Control, 31*, 1–13.

6 Cost of Quality

6.1 PRODUCTIVITY AND QUALITY RELATIONSHIP

Productivity can be defined as the ratio of the entire yield to total effort, i.e. input materials, manpower, investment cost, etc. Quality determines the conformance, performance, reliability, durability, and thus measures the overall performance. A positive correlation always exists between quality and productivity. Product sales can be increased by increasing quality. It also results in a defectless product, enhances efficiency, decreases the replacement of products, and improves customer satisfaction. In fact, better quality acts as the best advertisement through customer satisfaction, and decreases the costs associated with the sales department. In the manufacturing sector, manual operations have been replaced by computerised operations to improve quality. In such a manufacturing environment, standardisation and precision will likely reduce production time and defects and enhance productivity. Increased productivity reduces costs and also obtained competitiveness for organisations. Consumers are also satisfied, as they get good quality products for their money. Thus, enhancing productivity is not only measured in labour performance, but also in other stakeholders of the organisation. It is the sum total of efficiency and the aim to develop a win–win situation for the organisation in inter- and intra-level conditions. The productivity and quality relationship have been shown in Figure 6.1.

6.2 COST OF QUALITY

The Cost of Quality (COQ) is defined as tangible costs, which are accounted based on the actual transaction costs of the production process. These costs involve the commonly used conventional Prevention–Appraisal–Failure (PAF) model projected by Feigenbaum. The theory of COQ has been executed effectively in manufacturing and service organisations. However, COQ has focused on inter-firm quality, but not the complete supply chain. COQ acts as an accounting method that conveys the effect of bad quality and the activities of a quality programme and efforts into a common language for managers. COQ is a language that each member of the supply chain can understand, which is essential as it affects processing costs and consumers' needs. Thus, it is critical to extend COQ as a peripheral measure and combine these costs into SC modelling. Obvious examples include:

1. The adaptation of a manufactured item.
2. The re-testing of an assembly.
3. The modernisation of equipment.
4. The rectification of a bank statement.

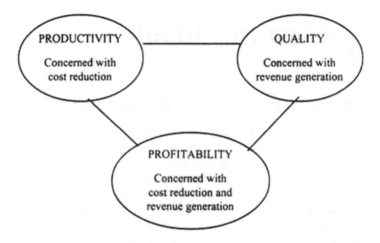

FIGURE 6.1   Productivity and quality relationship.

The cost of quality is generally classified into four categories:

1. External failure cost.
2. Internal failure cost.
3. Inspection (appraisal) cost.
4. Prevention cost.

The cost of quality classification is shown in Figure 6.2.

6.3   COST OF CONFORMANCE

Cost of conformance is defined as the element of cost to avoid poor quality of products. It consists of costs associated with quality-assuring activities, like process

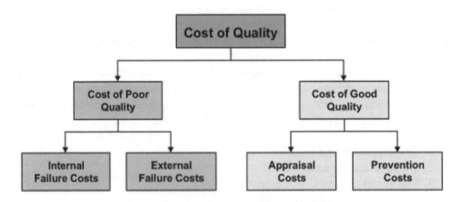

FIGURE 6.2   The cost of quality classification.

standardisation, training programmes, and costs associated with quality controlling activities, like reviewing, auditing, inspecting, and testing.

Cost of conformance is then divided into two types –

1. Prevention cost.
2. Appraisal cost.

The preventive costs are the costs due to enhancing the quality in production and servicing so that any fluctuation in process will be accepted either on upper or lower range of control charts. These costs generally consist of workers' guidance costs and equipping the workplace with advanced machinery and technologies. These also involve activities in the documentation process. These are the activities that costs are associated with and incurred:

a. Collecting information on consumers' needs by proper surveying.
b. Transfer of consumers' needs into the design and documentation stage.
c. Checking the authentication of suppliers.
d. Proper training of employees to enhance their capabilities.
e. Quality administration.

Appraising cost is another element in this category. This cost includes standardisation of the processes and activities so that a high level of quality in products and processes can be achieved. These costs are further incurred by the following activities or processes as elaborated below.

a. Testing and inspecting the data.
b. Inspecting the facilities provided by the suppliers.
c. Evaluating the quality during packaging and dispatching.
d. Performing different types of non-destructive testing.
e. Field trials of new products.

6.4   COST OF PREVENTION

One of the easiest ways to reduce the quality cost is to avoid defects before the first stage of production. This is very much less expensive, as it is easier to prevent a defect than finding and correcting the defect after it has happened. Costs associated with this are mainly focused on activities whose function is to avoid the defects. Organisations adopt some methods to avoid defects, for example, statistical quality control, value engineering, proper training of workers, and a number of techniques from TQM.

In this, there are costs incurred in QCs and statistical quality control. QCs involve groups of workers so that they can get together on continuous basis and debate some special issues to improve the quality awareness programme. Both managers and other employees can participate in this circle.

Statistical Quality Control (SQC) is one of the methods to avoid defects in products by improving processes. SQC basically involves seven principles. The first four techniques are non-statistical, and the other three are based on statistical processes:

1. Pareto diagram.
2. Process flow diagram.
3. Cause-and-effect diagram.
4. Check sheets.
5. Histogram.
6. Control chart for variables and attributes.
7. Graphs.

Some organisations offer technological help for their suppliers in avoiding raw material defects. Mainly in the case of just-in-time (JIT), this type of help is necessary for suppliers. In a JIT purchasing system, all vendors and suppliers operate by supplying at just the correct time, in the right situation, and in the right quantity to meet the consumers' needs. There are advantages of using JIT system to reduce prevention cost, as follows:

1. Reduced inventory cost.
2. Reduced material handling cost.
3. Reduced manpower and other facility at the time of production.
4. Easy to maintain a level of quality with lower costs.
5. Reduced inspection cost of supplier raw materials.

6.5   APPRAISAL COST

This cost is another element of quality control cost. Appraisal costs are a specific category in cost estimation. Organisations incur this cost to ensure their products and services are up to the expectations of consumers and other regulatory bodies of their country. These costs also consist of testing and inspecting expense.

Appraisal costs may include following categories:

1. Inspection on job floor.
2. Following international standard in processes.
3. Laboratory inspection.
4. Sharing technologies with other firms.
5. Continuous meetings of top management.

6.5.1   APPRAISAL APPROACH

The appraisal approach values assets based on the below factors:

1. Quality of services.
2. The income generated from the products and services through consumers.
3. Market value of asset, especially when consumers may pay more or less than actual value.

6.6 FAILURE COST

This cost has a great and immediate impact on any organisation's performance. Whenever a breakdown occurs, there will always be lost profit. This cost may include following elements

4. Lost profit.
5. The cost of the repair.
6. The constant and unpredictable operational wages exhausted during the downtime.

Usually these costs are huge for any organisation per year. These costs are normally recognised by top management even after bankruptcy. Failure costs are mainly incurred as during failure, whether it is of machinery or manpower, no production takes place, though inventory carrying costs and other maintenance costs or repairing costs are incurred continuously. Thus, fixed costs are continuously increasing, but there is no production taking place. Sometimes these costs are difficult to avoid for department managers and other top management.

There are two type of elements into which failure cost can be classified namely:

1. Internal failure cost.
2. External failure cost.

Total external and internal cost includes the following elements:

1. Labour: Both direct and indirect.
2. Product waste: This includes product repair and rework costs.
3. Services: This includes servicing of failed machinery and equipment cost.
4. Cost incurred due to inadequate materials supplied by suppliers.
5. Some additional costs of miscellaneous failures.

6.6.1 INTERNAL FAILURE COST

This cost occurs with non-conforming products and services namely:

1. Product scrapping costs: This cost is associated with non-usable products.
2. Product or machinery repair costs.
3. Work environment reconditioning costs.

Internal failure costs consist of the following elements of non-conformance costs:

a. Failure cost during the designing phase of the products: This cost is mainly incurred due to inadequate design, reworking on design changes, and scrap produced due to design changes of products.
b. Failure cost due to purchasing: This cost is mainly incurred due to rejection of outsourced equipment and other raw materials, replacement of outsourced facilities, suppliers' action correction, etc.

c. Operational failure cost: This cost includes a major portion of internal failure cost due to operationally unsuitable products or services, resource reviewing, product scrapping costs, internally active labour costs, etc.

6.6.2 EXTERNAL FAILURE COST

This cost is mainly incurred after products or services have been delivered to consumers. This cost may include the following elements:

1. Eliminating customers' complaints, and providing home services.
2. Back-ordering products for the consumers.
3. Redesigning costs due to faulty design steps.
4. Warranty costs paid by the organisation for repairing, cleaning, and poor working condition of the product.
5. Costs paid for damage and destruction to consumers and workplaces by products delivered by the organisation.
6. Penalties imposed by government regulatory bodies on the organisation due to its poor performance.
7. Cost paid to the dissatisfied consumers in the form of rewards or cashback.
8. Costs incurred by the organisation to prevent the loss due to fall in sales.

6.7 QUALITY COST ESTIMATION IN ENGINEERING AND SERVICE INDUSTRIES

Quality cost estimation in engineering and service industries includes managing of activity expenditure; it is estimating and management with proper monitoring, appraising the processes and facilities, and finally, risk analysis. The cost estimation process balances between expenditure, cost, and the period of estimation. They seek the optimum balance between cost, quality, and time requirements. Cost engineers play a very important role in cost estimation, as their practical knowledge and information helps in analysing all elements of cost estimation as discussed above (Figure 6.3).

6.7.1 COST ESTIMATING METHODS AND BEST PRACTICES

Estimation of quality is the description of quality enrichment as per the estimation. These enrichments have to function according to the benchmarks set by government organisations based on various quality standards or Indian standard organisation standards. There are other aspects of quality estimation other than its enrichments for the consumer's satisfaction. Some of the general scope of estimation includes proper documentation of all the information and quality assurance standards, uniform quality standards, etc.

Developing different facilities for cost estimation is the critical section of quality cost estimation. Early on, estimating follows different techniques by agencies. One of the best techniques is the estimation of resources requirements, e.g., estimating raw materials in manufacturing organisations or requirements of manpower in

FIGURE 6.3 Quality cost estimation.

small–medium enterprises, and then estimating cost associated. One of the returns of cost estimation is the segregation of quantities and costs.

6.7.2 METHODS FOR ESTIMATING COST

The following are cost estimation techniques used in the engineering and service industries:

1. Compilation of costs by the accounting method. It includes estimation by calculating different cost in different activities viz. travelling, telephone bills, etc.
2. Compilation of costs on the basis of workers involved in any activities, especially in designing and training activities.
3. Calculation of costs on the basis of working hours spent by manpower. Cost is calculating by multiplying the wage rate.

6.8 CONCLUSION

The Cost of Quality (COQ) is defined as tangible costs, which are accounted based on the actual transaction costs of the production process. Cost of conformance is defined as the element of cost to avoid poor quality of products. Costs associated with prevention are mainly focused on activities whose function is to avoid the defects. Appraisal costs are a specific category in cost estimation. Failure cost has a great and immediate impact on any organisation's performance. The cost estimation process balances between expenditure, cost, and the period of estimation.

6.9 CASE STUDY: A FOUNDRY SHOP

This is a case history of a foundry shop, which makes casting products by performing foundry operations. This shop has to produce 10,000 kg of its product in the foundry shop. Now, the next step is to estimate the cost of quality.

Fixed data:

Sales price of casting product is Rs 30/Kg.
Scrap value of casting product is Rs 10/Kg.
Net worth loss in sales is (30−10) = Rs 20.
Now taking various type of cost:

1. Preventive cost: This includes costs associated with the product design stage, process control stage, etc.
   Therefore, PC = Rs 1000.
2. Appraisal cost: This cost includes costs of inspection of casting products, quality engineering costs, etc.
   Therefore, AC = Rs 2000.
3. Internal failure cost: This cost includes cost lost in workers and machine extra works in scrap products, cost of rework etc. For this shop, it is 10% rejection of the total production, i.e. 1000 Kg.
   Therefore, IFC = 1000* 20 = Rs 20000.
   Other cost (OC1) = Rs 5000.
4. External failure cost: This cost includes costs lost in handling customers' complaints, loss of sales due to lack of advertisement, etc. For this shop, it is 5% of the total production, i.e. 500 Kg.
   Therefore, EFC = 500* 20 = Rs 10,000.
   Other costs like customer goodwill lost (OC2) = Rs 2500
5. Hidden cost: This cost includes intangible costs of visit to customer, extra manufacturing costs due to defects, scrap not reported, etc.
   Therefore, HC = Rs 5000.
   Now calculate the total cost of quality = 1000+2000+20000+5000+ 10000+2500+5000/10000 = Rs 4.55 per Kg of casting product.

POINTS TO REMEMBER

- **Failure:** This cost is incurred due to defective items produced by any organisation. This cost is zero when product is 100% good, and infinity when product is 100% defective.
- **External failure cost:** Costs associated with defects found after the customer receives the product or service. Example: Processing customer complaints, customer returns, warranty claims, product recalls.
- **Internal failure cost:** Costs associated with defects found before the customer receives the product or service. Example: Scrap, rework, re-inspection, re-testing, material review, and material downgrades, etc.
- **Inspection (appraisal) cost:** Costs incurred to determine the degree of conformance to quality requirements, such as measuring, evaluating, or auditing. Example: Inspection, testing, process or service audits, calibration of measuring and test equipment.

- **Prevention cost:** Cost incurred to prevent (keep failure and appraisal cost to a minimum) poor quality. Example: New product review, quality planning, supplier surveys, process reviews, quality improvement teams, education and training.
- **Total quality cost curve:** This curve represents the total cost of quality per unit product. It is given as sum of failure and appraisal cost.
- **Cost of conformance:** This is that element of cost which avoids poor quality of products. It includes preventive and appraisal costs.

SELF-ASSESSMENT QUESTIONS

1. Define the different types of cost of quality with examples.
2. Explain the external failure cost with some example. Also, elaborate the area of the organisation which is associated with this cost.
3. Explain the internal failure cost with examples.
4. Discuss the different type of appraisal or inspection cost.
5. Discuss the quality cost estimation in the engineering field.
6. Write down different methods of cost estimation.
7. Elaborate the relationship between productivity and quality with examples.

BIBLIOGRAPHY

Carr, L. P. (1992). Applying cost of quality to a service business. *MIT Sloan Management Review, 33*(4), 72–77.

Dimitrantzou, C., Psomas, E., & Vouzas, F. (2020). Future research avenues of cost of quality: A systematic literature review. *The TQM Journal.* doi:10.1108/TQM-09-2019-0224.

Feigenbaum, A. V. (1956). Total quality-control. *Harvard Business Review, 34*(6), 93–101.

Malik, T. M., Khalid, R., Zulqarnain, A., & Iqbal, S. A. (2016). Cost of quality: Findings of a wood products' manufacturer. *The TQM Journal, 28*(1), 2–20.

Plewa, M., Kaiser, G., & Hartmann, E. (2016). Is quality still free? *International Journal of Quality & Reliability Management, 33*(9), 1270–1285.

Ramudhin, A., Alzaman, C., & Bulgak, A. A. (2008). Incorporating the cost of quality in supply chain design. *Journal of Quality in Maintenance Engineering, 14*(1), 71–86.

Srivastava, S. K. (2008). Towards estimating cost of quality in supply chains. *Total Quality Management, 19*(3), 193–208.

7 Organising for Quality

7.1 CONTINUOUS IMPROVEMENT

Another theory of the TQM philosophy is the concentration on continuous improvement. Conventional methods mainly depend on the hypothesis that once an organisation has obtained a definite stage of quality, it has to be treated as a measure of success for the organisation.

Generally, improving behaviour of any organisation is measured in terms of reducing defects of the products manufactured by it or passing of government-certified standards. Conventionally, in the US, quality improvement involves a major behaviour change for top management or a firm level reformation. In contrast with the US, the Japanese think that the most excellent and long-term changes can be obtained from continuous improvements. This can be better understood by taking an analogy that minute-sized doses of healthcare drugs are more effective than one large dose. Continuous improvement, termed 'kaizen' by the Japanese, demands that an organisation should continuously attempt to be superior in its culture and problem-tackling behaviour. Since, a company cannot reach perfection, therefore, an organisation should always estimate its performance and take continuous actions to advance it. Table 7.1 explains the concept of continuous improvement.

7.1.1 EXAMPLE OF CONTINUOUS IMPROVEMENT

In a district, it is observed that teachers of Science, Technology, Engineering, and Math (STEM) leave that district more than peers from other domains. Also, it is happening at a rapid rate. A continuous improvement approach is planned by the leaders of the district for retaining STEM educators. How does the district do this? Let's discuss it for three questions:

- What is the problem at hand? The district wants to increase the retention of STEM teachers.
- What are the plausible changes to be introduced with reasons? The district might introduce additional coaching supports or financial incentives to retain STEM teachers.
- How will we know what change has actually resulted in improvement? The district will collect data that provides information about whether and how it is succeeding in retaining STEM teachers. The district will identify clear and specific measures – such as coaching logs, teacher satisfaction surveys, or teacher retention data – to capture both the processes and the outcomes that are critical to the continuous improvement process.

TABLE 7.1
Concept of Continuous Improvement

Concept of continuous improvement	Main idea
1. Focusing on customer	Main concept is the identification of customer need in advance for their satisfaction. It is a first step in continuous improvement for any organisation.
2. Continuous improvement	This is a never-ending process in term of process and culture improvement. Since 100% improvement is not possible, continuous effort is required for enhancing performance and reliability.
3. Employee training	This involves complete awareness of each employer in the organisation by using quality awareness programmes and training of workers on a regular basis for their skills enhancement and adaption of technologies.
4. Use of quality tools	In this, different techniques have to be used for improving quality and avoiding defects, e.g., quality cycles, different statistical methods to follow different standards.
5. Designing of products	In this, different products have to be designed as per specifications of customers' needs by following different designing parameters set by the organisations based on some standards.
6. Quality management	Quality should be improved during the manufacturing stages. Reason for quality problems should be found out and proper actions taken to avoid it.
7. Suppliers' management	This takes care of proper supplying facilities of raw materials and machineries. Therefore, this takes corrective action for enhancing supplier's capabilities.

7.2   JOSEPH M. JURAN PHILOSOPHY

Next to W. Edwards Deming, Dr. Joseph Juran considered as having the most influence on total quality management. Juran initially focused on a quality plan at Western Electric. He was basically recognised because of his *Quality Control Handbook* in 1951. In 1954 he went to Japan to team with manufacturers and gave lectures on quality. But his concept is comparable to Deming's theory, with a few disagreements. Deming focused on transforming the behaviour of any firm, but Juran focused on quality implementation without caring about the transforming of the firm in quality managing. Juran's most important assistance is the defining of quality and its cost. Juran is recognised for introducing quality as a strength in utility, but not just as per design terms and condition of products. In other words, quality can be defined as the strength which has to be taken care of in the manufactured goods' utility for the consumers, rather than concentrating on it for technical constraints. Juran also recognised for the theory of the cost of quality – this permitted computing quality in terms of dollars without considering biased measures. Juran was also acknowledged for his quality trilogy ideologies: planning, controlling, and finally improving quality by following the above two ideologies. The first element of the trilogy, quality planning, is essential for the organisation for the identification of its consumers and product demand, and for setting the industry aims. In this context, some procedure has to be followed for achieving different quality standards which have been set by organisations prior to actual production. The second element of the trilogy is quality control; in this, different statistical techniques have to be used for ensuring quality standards variations within permissible limits or within consumers' acceptable level. Finally, quality improvement is the third element of the trilogy. As per Juran, improvement in quality must be done in a continuous manner, along with Deming's philosophy. To achieve this, training and awareness programmes should be organised on continuous basis for workers by organisations.

Juran's Trilogy is probably one of the easiest overall frameworks for quality management. Juran noticed that it is a common language which can be easily recognised by managers of the organisation for use in financial management. Financial management is executed by implementation of three managerial techniques for finance, namely planning, controlling, and improving. Quality management also utilises these three basic activities of planning, controlling, and improving. The trilogy explains the requirement of quality management by achieving the goals with effectiveness and efficiently.

According to Juran's Trilogy, the three elements of quality management can be briefly explained as follows:

* Quality planning: This includes procedures of product design, servicing, and processing to attain target goals.
* Quality controlling: This includes procedures which have to be followed throughout the operation for achieving the desired goals.
* Quality improving: This includes various techniques which are used for improving quality in a continuous manner.

Basically, Juran's Trilogy is three directional philosophies with number of layered activities, as it needs the above three elements for its proper implementation in quality management and its improvement, e.g., the proper quality planning stage of any innovative product consists of planning distribution of products, supplier selection, etc. Another element of the planning phase explains data collecting techniques, involvement of the public and technology, etc.

7.3 THE PLAN–DO–STUDY–ACT CYCLE

The plan–do–study–act (PDSA) cycle explains the actions that an organisation has to execute for attaining continuous improvement of operations and work culture. The outline of this concept is given in Figure 7.1. This is also termed a Shewhart cycle or a Deming wheel. The circular behaviour of this cycle shows that improving in a continuous manner is a never-ending development. These are the steps involved in the PDSA cycle:

* **Plan:** The first procedure of the PDSA cycle is planning. In this procedure, top management have to examine the running activities and set a plan if any problems are encountered. They require proper documentation of current activities for up-to-date debugging of the procedure by proper

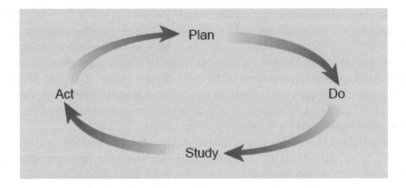

FIGURE 7.1   The concept of PDSA.

data-collection and problem identification. All of the collected data is examined and utilised to construct an efficient and effective plan for upgrading and precise actions to assess performance.

- **Do:** The second step of the PDSA cycle is proper implementation of the plan activities or the execution of the plan operations. Throughout the implementing stages, top management must change all the documentation work after collection and evaluation of the data or information.
- **Study:** The third step is for improvement of data-collecting methods and analysis of them. The collected information is analysed to confirm that the plan is achieving the desired aim which was set during the planning stage.
- **Act:** The last step of the PDSA cycle is continuous improvement. This process involves acting depending on the output of the previous stages. One of the best ways to achieve this is communication of the results to each and every employer of the organisation. After this, implementation of new procedures will take place which has been successful in the past. As all operations of evaluation and planning act in a cyclic manner, this will be repeated again and again for achieving continuous improvement.

Figure 7.1 explains the concept of PDSA.

7.3.1   EXAMPLE OF THE PDSA CYCLE

An individual is planning to schedule all the operations or tasks which are being repeated in every week. To complete the cycle, the PDSA cycle has been implemented.

Plan: In planning activities, a person can use a blackboard to write down the basic activities of all three shifts, i.e. morning, afternoon, and evening, which are repeated every week. For making such kinds of plans, it must be noted that the schedule of planning does not coincide with family activities.

Do: After planning of activities, the next step is the following of a planned schedule for actually performing the task. In this regular review of tasks performed, it is essential to find any missing task.

Study: After performing the actual tasks, the next step is to analyse all the previous tasks and re-allocate the time to all the tasks which have not been satisfactorily performed so as to achieve better results next time. This time, distribution can be discussed with the family and other close friends.

Act: Based on the above analysis, again tasks are performed as per the changed schedule according to the priorities set for each activities. In this, an individual must act in a positive manner, as sometimes results do not meet expectations. In this situation, the PDSA cycle can be repeated two to three times to improve the results.

7.4 SIX SIGMA

Before understanding Six Sigma, let us first describe briefly the terms associated with it and statistics like sigma and standard deviation.

Sigma: The word sigma means standard deviation. Standard deviation determines what variation may exist in a data distributing system. It is a critical aspect of the calculation of the tolerable amount of faulty units created in a sample population. Six Sigma concepts are not suitable for more than 3.4 defects parts per million.

Standard Deviation: Standard deviation means distribution of data around the mean data of the entire sample, or it represents clustering of data which is very close to the middle of a distribution. Normal distribution is the bell-shaped curve, which is balanced about the mean or average line of a sample population as shown in Figure 7.2.

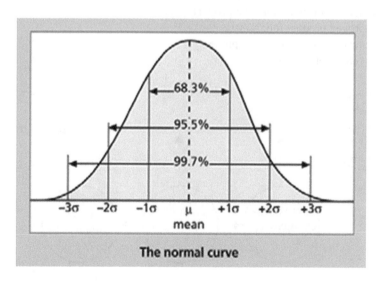

FIGURE 7.2 Normal distribution curve.

7.4.1 HOW TO USE IT?

Six Sigma concentrates on improving process quality. Therefore, it is considered a process capability tool. Conventionally, a process is called 'capable' if the natural extent, positive and negative three sigma, i.e. accuracy of 99.73%, is not more than the engineering standards. Six Sigma states that processes perform according to the engineering requirement, i.e. at least positive or negative six sigma from the process mean. This needs huge efforts for scientific and inspecting measures. Normally, numbers of tests are performed on different variables for better knowledge of what is happening during a process or operation. Once the operational variables have been determined, the next step is the identification of critical variables which are affected most. After identification, make the variable more effectively controlled to improve process capabilities index. Six Sigma consists of following elements, which are also explained in Figure 7.3.

- Proper understanding of customers and their requirements from the product.
- Review customers' reports and other data.
- Screening and prioritising of issues according to their impact and occurrence rate during the process.
- Determination of inter-firm activities which affect the organisation most.
- Identification of stage where the defects are occurring more frequently.
- Develop methods to tackle the defects effectively (Figure 7.3).

7.4.2 BENEFITS OF SIX SIGMA

- Reduction of process cycle time.
- Enhanced production and added value.
- Improved capacity and output.
- Reduction of total defective products.
- Improved product reliability.
- Reduction of lead times of process.
- Smothing of process flow.

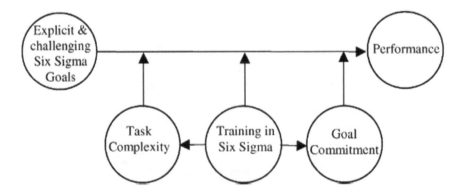

FIGURE 7.3   Six Sigma elements.

- Increased return on investment.
- Improved overall customer satisfaction.

7.4.3 Examples of Six Sigma

Sigma tools have been found to be beneficial in reducing errors and finding optimum benefits from various projects:

Affinity diagram: The tool helps in identifying the best ideas out of the ideas provided by the people.

Histogram: A bar chart to estimate and evaluate the data collated from various aspects of a system.

Pareto charts: This short-lists causes of various problems. It is one of the easiest ways to solve problems.

Brainstorm: Usage of this tool involves employee participation where they think innovatively and come up with variety of ideas and suggestions for the purpose of improvement. Effective solutions are arrived at in the culmination of this phase in critical situations.

There are numerous organisations that feature the examples of Six Sigma implementation. Examples of Six Sigma companies:

Motorola: This is the inventor of the Six Sigma system. Its implementation was on an experimental basis to resolve the frequent quality issues in the company. The yield of implementation of this system was brilliant, and it was evident from the performance of the organisation.

Satyam: Satyam, a prominent company in the software domain, became one of the most popular companies in the area after implementation of the Six Sigma infrastructure.

Microsoft: A popular company, and one of the highest revenues-generating organisations, had a secret of implementing Six Sigma behind near-perfect service deliveries. In fact, Microsoft is considered an ideal example of Six Sigma implementation.

7.5 APPROACHES TO QUALITY – KAIZEN

Kaizen is a Japanese word which means continuous improvement of the process, work culture, and other aspects of the organisation for continuous quality improvement. One of the important concepts of kaizen is the ongoing, endless continuous improvement process. It should be noted that introduction of some innovative product or technology in any organisation is not a difficult task. The difficult task is keeping and maintaining the whole procedure which has been set once, and also following continuous improvement on a regular basis. Many organisations have tried to initiate such initiatives like QCs, re-engineering, and lean manufacturing, etc. However, only some of them have been successful; most of them failed to initiate the above projects due to obvious reason. For example, many foreign organisations have introduced QCs by linking workers, but most of the organisations have simply failed to adopt this concept. This occurred due to the requirements of new infrastructure of internal facilities, systems, and measures which would guarantee the continuation of QC actions. This has happened as most foreign organisation lacked the idea of kaizen. Kaizen basically involves six elements or pillars on which kaizen philosophy work. The six pillars of kaizen are shown in the form of an umbrella, as shown in Figure 7.4.

These are the basic elements of kaizen:

- Kanban includes customer focus.
- Systematic approach for managing quality programmes.
- Continuous improvement of processes.
- Zero-defects policies for defect reduction.
- Effectiveness of procedure activities for quality improvement.
- Proper networking of each facility of the organisation.

For proper implementation of above elements, the following activities must be carried out in the kaizen philosophy:

- Proper customer orientation.
- Implementation of Six Sigma.
- Total productivity maintenance for continuous improvement.
- Just-in-time approach.
- Automation of organisation facilities.
- Poka yoke, which means flexibility.

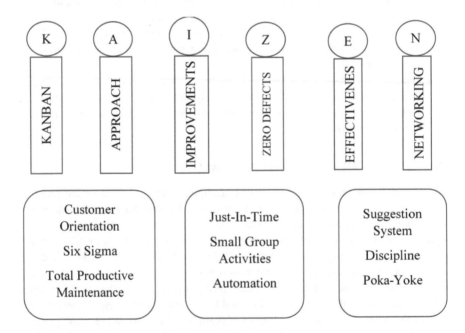

FIGURE 7.4 The six pillars of kaizen.

7.5.1 KAIZEN AND INNOVATION

The basis of kaizen is the '5S' model, as introduced by Japanese experts as a combination of goods, customs, and behaviour, taken from the conventional approach to behaviour in home and education institutions. Basically the '5S' concept is taken from the five Japanese words. The five 5S concept is explained briefly as follows:

- Seiri means selection: This includes appropriate selection of a place of work, behaviour, and proper instrumentation facilities of work, with the removal of everything which is unwanted or useless.
- Seito means a proper ordering system or systemic approach: Compactness of a workplace and having every necessary tools and technique for making them simple and quickly used.
- Seiso means clearness or cleaned-up work environment: A clean work environment enhances work safety to avoid injuries, and gives better control of equipment and enhanced accountability for the resources of manufacturing.
- Seiketsu means standardising: There should be set of standards for an organisation for its culture and facility utilisation based on which each worker performs their duties. It helps in taking care of equipment and maintaining workplace in order.
- Shitsuke means sustain: This is the capability of workers to maintain self-discipline without managing by the top authority. Adjustments by workers based on the standards followed by the organisation will definitely avoid bad habits and give guidance.

The proper adoption of the 5S concept allows the perfect implementation of the kaizen philosophy. In this, continuous improvement performed by all the workers participates in practices of changing the whole organisation. The block diagram of the 5S concept based on innovation is shown in Figure 7.5, and is also explained in tabulated form below.

The comparison of the basic features of kaizen philosophy and innovation is demonstrated in Table 7.2.

7.5.2 KAIZEN AND PEOPLE

The exact behaviour of kaizen is the involvement of individual in various functional activities. Improving through kaizen philosophy needs deep, organised, and continuous participation of the public by adopting specific programmes, but mostly developing their brains, leading to a process of development to initiate improvement which will never end. Kaizen's aim is 'today is superior with respect to yesterday, tomorrow is superior with respect to today.' This theory of regular enhancement is implemented in every direction. Organisational processes and functioning methods can be enhanced, quality defects can be avoided, and reduction of waste is also possible through waste management techniques. Customer satisfaction can be improved by improving quality or service. The work culture can be improved and relationships within the organisation can be improved. Kaizen is enhancement by using the 'poor man approach.' According to this approach, a poor man does not waste capital on

FIGURE 7.5   5S.

TABLE 7.2
The Comparison of Basic Features of Innovation and Kaizen Philosophy

Innovation	Kaizen
1. Creative form of production	1. Capable of adapting
2. Needs individual work	2. Requires teamwork
3. Needs specialist worker	3. There is no such need
4. Needs great knowledge on general topics	4. Needs great knowledge of details
5. Focused on techniques	5. Focused on workers
6. Information will flow toward a specific person	6. Information will flow through a specific channel
7. Focused on individual section	7. Focused on entire department
8. Searching for new technologies	8. Based on existing technologies
9. Limited feedback	9. Strong feedback
10. Short-term effect	10. Long-term effect
11. Involvement of specific chosen top management	11. Involvement of all workers
12. Adapting to fast-rising market of any country	12. Adapting to slow-rising market of any country
13. Requires huge investment	13. Requires small investment
14. Results are in the form of specific benefits	14. There is no specific output or unpredicted benefits

improvements as they have no money to waste at it. They rather use their knowledge, mind, imagination, capacity, and patience.

7.5.3   EXAMPLES OF QUALITY KAIZEN

The kaizen approach is beneficial for designing manufacturing systems. Chen et al. (2000) focused on a project of meat tenderiser manufacturing equipment. To address the issue of the current expensiveness of the equipment, the help of a design engineer, a manufacturing engineer, a quality engineer, and machining operators is sought. They are invited onto the team for this kaizen project. Once the problems are identified and information from various sources is obtained, a brainstorming process is used to explore the team goals. A cellular manufacturing system reduces the cost of production. Kaizen brings CI which helps in reducing the per unit cost by 25%; further, it reduces the floor space requirement by 15%. The communication network across the organisation is significantly improved as well.

Kaizen finds a use in a study by Chandrasekaran et al. (2008) to solve the 'part mismatch problem' on an assembly production line in the automobile industry. The process follows a technique to solve the problem by collecting data, then analysing the root cause. It then finds the best solution and after taking the corrective steps, documentation is prepared. The benefits of kaizen include the elimination of a major functional problem and a reduction in quality rejections and re-work processes, with significant reduction of costs.

7.6 AWARDS IN QUALITY MANAGEMENT

During the early 1980s there were two main standards for quality in an organisation, which have been recognised throughout the world – ISO 9000 and TQM. The first comprises certain quality standards based on which process and product standardisation has taken place. The level of conformity of a business to ISO 9000 can be estimated by using a confirmatory inspection, which process itself is regulated by published ISO standards. Organisations that effectively follow such standards would attain an international recognition and hold an ISO 9000 registration position. The second standard of quality check is TQM. It is a procedure which has a total orientation toward quality. It consists of certain quality managing tools for the entire organisation with the goal of increasing profit margins through proper focus on customers. There is no quality standard which has been internationally accepted. There is no consistent set of guiding principle for measuring the relevance of TQM. There are also no registration agencies that can provide recognised international standards for indicating the benefits which can be achieved by proper implementation of TQM. However, it is extensively acknowledged in the area of management that growth occurs by following the TQM principle. There exists no commonly applicable set of standards. In TQM, improvement by the application of TQM procedures can be only estimated by controlling the process enhancement and the deviation of outcomes and results. Therefore, the assessment of the extent of achievement by TQM involves the evaluation of the entire organisation's success.

With globalisation and rise in transnational trade, government agencies in many nations have realised the necessity of competing on a global scale. Identification of key elements of success and ways to propagate the body's knowledge of business entities are some initiatives that are funded to aid local groups of industries to gain a competitive advantage. Government agencies emphasise the importance of world-class standards of quality for surviving market competition by sponsoring the National Quality Awards. Specific guidelines enumerating the criteria for evaluation of an organisation are provided and publicised to measure progress. The sole idea here is to publicly recognise remarkable accomplishments, to put them forth as role models, and to show the benefits of employing the principles of Total Quality Management to others.

7.6.1 JAPANESE DEMING PRIZE

Japan acknowledged in the early 1950s the advantages of applying a quality-based approach as a competitive advantage in the international market. Manufactured goods' quality and the orientation towards the fulfilment of customer's demands have pushed the Japanese customers' products from cameras and electronic devices to complete automation so that their organisation emerged as a benchmark setter at globalised level. Due to above initiative, the profits of Japanese organisations have increased to a large extent which ultimately enhanced their economy. The Japanese Deming Prize is an award which is given to organisations for their growth in the application of the PDCA (Plan–Do–Check–Act) cycle. The efficiency of an organisation is analysed based on the following checkpoints: Proper planning, which includes policy-making, organising and managing, and training; proper implementing of turnover management and controlling of price; standardising the processes; quality assuring, etc. These processes result in future forecasting. It is clear that the Japanese Deming Prize criteria consist of all business functions. An award-winning position is fixed for organisations which exhibit success at different levels of business processes. This prize is not restricted only to certain aspects in segregated manner, like manufactured goods' quality or profitability. For example, the concept 'total quality management' was formerly known as 'total quality control' and was given when the Japanese Deming Prize acknowledged the presence of quality behaviour through the entire organisation.

7.6.2 MALCOLM BALDRIGE NATIONAL QUALITY AWARD – US

On August 20, 1987, US President Ronald Reagan accepted and signed the Malcolm Baldrige National Quality Improvement (MBNQI) Act of 1987. This Act later included the following text: 'the management of the United States in product and practice quality has been challenged powerfully (and sometimes effectively) by overseas competitors, and our country's production expansion has enhanced less than our competitors in the recent two decades.' The Act of Congress then comprised detailed mention of poor quality expenses, quality upgrading and enhanced productivity, strategic planning for quality and quality development programmes, assurance of good quality, better management understanding, and other concepts that are well-known to the experts of quality and management publications. American organisations were vulnerable to worldwide competition and were required to protect them – the US Government business advisors suggested the applications of quality management tools and techniques. This Act was fundamentally an announcement of war on bad quality and its management by the US Government. American organisations were affected to a large extent by globalised competition and there emerged a requirement of setting quality standards for improving their quality. The US Government's organisational advisors recommended the use of certain quality management tools or techniques. There was huge publicity coverage of these awards, and a number of copies of the criteria were distributed to the different organisations for the purposes of information, self-assessment, or its utility as the guidance for the award. Through this extensive publicity, the MBNQ Award criteria became recognisable to the experts who were concerned with the criteria for the assessment of TQM development even outside the US. The MBNQ Award criteria structure has seven groups having four basic elements, namely, driver which means guidance; system which involves data interpretation and their analysis; strategic quality planning; developing human resources and their organisation; managing process quality; measures which consists of quality and operations management; and finally, goal which means satisfying the customer needs. The award criteria are planned to highlight the key necessities of better value for customers by optimising the overall production within the business.

7.6.3 The Rajiv Gandhi National Quality Award (RGNQA) 1994

Named after India's late Prime Minister Shri Rajiv Gandhi, the Rajiv Gandhi National Quality Award was initiated by the Bureau of Indian Standards in 1991. Its evaluation procedure is very much comparable to that of the MBNQA. There are four award categories: 'large scale manufacturing units,' 'small scale manufacturing units,' 'service sector organisations,' and 'best of all'; one award for each of them. There are six commendation certificates each for the large- and small-scale manufacturing units. One commendation certificate is given to a service sector organisation.

7.7 CONCLUSION

The concept of Continuous Improvement (CI) has been explained in the chapter. CI is a never-ending process for quality improvement in total quality management philosophy and includes seven basic processes, namely: focus on customers, continuous process improvement, employee training, implementation of quality tools, proper product design, and finally, quality and supplier management. In this chapter, various concepts related to CI such as Juran's Trilogy, Six Sigma, kaizen, kanban, poka yoke, and JIT approaches have been explained in detail.

7.8 CASE STUDY: THE SCHOOL FOR QUALITY EDUCATION IN AMERICA

In 1995, the American Education Society realised that the current education system did not focused on quality education and its continuous improvement. Some of them suggested that proper implementation of TQM could be the best possible philosophy for creating a new education system which would suit the 21st century, rather than depending on the factory-based system of schooling in most of the countries of the world.

The following questions can be asked based on this case study:

- What are these kinds of school based on TQM?
- How this school different from current schools?
- How can TQM be implemented in the current education system?
- What will be the result of adopting TQM philosophy?

This new type of education system is mainly based on the four pillars of TQM:

Customer and supplier relation: In this, the whole school system must be focused on building proper relations between people. The people may belong either inside or outside the school. In the system, students play the dual role of both customer and supplier. As a supplier, students pursue their individual growth with continuous feedback to the teachers, which will also improve teacher's skills. As a customer, a student can expect a high quality of teaching with complete facilities and security of study in the school. In this kind of system, exam and test results are indicative of the faculty's success through students' performance.

Continuous improvement: This involves inch by inch improvement through proper collaboration of teaching staff and students. In this, both the teacher and the student groups act as a mutual support system at academic and personal level on a continuous basis. This type of system can exist only when people share their experience with ease. By implementing the PDSA cycle within the organisation, this type of continuous improvement can be possible.

Process/system approach: This approach is based on Deming's theory, which stated that 80% of things that have gone wrong within an organisation are the result of the entire system. Individual contributions of the teachers and the students are necessary, but this could not succeed without proper support of the top administration, parents, and business leaders. Therefore, a collaborative system effort is essential for achieving such a type of education system.

Consistent quality leadership: This is the most critical pillar for developing a new education system based on TQM. The complete success of any system depends on its top management capability of creating a competitive and innovative work environment. In the school system, e-learning and online teacher meetings can be seen as one of the initiatives in this direction. By implementing kaizen philosophy with people and innovation, this can be achieved easily.

POINTS TO REMEMBER

- **Continuous improvement:** It is a never-ending process for quality improvement in TQM philosophy. It includes seven basic processes, namely: focus on customers, continuous process improvement, employee training, implementation of quality tools, proper product design, and finally, quality and supplier management.
- **Juran's Trilogy:** This is a three-dimensional philosophy of continuous improvement. This includes planning, controlling, and improving of quality.
- **Six Sigma:** This is a disciplined, statistical-based, data-driven approach and continuous improvement methodology for eliminating defects in a product, process, or service.
- **Kaizen approach of quality improvement:** This is the Japanese word for 'improvement.' In business, kaizen refers to activities that continuously

improve all functions and involve all employees from the CEO to the assembly line workers. It also applies to processes, such as purchasing and logistics, that cross-organisational boundaries into the supply chain.

- **Kanban:** This is a scheduling system for lean manufacturing and JIT manufacturing. Taiichi Ohno, industrial engineer at Toyota, developed kanban to improve manufacturing efficiency. For many in the automotive sector, kanban is known as the 'Toyota nameplate system,' and as such the term is not used by some other auto manufacturers.
- **Poka yoke:** A poka yoke is any mechanism in any process that helps an equipment operator avoid (yoke) mistakes (poka). Its purpose is to eliminate product defects by preventing, correcting, or drawing attention to human errors as they occur.
- **JIT approach:** This is a methodology aimed primarily at reducing times within production system, as well as response times from suppliers and to customers.

SELF-ASSESSMENT QUESTIONS

1. Explain the role of continuous improvement in total quality management. Write down its basic elements.
2. State Juran's Trilogy. How does it help in quality improvement?
3. Briefly explain the PDCA cycle with examples.
4. What is the significance of Six Sigma? Explain with examples.
5. Briefly explain the benefits of Six Sigma.
6. Explain the kaizen philosophy with the help of the 5S concept.
7. How kaizen is related to innovation?
8. Briefly explain the role of people in the implementation of the kaizen approach for quality improvement.
9. Explain the role of various quality awards in continuous quality improvement.
10. What are the different types of quality awards that have been implemented across different countries for improving quality?

BIBLIOGRAPHY

Carnerud, D., Jaca, C., & Bäckström, I. (2018). Kaizen and continuous improvement–trends and patterns over 30 years. *The TQM Journal, 30*(4), 371–390.

Chandrasekaran, M., Kannan, S., & Pandiaraj, P. (2008). Quality improvement in automobile assembly production line by using Kaizen. *Manufacturing Technology Today, 7*(3), 33–38.

Chen, J. C., Dugger, J., & Hammer, B. (2000). A kaizen based approach for cellular manufacturing system design: A case study. *The Journal of Technology Studies, 27*(2), 19–27.

Dadi, G., & Azene, D. (2017). A TQM and JIT integrated continuous improvement model for organizational success: An innovative framework. *Journal of Optimization in Industrial Engineering, 10*(22), 15–23.

Ershadi, M. J., Najafi, N., & Soleimani, P. (2019). Measuring the impact of soft and hard total quality management factors on customer behaviour based on the role of innovation and continuous improvement. *The TQM Journal, 31*(6), 1093–1115.

Jimoh, R., Oyewobi, L., Isa, R., & Waziri, I. (2019). Total quality management practices and organisational performance: The mediating roles of strategies for continuous improvement. *International Journal of Construction Management, 19*(2), 162–177.

Jurburg, D., Viles, E., Tanco, M., & Mateo, R. (2017). What motivates employees to participate in continuous improvement activities? *Total Quality Management & Business Excellence, 28*(13–14), 1469–1488.

Matthews, R. L., & Marzec, P. E. (2017). Continuous, quality and process improvement: Disintegrating and reintegrating operational improvement? *Total Quality Management & Business Excellence, 28*(3–4), 296–317.

McLean, R. S., Antony, J., & Dahlgaard, J. J. (2017). Failure of continuous improvement initiatives in manufacturing environments: A systematic review of the evidence. *Total Quality Management & Business Excellence, 28*(3–4), 219–237.

Prashar, A., & Antony, J. (2018). Towards continuous improvement (CI) in professional service delivery: A systematic literature review. *Total Quality Management & Business Excellence, 29*, 1–29.

8 Human Aspect in Quality Management

8.1 HUMAN ROLE IN AN ORGANISATION

Human resources in an organisation handle the physical resources, e.g., money, materials, machinery, etc. to perform various functions by which an organisation achieve their goals. Each individual in the organisation is related to the others and his functioning affects others and, in turn, is affected by others. Thus, in a large organisation, the collaboration of individuals' efforts becomes a complex problem for management. For effective and successful business, a manager should understand the nature of human beings. Management should take care of various factors (human and non-human) of production in such a way that these factors help to achieve maximum efficiency of the organisational goal.

Human aspects are the characteristics of human beings that determine the way in which they perform tasks, or their ability to perform tasks, their interests, and their relationships (e.g., social behaviour). In psychology studies, the characteristics of human beings have been addressed as follows:

Cognitive system: This may be defined as the way of understanding, learning, processing, and executing tasks. Humans are able to work with their stored memory for information on various tasks and also capable of doing work by eliminating the difficulties which can affect the task.

Motivation: Motivation may be defined as the factor which guides a human being to achieve new things, desires, and goals. Motivation is classified as intrinsic and extrinsic. Intrinsic motivation may include internal factors and extrinsic motivation includes external factors related to the worker.

Preferences: Humans have their personal preferences, which are based on their experiences and on others' experiences which are observed by them. For example, when a worker is feeling bored when executing time-consuming tasks, he will choose less time-consuming tasks.

Social behaviour: Social behaviour means a group/community organising to perform activities. The sense of community theory develops social behaviour based on membership, integration, and shared emotional connection. This behaviour may describe the way community members behave and execute tasks in the system.

Emotion: Emotion may be defined as a physiological state of a person by which humans can sense whether a task is desirable or not. Emotion is related to mood, affection, feeling, and opinion. For example, it affects the functions of learning, perception, and reasoning.

Individual differences: Humans are different from each other in various factors such as decision-making, problem-solving, and performance. The main differences are knowledge, skill, and mental ability.

This chapter will provide the ability to understand human aspects, their effects on quality management in industry, and benefits of them to the reader. They will be able to understand the concept of employees' involvement in quality management practices, the QC concept, and the zero-defect concept.

8.2   COMMITMENT

Commitment is the state/promise/agreement/quality of being dedicated to a cause, activity, etc. For example, marriage is a commitment. Commitment is the feeling of responsibility of a person towards the work area, the objectives of the organisation, and the mission of their organisation; this is known as job commitment. For example, when someone has job commitment, they are committed to perform tasks and responsibilities that will help an organisation to achieve their goal. *Commitment is an important factor in management.* Commitment helps an organisation to secure their resources for survival. There are three main types of commitment as follows:

Affective commitment: This is due to affection/emotional attachment to your work and organisation. This is because of satisfaction with work, environment, and firm. You have feelings for all of these, and it will increase your affective commitment.

Normative commitment: This is due to feelings of obligation. This means you feel an obligation because an organisation provided you training, an education loan/fees for study, an advance bonus, etc. It is also due to loyalty towards the firm which comes from upbringing.

Continuance commitment: This occurs due to the comparison of advantages and disadvantages of leaving the present organisation, for example, loss of increments, loss of seniority, loss of friends, and loss of experience, etc. This comparison may increase the commitment to the present organisation.

8.2.1   FIVE STEPS TO INCREASING COMMITMENT

1. **To set achievable goals:** The first thing that increases commitment is to set a goal that can easily be achieved. For example, setting the goal according to your capacity is much better, and then increase it slowly.
2. **To set a specific goal:** The second step is to set your goals specifically, which will tell you that what you need to do. Your goal is very clear to you – that is, what is to be done and how.
3. **To write goals on a paper:** The third step is to write your goal on paper. According to Dr. Robert Cialdini if you put something on paper, it remains in your mind – that commitment is something that is much bigger.
4. **To present your goal publicly:** The fourth step is to share your goal publicly. Discussing your goal with at least one person will make your

commitment much stronger. If you tell your goal to someone, there is a higher probability that you will really do it.

5. **To make your to do list:** After doing these four steps, you know what to do and how. Now make a list of the activities that form your to do list and start your actions as soon as possible.

If you follow these steps in setting and achieving your goals, your commitment will be much stronger, and your productivity will also be much higher.

8.3 MOTIVATION

Motivation is the force behind each and every action, willingness, and goal of any person. Motivation comes from the word *motive* which means a need that requires satisfaction. Motivation is the most important factor that pushes or inspires a person to move ahead. It may be affected by external factors (extrinsic motivation) or it may exist within the person (intrinsic motivation). There are some forces which drive the motivation externally and internally. These forces are:

- Interest.
- Needs.
- Incentives.
- Fears.
- Curiosity.
- Beliefs.
- Values.
- Social pressure.
- Self-confidence.
- Expectations.

Some psychologists have considered motivation as a personal trait of human beings or an individual characteristic. Some state that motivation is nothing more than a temporary state or situation. Some says that motivation depends on internal, personal factors. Other says that it relies on external factors such as rewards, punishments, social pressure, and so on, as shown in Figure 8.1.

8.3.1 CHARACTERISTICS OF MOTIVATION

- Personal feelings.
- To produce a goal.
- Type of bargaining.
- System-related.

Some important types of motivation are as follows:

1. Achievement motivation: This is a force to attain a goal.
2. Affiliation motivation: This is a desire to get a status socially.

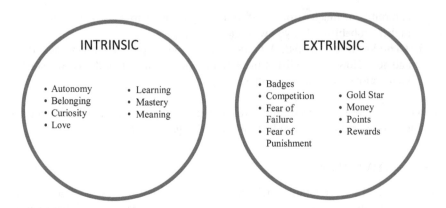

FIGURE 8.1   Intrinsic and extrinsic motivation.

3. Competence motivation: This is a force to compete and get success.
4. Power motivation: This is a drive to have a sense of power.
5. Attitude motivation: This is a drive to have self-confidence.
6. Incentive motivation: This is an external or internal force to achieve a goal.
7. Fear motivation: This is a fear of punishment if the goal is not achieved.

8.3.2   INTRINSIC MOTIVATION

Intrinsic motivation has been studied since the 1970s. Intrinsic or internal motivation is the self-desire to know different things, innovate and accept challenges, to study, to observe, and to gain knowledge. It presents within the human being rather than depending on external forces or a desire. It is due to an interest or enjoyment in doing things of interest. The phenomenon of internal motivation was first introduced within animal behaviour. According to this study, animals would enact playful behaviours even in the non-availability of rewards if they don't know about rewards. Salient features of intrinsic motivation are:

- It is a natural motivational tendency.
- It is a critical element in cognitive, social, and physical development.
- Self-determination and an increase in competence are two important elements for intrinsic motivation.

An example of intrinsic motivation: Someone becomes an engineer in an IT department as they want to do that, or to learn about the computer and interact with computers as a user. This is the internal motivation of employee to gain knowledge on these terms.

On the other side, internal motivation may be used to assist external motivation to achieve a goal. For example, a child wants to achieve the goal of playing with a toy, but he has autism and difficulty communicating. His desire to play with toy is his strong internal motivation, and his desire to communicate with his therapist to get the toy is external motivation.

Advantages:

- Self-sustaining and long-lasting.
- Promotes student learning.
- Focus on the subject, not on rewards or punishments.

Disadvantages:

- Slow process and needs special and time-consuming preparation.
- For variety of students, a variety of approaches may be needed.
- It helps only when there is interest in the subject.

8.3.3   EXTRINSIC MOTIVATION

Extrinsic motivation is the external force which affects the actions of human beings. The main questions come from finding where people get motivation. Extrinsic motivation is used to attain results that intrinsic motivation not get. External motivations are rewards to give desire, and also there is the possibility of punishment in case of misbehaviour. Another external motivator is competition which pushes the person to win by beating others, not only for rewards of the activity. A cheering crowd and the desire to win a trophy are examples of external incentives.

Salient features of extrinsic motivation are:

- It is the external force which affects the individual action.
- Rewards, threat of punishment, and competition are common extrinsic motivators.
- The difference between external and internal motivation – nature of reasons or goals that lead to action.

Social psychological research has explained that extrinsic motivation has a drawback; that is, rewards may lead to over-justification, and secondly, it reduces the intensity of intrinsic motivation.

Advantages:

- External force such as punishment, rewards have increased the intrinsic interest.
- Threat may create desire for that task. For example, when we threaten a child against something like playing with a toy, than it increases the desire to playing with that toy.

Disadvantages:

- Extrinsic rewards might reduce the ability to desire to do a task.
- Rewards may lead to over-justification and secondly, it reduces the intensity of intrinsic motivation.

8.3.4 THEORY OF MOTIVATION

There are some theories that have developed to understand the concept of motivation called theories of motivation. Motivation is the energy to push us to do hard work to achieve goals, even in tough situations. These theories are categorised into two groups on the basis of content and process, then again into eight sub-groups under these two groups of theories, as shown in Figure 8.2.

Motivation theories are divided in two groups consisting of four theories in each group and these are:

1) Content theories.
2) Process theories.

Various motivation theories on the basis of content and process are:

1. Maslow's Hierarchy of Needs.
2. Alderfer's ERG Theory.
3. McClelland's Needs Theory.
4. Herzberg's Two-Factor Theory.
5. Skinner's Reinforcement Theory.
6. Vroom's Expectancy Theory.
7. Adams' Equity Theory.
8. Locke's Goal-Setting Theory.

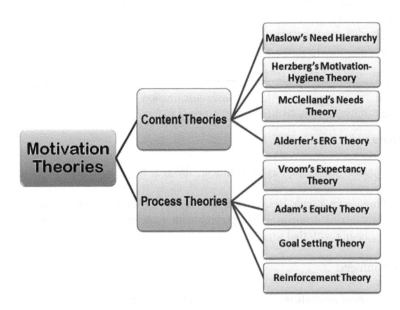

FIGURE 8.2 Motivation theories.

8.4 MANAGEMENT AND WORKER PARTICIPATION IN QUALITY MANAGEMENT

For effective and efficient management of an organisation, people's involvement is necessary. Workers' participation, recognition, empowerment, and enhancement of competence provides the involvement of people in achieving the organisational goals.

In the global market, there is a tough competitive environment in the industrial arena. The new organisations entering into the market, locally and globally, have provided the customer with a wide variety of choices for products. To grow and succeed in a competitive market, every organisation needs to focus on quality improvement in problem-solving and processes used for it. Total Quality Management (TQM) is a continuous process that strives to increase customer satisfaction, lower costs, and minimise defects and variations in every aspect and every process of the business

8.4.1 SALIENT FEATURES OF TQM

- To involve every employee in the organisation to improve quality and customer satisfaction.
- Managers take decisions and send them to workers.
- Top to bottom management system.
- Slow and inflexible.
- Focuses on the importance of employee involvement.

8.4.2 EMPLOYEE INVOLVEMENT

This is a system for direct participation of employee by giving them responsibilities for organisational success. Many companies have started involving their employees in the problem-solving and decision-making process of the firm. It is one participative style of management.

For example, we consider the case study of Ford: A problem arises in Ford – they suffer from a competitive threat from car manufacturers in Japan, and a study has been carried out on their performance efficiency. After this study, they found that performance and efficiency was high because of their empowered workforce and the teamwork they have. Employers gave the responsibility for the relevant process to the workers themselves so that if they found the quality failed to meet the standards specified, they could stop the process. This gave them a feeling of being an owner not an employee, which pushed them to do their best to achieve quality work.

8.4.3 PRINCIPLES OF TQM

- Teamwork.
- Training.
- Motivation.
- Recognition and rewards.

- Feedback.
- Praise for good work.
- Empowerment.

8.4.4   Key Barriers in Implementation of Employee Involvement

1) Lack of experience of workers.
2) Resistance to change from traditional to new system.
3) Lack of trust of workers for management's motives.
4) Lack of management commitment to employee involvement.
5) Lack of experience in participative activities.

Most of the companies have achieved a strong bond between workers and managers. These companies attain that level through the policies and standards set for TQM. Even this transformation from traditional practices to the new system was a long process. It requires a lot of effort and time, and it is a slow process.

8.5   TOP MANAGEMENT COMMITMENT

Top management is the uppermost level of management in an organisational system. There are three levels of management – low-level management, middle-level management, and top-level management. Top-level managers are responsible for controlling and overseeing the entire organisation. Top management is made up of the senior officers of an organisation, like the Chief Executive Officer (CEO), President, or Vice-President. Top-level management is focused on market position through long-term planning. Middle-level managers deal with decision-making processes of their area of responsibility and meet the objectives of the organisation.

According to the ISO 9000 series of standards, 'Top management may be defined as the person or group of people who directs and controls an organisation at the highest level.' The implementation of a management system should be a decision by top management. But top managers' commitment is not always clearly understood by the employees. Top management is the board of directors. They make the vision and mission of the company and set the objectives of the company.

8.5.1   Top Management Responsibilities

- To set the policies and objectives of the organisation.
- To focus on customer requirements.
- To make sure that appropriate processes are implemented for achieving objectives.
- To check the quality management system is established, implemented, and maintained and is effective and efficient at reaching the quality objectives.
- To make sure that the availability of resources is sufficient.
- To review the effectiveness of the system on a regular basis.
- To set an action plan for the quality policy.
- To set actions for system improvements.

8.6 QUALITY CIRCLE

A QC is a group of workers who do the same or similar work and meet regularly to identify, analyse, and solve work-related problems A QC group is small in size and led by a supervisor or manager. The results or solutions they find are finally presented in front of management. Even then, wherever possible, workers independently implement the solutions to improve performance, which motivates other employees/workers. The QC concept is based on respect for the individual. It builds mutual trust and understanding between workers and management. QCs were most popular during the 1980s. QC involves paying attention to major topics like improving safety and health, improving product design, and making improvements in the workplace and processes used in production. The structure of a QC is shown in Figure 8.3.

The QC concept was introduced in 1962 by a Japanese Company named Nippon Wireless and Telegraph. QCs are formal groups of employees. They meet regularly during working hours and are trained by experts (known as facilitators) who may be industrial experts and specialists in the basic skills of problem identification, information gathering, analysis, statistics, and solution generation. QCs are free to select any topic they wish (other than those related to salary and terms and conditions of work). QCs have the advantage of continuity, meaning the circle remains intact from project to project.

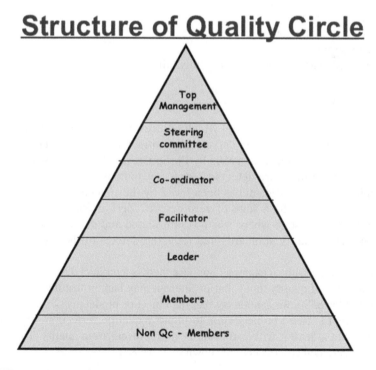

FIGURE 8.3 Structure of a quality circle.

8.6.1 SALIENT FEATURES OF A QUALITY CIRCLE

- QCs are formal groups of employees.
- QCs are free to select the topic of their choice.
- It provides an opportunity to the members of the QC to use their creativity, wisdom, and experience for making improvements in the work.
- It builds trust and understanding among employees and management.

8.6.2 OBJECTIVES OF A QUALITY CIRCLE

- To improve productivity, quality, and safety, and reduce costs.
- To provide an opportunity to the members to use their wisdom and creativity.
- To enhance self-development, such as leadership qualities.
- To support the motivational needs and self-esteem of employees.
- To improve the quality of life of members.

8.6.3 BENEFITS OF A QUALITY CIRCLE

- Cost reduction.
- Increase productivity.
- Improve quality.
- Better communication.
- Increased teamwork.
- Smooth working.
- Great sense of belonging.
- Increase safety.
- Knowledge and skills of workers fully utilised.

8.7 ZERO DEFECTS

Zero defects is a management tool which reduces defects through prevention. It may be defined as a state where defects are eliminated and reduced to zero. This philosophy was introduced in 1960s by Philip Crosby. It is used by automobile industry for first time. Zero defects concepts mean no wastage in production. A lot of objections and criticism has been faced by the concept. Some researchers say that there cannot be a state of zero defects. Zero defects in quality management refers to a state where waste is eliminated and defects are reduced. It means ensuring quality standards and reducing defects to the level of zero in projects.

Let us explain it with an example. Suppose there is a product developed with zero defects in terms of quality today, but in future it may lack in features that the new product will have. So, we cannot say that the object or product is perfect. The zero defects concept is based on perfection to improve quality. Perfection might not be achievable, but at least it will lead towards an improvement in quality. The parameters of the zero defects concept are shown in Table 8.1.

TABLE 8.1

Parameters of Zero Defects Concept

S. No.	Parameter	Zero Defects Concept
1	Objective	Prevention of defects
2	Key idea	Works right the first time and every time
3	Cost	Higher cost
4	Instruments	Continual improvement through leadership
5	Standards	No defects are acceptable
6	Scope	Applicable to every job
7	Workers' involvement	Worker can identify the problem
8	Manpower	Limited employees needed

8.7.1 PRINCIPLES OF ZERO DEFECTS

- Quality is conformance to requirements.
- Prevention of defects is preferable.
- The standard of quality is always zero defects.
- Quality is measured on the basis of price.

8.7.2 ZERO DEFECTS THEORY

Zero defects theory means that there is zero waste in a production system. Waste applies to all unproductive processes, tools, and employees, etc. The unproductive things that do not add value to a project should be eliminated from the work or production system. This is the process of elimination of waste, waste reduction, and reduction of costs involved in waste. This is the move towards perfection. Zero defects theory works on the fact that all work should be perfect the very first time. Zero defects theory is based on four elements for implementation in the system. They are:

- Quality is a state of assurance.
- Zero defects.
- Quality comes first.
- Quality in terms of money.

Advantages:

- Cost reduction.
- Waste reduction.
- Improves services.
- Improves quality.
- Customer satisfaction.

Disadvantages:

- Increased costs in defect finding.
- Work environment and production may be affected by strictness.

8.8   SMALL GROUP ACTIVITY

Small group activity is also known as continuous improvement. It is a method for problem-solving by making a team of some members who search for the root causes of problems, and solutions to eliminate them. In manufacturing plants, solving problems is limited to the removal of the symptoms, and does not go into the root cause of the problem. We have a tendency to spend more time on solving the problems, and forget about the complete study of the problem. The root causes are not removed. Therefore, the problem will be repeated. With the help of the SGA, you first find the root cause and remove it completely. The final solution is standardised, which prevents the recurrence of the problem. For all this process, team members should learn the use of techniques like cause-and-effect diagrams or fishbone diagrams. The team members should also learn communication skills, teamwork, and decision-making in order to use their knowledge and experience.

8.8.1   CONTINUOUS IMPROVEMENT

Continuous improvement is based on a Japanese concept called kaizen, which is the philosophy of continually seeking ways to improve operations' (as shown in Figure 8.4). It includes identification of standards of excellent practices and developing a sense of ownership of the process among employees.

8.8.2   CAUSE-AND-EFFECT DIAGRAM

In the year 1950, Ishikawa first developed this tool in Japan, to explain the causes that affected the production of steel. This was further developed by Ishikawa in the early 1950s in Japan. It identifies all the probable reasons/causes of an effect or problem. It provides a basis for brainstorming sessions and has the power to categorise ideas to form useful solutions. It gives a systematic representation of causes and their effects on a problem. A cause-and-effect diagram is also known as a fishbone diagram, as shown in Figure 8.5.

8.8.2.1   How to Construct a Fishbone Diagram

Step 1: Define the problem statement, also known as the effect of a process.
Step 2: Conduct the brainstorming session to identify all the possible causes of a problem. The focus here is people, machines, materials, inspections and testing, maintenance, safety, and services, or the service after sales.
Step 3: Try to categorise all the possible causes.
Step 4: Again, try to identify all the sub-causes of the main cause by using the question 'why?' and develop a high level of understanding of all causes.
Step 5: Draw the causes and all possible sub-causes in a diagram.

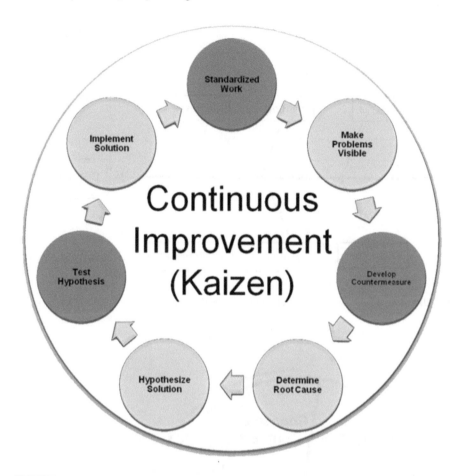

FIGURE 8.4 Continuous improvement (kaizen).

8.9 STRUCTURAL APPROACH

'SGA structure is taken from PDCA-circle given by Dr. W. Edwards Deming' (1982). It consists of eight steps on the basis of the SGA circle, as shown in Figure 8.6. The SGA team works independently. SGA will be used when the problem needs more than one person and no one answer for it is available.

The eight steps of the SGA process shown in Figure 8.6 are:

1. Identify and choose a problem.
2. Determine the objectives.
3. Analysis of the problem.
4. Finding solutions.
5. Data analysis.
6. Execution of solutions.
7. Solution checking (if it works or not).
8. Standardise the solution, which is final.

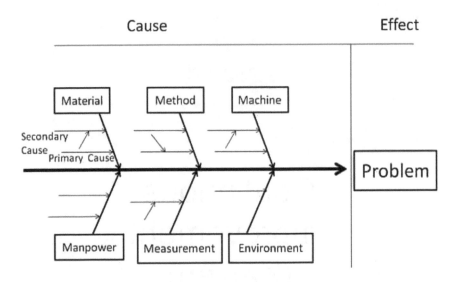

FIGURE 8.5   Cause-and-effect diagram (fishbone diagram).

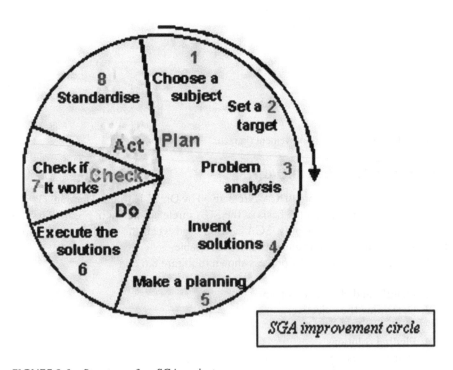

FIGURE 8.6   Structure of an SGA project.

Advantages of SGA:

- Team-owned solutions are always received with more enthusiasm than imposed solutions.
- Improves the relationships between the participants.
- The group usually generates better solutions than solo person.

8.10 CONCLUSION

After this chapter, the reader will be able to understand the concept of human aspects of the management of quality and the success of a business. Organisations who want to gain profit and sustainability in business have to focus on customer satisfaction, continuous improvement, and development of their human resources. TQM can change the working of an organisation by adopting new techniques, education, and training. The total quality management system works for continual improvement at all levels, and also is constantly upgrading the skill levels of all employees, which can only happen through continuous education and training. Top management and all the other employees play a vital role in providing quality products and services to customers. Therefore, to achieve overall performance excellence, organisations need to input Total Employee Involvement (TEI). Employees are the main force who makes the difference between a world-class organisation and an ordinary organisation.

8.11 CASE STUDIES

8.11.1 CASE STUDY 1: AEROSPACE MANUFACTURING COMPANY

Customer: Global supplier of aircraft titanium casting parts.
Purpose: Producing zero-defect aircraft parts.
Situation:

Customer's requirement:

- Overall aircraft safety and producing zero-defect parts.
- Also wants costs associated with expensive production of titanium casting parts as well as costs associated with assembly to be managed.

Challenges

The challenges facing them:

- Management of production costs, as titanium casting parts are expensive to produce.
- Management of delivery times, as parts needs to be produced on time because they are part of a complex assembly process.
- Maintain quality with zero defects.
- Creation of a production model.
- Customer satisfaction with quality and work.

Actions

The actions taken to solve the challenges:

- Costs: They adopted a production process to produce parts in machines which allowed faster and more efficient inspection.

- Delivery time: They made improvements in technology, machines, equipment, and continuous improvement processes that provided a shortened lead time.
- Zero defects: They made new fixtures and using them eliminated hand intervention.
- Model: They received the customer's permission to use a digitised part for programming a model to use in production.

Results
- High quality of parts produced.
- Less human intervention.
- Better tool life and management of that tool for other manufacturing techniques.

8.11.2   Case Study 2: Quality Circles Programme at Hughes Aircraft17

Objective: To promote workers' participation in management.
Area: Hybrid microwave devices manufacturer.
Problem: Excessive errors in assembly, part scrapping, re-work.
Challenges:
- Insufficient lighting, dirty projector screens, and lack of colour-coded documents.
- Minor changes in the assembly planning documents.
- To study the documents on assembly errors, part scrapping, and re-working.

Actions:
- Send a request to the environmental health and safety department to conduct a lighting check, set overhead lighting, and replace the existing station lighting.
- Clean screens on projector and warped slides were replaced and all assembly documents were coloured.

Results:
- Provided for the growth and development of individual workers.
- Created a more viable and collaborative work group.
- Increase in information-sharing among their staff, increased cooperation, and willingness to make an extra effort.

POINTS TO REMEMBER

- **Motivation**: Motivation is the force behind each and every action, willingness, and goal of any person.
- **Quality circle**: A quality circle is a group of workers who do the same or similar work and meets regularly to identify, analyse, and solve work-related problems.
- **Zero defects**: Zero defects is a management tool which reduces defects through prevention.

SELF-ASSESSMENT QUESTIONS

1. What do you mean by human aspects?
2. What are the main human aspects in management?
3. What is commitment?
4. What are the types of commitment?
5. What is job commitment?
6. What do you mean by motivation?
7. What are the types of motivation?
8. Differentiate between intrinsic and extrinsic motivation.
9. Explain various theories of motivation.
10. What do you mean by employee involvement in quality management?
11. What do you mean by continuous improvement?
12. Explain the structure of top management.
13. List the various responsibilities of top management in quality improvement.
14. What is a quality circle? Explain its structure, advantages, and disadvantages.
15. What do you mean by zero defects?
16. Explain the steps involved in making a cause-and-effect diagram.
17. What is a fishbone diagram? What is it used for?
18. Explain small group activities. What are its advantages?

BIBLIOGRAPHY

Ali, P. M., Raju, R., & Murugesan, T. K. (2016). The impact of human factors on effective implementation of TQM in South Indian manufacturing industries. *Asian Journal of Research in Social Sciences and Humanities*, 6(7), 517–536.

Deming, W. E. (1982). *Out of the Crisis*. Center for Advanced Engineering Study, Cambridge, MA.

Eklöf, J., & Selivanova, I. (2008). Human aspect in service quality: EPSI benchmark studies. *Total Quality Management*, 19(7–8), 827–841.

James, P. (2017). Total quality environmental management and human resource management. n: *Greening People*, Wehrmeyer, W. (Ed.) (pp. 35–48). Routledge, London.

Kufidu, S., & Vouzas, F. (1998). Human resource aspects of quality management: Evidence from MNEs operating in Greece. *The International Journal of Human Resource Management*, 9(5), 818–830.

Lenka, U., Suar, D., & Mohapatra, P. K. (2010). Soft and hard aspects of quality management practices influencing service quality and customer satisfaction in manufacturing-oriented services. *Global Business Review*, 11(1), 79–101.

Ponciano, L., Brasileiro, F., Andrade, N., & Sampaio, L. (2014). Considering human aspects on strategies for designing and managing distributed human computation. *Journal of Internet Services and Applications*, 5(1), 10.

Tarí, J. J., & Sabater, V. (2006). Human aspects in a quality management context and their effects on performance. *The International Journal of Human Resource Management*, 17(3), 484–503.

Turuthi, D. G., Njagi, K., & Chemwei, B. (2018). How does technology influence students' motivation towards learning kiswahili proverbs? In: *Handbook of Research on Pedagogical Models for Next-Generation Teaching and Learning*, Keengwe, J. (Ed.) (pp. 361–390). IGI Global, University of North Dakota.

9 Total Productive Maintenance (TPM)

9.1 TOTAL PRODUCTIVE MAINTENANCE

The Preventive Maintenance (PM) concept came from the US. Total Productive Maintenance (TPM) originated in 1951 in Japan where the PM concept was introduced. The first company that adopted PM in the 1960s was the Toyota Group company, Nippondenso. This organisation required more maintenance employees for automation. The management had taken a decision to reduce the requirement of employees in the maintenance department and that the small maintenance work on the machines would be carried out by the machine operators itself. This is also a major feature of TPM, as Autonomous Maintenance (AM). As a result, the first organisation obtaining the certificate of TPM was Nippondenso in 1971. This award is for maintenance, operations, and quality of product and performance. It has been known as a tool for better maintenance planning through employee involvement since 1988. Due to this competitive environment, manufacturing organisations are adopting improvement strategies like TQM, TPM, CI, and JIT to improve the manufacturing performance.

In today's competitive environment, organisations force themselves to modify their manufacturing processes regularly. TPM has been considered a most acceptable plan to improve maintenance performance (Nakajima, 1988). TPM is the most popular system of maintenance and was developed by the Japan Institute of Plant Maintenance (JIPM). The following are the definitions of TPM:

1. Hartmann (1992) described how overall effectiveness of equipment can be improved by using TPM.
2. Willmott (1994) defined the TPM process as how maximum output can be achieved by keeping all assets in optimum condition.
3. JIPM (1996) elaborated on TPM being about the inclusion of corporate culture which will help in maximising the effectiveness of the production system and preventing losses.

According to Siiechi Nakajima, the father of TPM 'TPM is a system of maintenance covering the entire life of the equipment in every division including planning, manufacturing, and maintenance.' TPM has five key characteristics:

- High equipment effectiveness.
- TPM developed the Preventive Maintenance system.
- It is a system of cross-functions.
- TPM involves each employee.
- It is based on Preventive Maintenance via Group Activity.

Through the use of teamwork, group activities, and worker participation, an organisation can achieve the goals of improvement.

9.2 NEED OF TPM

Applications of TPM in the manufacturing sector help in enhancing competitiveness among the organisations and also change the work culture of the employees working in the organisation, thereby increasing the equipment effectiveness. These activities of TPM have made the transition from the maintenance department to business functions. Majumdar (1998) reported that application of TPM was helpful in preventing breakdown of equipment due to maintenance by the company. This will result in utilisation of machines running at full capacity. In an organisation, implementation of TPM reduces operating costs and overall maintenance costs, and also enhances the life of equipment.

9.3 TPM BENEFITS

The benefits of TPM are categorised as:

9.3.1 TPM – DIRECT BENEFITS

- Increased efficiency and production.
- Manufacturing cost reduction.
- Fewer accidents.
- Rectifying customer complaints.
- Customer satisfaction.
- Improving product quality.

9.3.2 TPM – INDIRECT BENEFITS

- Increasing employees' confidence and cooperation.
- Feeling of ownership of the machine by the worker.
- Clean and attractive workplace.
- Favourable attitude of operators towards the company.
- Sharing of knowledge and experiences of employees.
- Cooperative environment to achieve organisational goals.
- New and improved concepts are developed in all areas of the organisation.

9.4 OBJECTIVES OF TPM

- To increase employee involvement in all levels of the organisation.
- To enhance OEE of machines through total employee participation.
- To reduce total equipment maintenance expenditure.
- To create an enthusiastic work environment.
- To reduce total maintenance expenditure.
- To have zero pollution, losses, accidents, and failures

9.5 THE RELATIONSHIP BETWEEN TPM AND TQM

The aims of both TQM and TPM are to improve the efficiency of resources (man/machine) which can only be achieved by minimising waste through total employee participation and providing quality service to our customers. TPM is a maintenance approach while TQM is total quality control. Employee empowerment is a tool used in TQM implementation, while TPM uses optimisation. There are similarities between TPM and TQM as follows:

1. Both require the commitment of leadership for implementation.
2. Both take corrective action.
3. Employees must fully understand and accept their job responsibility.

9.6 OVERALL EQUIPMENT EFFECTIVENESS (OEE)

Measurement is a very important requirement in continuous improvement processes. OEE is necessary to establish suitable metrics for the purpose of measurement. According to a generic perspective, OEE is a set of maintenance operations, available resources, and management of equipment that together define TPM. According to Nakajima (1988), 'OEE measurement is an effective way of analysing the efficiency of a single machine or an integrated manufacturing system.' OEE can be used as a measuring tool of quantitative data in any production system to represent the success of kaizen implementation (Jeong and Phillips, 2001). 'It can also be defined as the ratio of actual equipment output to its theoretical maximum output.' It is a systematic method to fix some target for production to achieve the targeted availability, performance, and rate of quality. OEE also can be used to find the improvements in machines performance and associated processes. OEE can be understood as equipment being required to work at its maximum efficiency in order to get the actual output of machine. This is how OEE highlights the real 'hidden capacity' in an organisation. Operation time may face losses like scrap, changeover, breakdown, and slow speed. These losses can be overcome by adopting ergonomics. A graphical representation of OEE is as shown in Figure 9.1.

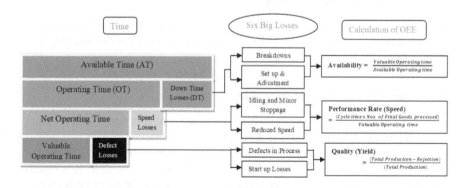

FIGURE 9.1 Graphical representation of OEE calculation.

OEE is a set of three functions as given below.

1. Availability.
2. Performance efficiency.
3. Quality rate of output.

$$OEE = Availability \times Performance\ Rate \times Quality\ Rate$$

OR

$$OEE = A \times PE \times Q$$

where

$$Availability\ of\ the\ machine = \frac{(Planned\ production\ time + unscheduled\ downtime)}{Planned\ production\ time}$$

$$Production\ time = Planned\ production\ time + Downtime$$

Total available hours for production (365*24*7). Planned downtime includes vacation and holidays. Availability losses include equipment failures and changeovers.

$$Performance\ efficiency\ rate = \frac{(Cycle\ time \times Number\ of\ products\ processed)}{Production\ time}$$

$$Quality\ rate = \frac{(Number\ of\ products\ processed - Number\ of\ products\ rejected)}{(Number\ of\ products\ processed)}$$

OEE used to find the hidden capacity of machine. Most of the machines work at 35% to 45% of the mentioned power or efficiency. If machine give 85% of real efficiency, then machines/equipment can give double of the productivity at the same cost.

9.7   TYPES OF MAINTENANCE

As discussed in the journey of TPM in the previous section, many maintenance systems or approaches or strategies have been evolved. Here we discuss only a few strategies which are very common.

9.7.1   BREAKDOWN MAINTENANCE (BM)

Breakdown maintenance is unplanned maintenance which is performed on equipment that has failed or broken down. This type of maintenance planning was adopted in the manufacturing sector around 1950. The basic concept behind this breakdown maintenance is not to do anything unless and until the machine fails. It is reactive maintenance in which machines are serviced only when special attention is required by the machines, that is, only in case of failure. To solve critical production problems,

BM is the best suitable maintenance strategy. This concept has several advantages and disadvantages, as given below.

9.7.1.1 Advantages of Breakdown Maintenance (BM)
- No planning required.
- No system required.
- No supervision required.

9.7.1.2 Disadvantages of Breakdown Maintenance (BM)
- Sudden breakdowns of machines.
- Serious damage.
- Unavailability of essential spare parts.
- More maintenance costs.
- High breakdown time.

9.7.2 PREVENTIVE MAINTENANCE (PM)

This maintenance strategy was proposed in 1951. PM is a maintenance strategy which is done through a daily routine like cleaning, inspection, oiling, tightening, etc. to keep the equipment in good condition and reduce the depreciation rate as well. The schedule for daily maintenance tasks of PM strategy is prepared as per the condition of equipment, say, weekly, monthly, half-yearly, or yearly. In this maintenance strategy, physical check-up of the machines is done to reduce machine breakdowns so as to maintain the flow of continuous production. This maintenance strategy has been divided into two types: Periodic and predictive maintenance. The life of equipment can be enhanced by using a PM strategy as same as human life is extended by using medicine. This concept has several advantages and disadvantages, as given below.

9.7.2.1 Advantages of Preventive Maintenance (PM)
- Planned stoppage.
- Spare part control.
- Reduced breakdowns.
- No waiting or delay time.

9.7.2.2 Disadvantages of Preventive Maintenance (PM)
- Increased maintenance costs.
- Required maintenance planning.
- Stopping running machines for maintenance.

9.7.3 PERIODIC MAINTENANCE (PERM)

Periodic maintenance is a Time-Based Maintenance (TBM) system. PerM is basically a technique of PM in which inspection, cleaning, replacement of parts, etc. is done at a pre-decided time period, which is independent of the condition of the part or equipment. PerM helps to keep equipment in a state of wellbeing so that the system may have the minimum possible downtime. In Periodic Maintenance, an old part is replaced when it fails or after given time period which comes first, for example, maintenance and servicing schedules of vehicles in the automobile industry.

9.7.4 Predictive Maintenance (PreM)

Predictive maintenance is condition-based maintenance (CBM). PreM is basically a technique of forecasting based on previous data and executive experience on the basis of conditions like different signs of abnormal behaviour (pressure, noise, vibrational analysis, erosion and corrosion, lubrication, etc.) of equipment or machines. A decision is then taken by the maintenance department to initiate maintenance of a particular machine. Predictive Maintenance works on the principle that 'Prevention is better than cure.' It saves lots of capital and avoids the chances of sudden failure of machines, which may be hazardous to the operators. Staff and employees associated with PreM must have a sound knowledge, rich experience, and strong background in the machines concerned. One of the major shortcomings of the PreM technique is that premature replacement of parts is also possible. This concept has several advantages and disadvantages, as given below.

9.7.4.1 Advantages of Predictive Maintenance (PreM)
- Less waiting time.
- Improved machine performance.
- Reduced maintenance cost.
- The breakdown is predicted before it occurs.

9.7.4.2 Disadvantages of Predictive Maintenance (PreM)
- High level of skills required for condition monitoring.
- Additional instruments required.
- High maintenance costs.

9.7.5 Corrective Maintenance (CM)

This is defined as maintenance work performed to put the equipment/machine in working condition through corrective action. It was introduced in 1957. This mainly deals with maintenance of equipment after failure by repairing equipment and returning it to the workplace with an improved condition. To improve reliability, the life of equipment and its safety is the aim of corrective maintenance, reducing breakdowns or failures of the equipment.

9.7.6 Maintenance Prevention (MP)

Maintenance prevention is an important concept for ensuring reliability and maintainability of manufacturing facilities that was introduced in the 1960s. Nowadays, MP is a leading technique which starts as early as the design of a machine or equipment. A machine is to be designed ergonomically under the rated conditions so that the chances of failure or breakdowns can be kept to the minimum possible.

Moreover, the recent advances in the field of material science have helped us in the selection of diverse materials which can withstand very high temperatures, pressure, and wear and tear. In MP, our approach is to avoid the maintenance of equipment as much as possible. This can be achieved only when we have followed all the quality perspectives in the design, production, inspection, and shipment of our machines.

9.7.7 Reliability Centred Maintenance (RCM)

This is a cooperative level maintenance strategy which was introduced in the 1960s. It is implemented to optimise the maintenance programme. The researchers Moubray, Agrawal, and Rausand have each defined RCM as follows:

- According to Moubray (2001), RCM is defined as 'a process which can be used to find out that a particular physical asset (machines and equipment) is fulfilling the requirements of the end user under the existing operating conditions.'
- According to Agrawal and Gandhi (1997), RCM is defined as 'a process used to find out whether a particular physical asset is meeting the intended use for which it was made.'
- According to Rausand and Vatn (2008), RCM is defined as 'a proper consideration of the functions and failures of a system keeping the priorities of safety and economics of a particular physical asset in the effective use of it.'

9.7.8 Productive Maintenance (ProM)

This is maintenance performed during production with the aim of increasing productivity during the various stages of processes like design, production, inspection, and maintenance for the total cost reduction of the production, as well as enhancing the life of the equipment. The main characteristics of productive maintenance are equipment reliability, maintainability, and cost-effective maintenance activities. Essentially, ProM was the stepping stone for Nakajima to develop TPM. The goal of ProM is profit. This requires avoiding machine breakdowns, reducing defects, and making the process more economical and efficient (Nakajima, 1988). Figure 9.2 illustrates the four master techniques to achieve this.

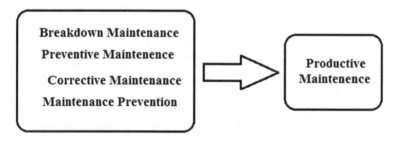

FIGURE 9.2   Various techniques involved in Productive Maintenance.

9.7.9 TOTAL PRODUCTIVE MAINTENANCE (TPM)

Total productive maintenance is a method used to maintain production with fewer losses/failure and increases in productivity and the quality of the product. It is a Japanese philosophy that was given by the M/s Nippondenso Co. Ltd of Japan in 1971.

'TPM is an innovative maintenance approach used to optimise equipment effectiveness eliminate breakdowns and promote autonomous maintenance by involving the total workforce' (Bhadury, 2000).

'TPM is a world class manufacturing (WCM) initiative that seeks to optimise the effectiveness of manufacturing equipment' (Shirose, 1995).

TPM tries to involve all manpower in departments and levels from lower workers to senior officers, to make sure of equipment effectiveness. It also tries to reduce waste, reduce the manufacturing cost, and increase equipment quality in a firm. TPM plays the role of mediator between maintenance and production functions.

9.8 PILLARS OF TPM

For the improvement of OEE, it needs the long-term commitment of employees in TPM. For this, it is required to train them for routine maintenance tasks. The 'TPM concept is built and stands on eight pillars' (Sangameshwran and Jagannathan, 2002) that are known as the basic practices of TPM implementation. The TPM model's eight pillars are shown in Figure 9.3.

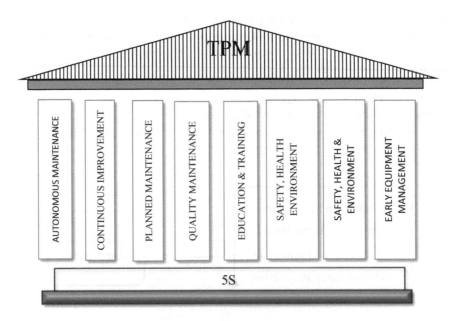

FIGURE 9.3: Eight pillars of implementation of TPM.

9.8.1   History of TPM Pillars

TPM activities are indicated and organised by 'pillars.' The number and name of the TPM pillars may differ slightly according to different authors. However, the most commonly used model is Nakajima's eight pillars (Nakajima, 1988), as shown in Figure 9.4. This Nakajima model has been simplified by some of the Western TPM experts.

Figure 9.5 shows a five-pillar model given by Yeomans and Millington in 1997. The researchers Yeomans and Millington eliminated three pillars, namely quality

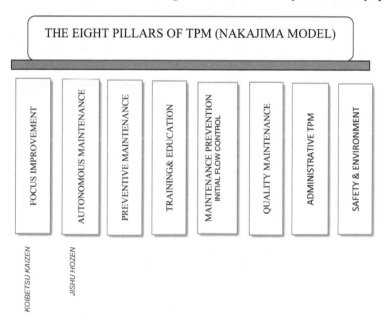

FIGURE 9.4   The eight pillars of TPM (Source: Nakajima Model).

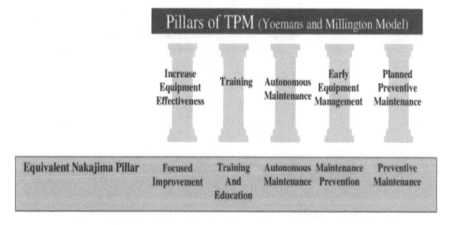

FIGURE 9.5   The pillars of TPM (Source: Yeomans and Millington Model).

maintenance, administrative TPM, and safety and environment, in a simplified Nakajima model in 1997.

Other Western practitioners called Steinbacher and Steinbacher also simplified the pillar model in 1993, as shown in Figure 9.6. This model is known as the Steinbacher and Steinbacher TPM model 1993.

The Society of Manufacturing Engineers in 1995 developed a new model for SMEs, which also includes five pillars as shown in Figure 9.7. This model is called the SME model.

Figure 9.8 illustrates the traditional TPM model which was developed in the 1960s. It also consists of eight activities or pillars, with the strong foundation of 5S.

TPM identifies the six big losses – set-up (initial) and breakdown time, speed losses, idle losses, start-up, and in-process losses. Machine operators of the

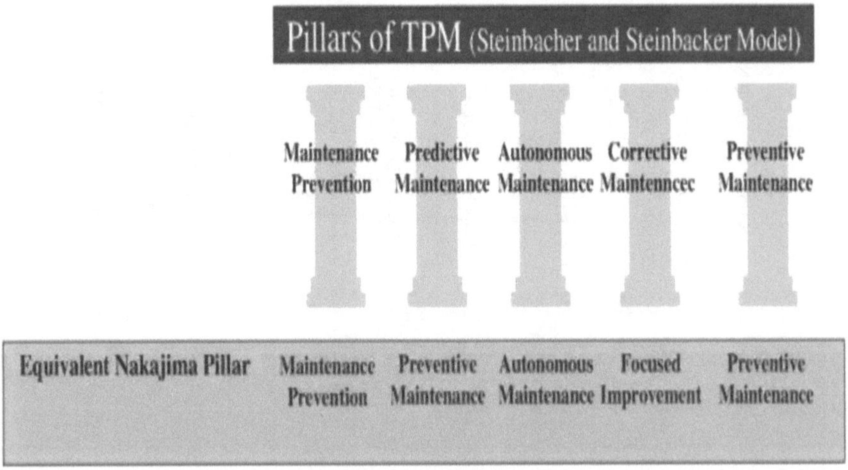

Pillars of TPM (Steinbacher and Steinbacker Model)

Maintenance Prevention	Predictive Maintenance	Autonomous Maintenance	Corrective Maintenncec	Preventive Maintenance

Equivalent Nakajima Pillar	Maintenance Prevention	Preventive Maintenance	Autonomous Maintenance	Focused Improvement	Preventive Maintenance

FIGURE 9.6   The pillars of TPM (Source: Steinbacher and Steinbacher Model).

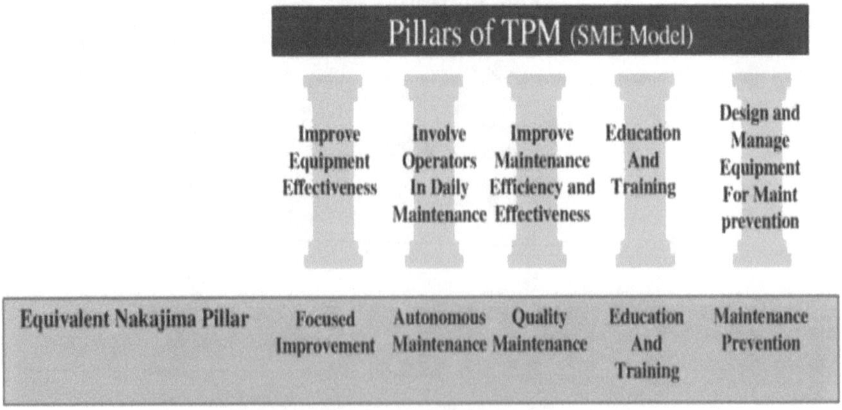

Pillars of TPM (SME Model)

Improve Equipment Effectiveness	Involve Operators In Daily Maintenance	Improve Maintenance Efficiency and Effectiveness	Education And Training	Design and Manage Equipment For Maint prevention

Equivalent Nakajima Pillar	Focused Improvement	Autonomous Maintenance	Quality Maintenance	Education And Training	Maintenance Prevention

FIGURE 9.7   The pillars of TPM (Source: SMEs Model).

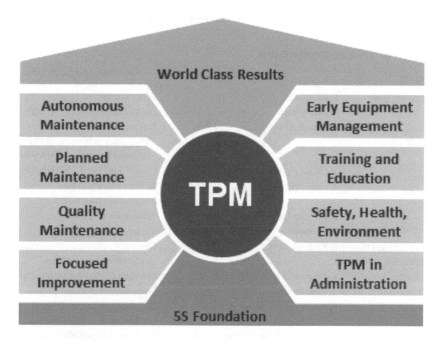

FIGURE 9.8   The pillars of TPM (Source: Traditional Model).

manufacturing cell must be involved in maintenance work and rectify the error as soon as possible to remove the losses or waste. The most important obstacles or barriers in implementing TMP are lack of top management interest, no support from the workers' union, a tight budget, organisational change, etc.

9.8.2   SALIENT FEATURES OF TPM

- TPM is a maintenance process.
- It is an advanced step of TQM.
- It is used to maintain the plant or equipment in good condition.
- The preventive as well as predictive maintenance step is needed for TPM.
- It can minimise failure of the equipment.
- The maintenance team and the production team have to work together for results.

9.8.3   12 STEPS OF TPM IMPLEMENTATION

The 12 Steps of TPM Implementation are categorised in Table 9.1.

9.8.4   PILLARS OF TPM

9.8.4.1   Pillar-1: Jishu Hozen

The first pillar is geared towards developing the ability of the operators to take care of small maintenance tasks by themselves, so that the experts of the maintenance

TABLE 9.1
12 Steps of TPM Implementation

Category	Step	Main Points
Preparatory stage	1. Introduction to TPM by top management	Announcement of TPM meeting according to company bulletin.
	2. Education and training on TPM	Training camp for officers in each level, and arrangement of slide screening for general employees
	3. Create organisation to promote TPM	Committees, special working groups
	4. Frame policies and goals of TPM	Benchmarks and goals, effectiveness forecasting
	5. Develop the TPM master plan formation	Assessment preparation
Commencement of introduction State of implementation	6. Kick-off TPM	Customers, affiliated companies, and cooperative companies
	7. Improvement of equipment effectiveness	Selection of model equipment and formation of team
	8. Autonomous maintenance set-up creation	Step-wise method, assessment, and certificate
	9. Create the planned maintenance set-up.	Predictive and periodic maintenance, management of spare parts, blueprints
	10. Training of modified operation and maintenance skills	Collective education of leaders, communicating this to members
	11. Create the initial set-up for management of equipment	Maintenance, prevention design, initial management, and LCC
Stages of firm establishment	12. Implementation of higher level TPM	For PM Awards do screening, challenging a higher goal

department are free to spend time on more value-added activity and special technical repairs. This pillar is called autonomous maintenance. The machine operators are responsible for maintenance of their machine/equipment to prevent failures.

Policy:

1. Smooth process.
2. Operator's flexibility.
3. Effective employee participation to remove defects.
4. Focus on small group activities.

Steps in autonomous maintenance:

1. Employee preparation.
2. Clean-up of machines initially.
3. Take countermeasures.

4. Standard fixing of AM.
5. Inspection generally.
6. Standardisation.

9.8.4.2   Pillar 2 – Continuous Improvement (Kaizen)

The second pillar is continuous improvement which is aimed at improving products, processes, and services by reducing waste in the workplace that affects efficiencies. It is known as 'kaizen.' Kaizen is a Japanese word for improvement. "Kai" means change, and "zen" means good (for the better), so kaizen means change for the better. These activities are not only for the production field, but can also be implemented at the administrative level in a firm. Kaizen refers to all activities that continuously make small improvements involving all people (from CEO to workers) in the organisation. Kaizen, unlike big innovations, requires little investment. Basically, large numbers of small improvements are more effective than a few large one.

Policy:

1. Zero losses concept.
2. To ensure cost reduction of resources.
3. To enhance machine effectiveness.
4. To eliminate losses with the help of the PM tool.
5. Ease of handling on machine by operators.

Tools used in kaizen:

1. Cause-and-effect diagram.
2. Gantt diagram.
3. Pareto chart.
4. Six Sigma.

9.8.4.3   Pillar 3 – Planned Maintenance

The third pillar is planned maintenance which focused on having failure-free equipment which produces error-free products for getting customer satisfaction. This is further divided into four sub-maintenance areas; these are:

1. Preventive maintenance.
2. Breakdown maintenance.
3. Corrective maintenance.
4. Maintenance prevention.

With the help of planned maintenance, we found a reactive to proactive method and use trained staff to help other staff to be trained for better maintenance of their machines.

Policy:

1. Sustain availability of machines.
2. Optimum cost of maintenance.

3. Reduce spares inventory.
4. Improve reliability of machines.

Six steps in planned maintenance:

1. Equipment evaluation.
2. Improve weakness by restoring deterioration.
3. System building for information management.
4. Set time-based information system.
5. Prepare a predictive maintenance system.
6. Evaluate the planned maintenance.

9.8.4.4   Pillar 4 – Quality Maintenance

Quality maintenance is the fourth pillar of TPM, aimed at assuring zero-defect manufacturing to ensure customer receives the best quality product. The main focus is on taking corrective actions in a systematic manner. The key factor of QM is to prevent errors from occurring in the product in the first place, rather than fixing produced ones.

QM is implemented into two phases. In the first phase, the quality issues are eliminated by analysing the defects, to prevent accruing the defects, then these improvements are implemented. The second phase is to ensure sustaining the quality through standard parameters and methods to achieve zero defects. The major benefits of QM are reductions in the cost of quality, re-work, consumers' complaints, and need for inspections.

Policy:

1. Control of equipment for defect-free conditions.
2. QM activities for quality assurance.
3. Defect prevention at source.
4. Detection of defects during production.
5. Segregation of defects within the production line.
6. Implementation of quality assurance to ensure operator effectiveness.

Steps related to product:

1. Product defects.
2. Check severity of the defect – whether it is major or minor.
3. Locate the defect with reference to the layout.
4. Check the magnitude and frequency of defect occurrence.

9.8.4.5   Pillar 5 – Education and Training

Education and training is the fifth pillar and is aimed at educating the workers to have multi-skilled staff whose morale is high, who work with eagerness, and who do all necessary functions independently with efficiency. The operators are educated to upgrade their skills. The operators gain an idea about 'know-how' from their experience and solve the problem without knowing the root cause of it. So, it is necessary to train them with 'know-why.' The staff should be trained with the aim of creating a firm with lots of experts. There are various phases of skills, like do not know; know theoretically, but not practically; can do, but cannot train others; and can do as well as also teach others.

Policy:

1. Techniques to improve knowledge and skills.
2. Training provides for self-learning.
3. Revitalisation of employees through training/assessment, etc.
4. Create a good work environment for reducing employee fatigue.

Steps involved in education and training activities:

1. Firstly, check present status of education and training and set new policies.
2. For upskilling, establish a training system for maintenance.
3. Prepare a calendar schedule for training.
4. Start the training systems.

9.8.4.6 Pillar 6 – Safety, Health, and Environment

Safety, Health, and Environment (SHE) is the sixth pillar of TPM, which focuses on providing a safe workplace and a healthy environment for employees. This pillar aims to cultivate continuous improvements to achieve a sustained and excellent record of safety, health, and environment. A committee is constituted involving all level staff/officers/workers and is headed by a technically senior person. Safety is the top-most factor in the plant. For this, there should be a need to create awareness among employees through various steps, e.g., quizzes, dramas, slogans, and posters, etc. on safety can be organised by the firm from time to time.

9.8.4.7 Pillar 7 – Office TPM

This pillar concentrates on all administrative activities and support functions in the organisation. It starts working after the first four pillars of TPM come on track. The main aim of this pillar is to identify and eliminate waste and losses, to improve efficiency in the administration work. To improve automation in the office, it includes a detailed analysis of the processes and procedures of work used in it.

Office TPM and its benefits:

1. Better work area utilisation.
2. Reduced repetitive work.
3. Reduced inventory levels.
4. Reduced cost of administration.
5. Reduced inventory carrying cost.
6. Reduce paperwork.
7. Reduction of overhead costs.
8. Reduction in breakdown.
9. Clean and attractive workplace.

9.8.4.8 Pillar 8 – Early Equipment Management

The last pillar of TPM is early equipment management. It uses the experience collected from previous maintenance activities to make sure that new machinery reaches its maximum performance. The output of a machine is guaranteed from the first day when machine starts. By taking input from the people who work on that machine on a daily basis and from suppliers, you can improve the maintainability and operability of the machine.

Steps involved in early equipment management:

1. Easy cleaning and inspection.
2. Lubrication.
3. Accessibility.
4. Improving operability through ergonomics.
5. Feedback mechanisms.
6. Increased safety features.

9.9 STATUS OF TPM IN INDIAN MANUFACTURING INDUSTRIES

Nowadays, most Indian organisations are planning to implement TPM, but only few organisations had implemented it in the last few years. The TPM Club India was established in 1998 under the Confederation of Indian Industries (CII) to promote the TPM concept and practices in Indian enterprises. The TPM Club India has become one of the most effective interventions for manufacturing industries. The TPM Club India has facilitated more than 100 Indian organisations to receive TPM excellence awards and made India the second-largest country for receiving TPM awards after Japan. During the course of development, many organisations have become members of CII to take training from CII-trained counsellors. The status of TPM award-winning organisations was very critical in the year 2009. 2010 was a little better in results.

During 2009–2010, most of the companies across the world entered the TPM Awards. The results show the importance of TPM and its supportive nature towards companies in critical situations. The award function was organised in Japan on March 11, 2010 for the winners of TPM awards. The award function was attended by more than 310 people to make it special. Table 9.2 illustrates the number of award-winners by various countries in 2009.

Seth and Tripathi (2005, 2006) and Ahuja and Khamba (2007) have highlighted TPM accomplishment in Indian organisations in their studies, and also validate the increasing acceptance of TPM concepts and philosophies in the context of improving performance in Indian organisations. Indian organisations received a lot of TPM awards and maintained the trend of the high number of companies outside Japan this year and remain competitive with Japan to now, as shown in Table 9.3.

9.9.1 TPM Award-Winning Indian Organisations

There are various categories of TPM awards such as 'Award for TPM Excellence-First Category,' 'Award for Excellence in Consistent TPM Commitment-First Category,'

TABLE 9.2

TPM Award-Winners' by Country for the Year 2009

Country	No. of Awards	Country	No. of Awards	Country	No. of Awards
Japan	27	Argentina	2	Poland	1
Thailand	18	Brazil	2	Sweden	1
India	9	Spain	2	Hungary	1
Turkey	8	Belgium	1	Israel	1
China	7	Canada	1	Mexico	1
Taiwan	5	Colombia	1	Netherland	1
Germany	5	Ecuador	1	Pakistan	1
USA	3	Egypt	1	Total	100

Source: Confederation of Indian Industry Website, www.cii.in.

'Award for TPM Excellence – Second Category,' 'Award for TPM Excellence Special Award Category,' etc. Table 9.4 illustrates the details of Indian organisations who received various TPM awards from 1995 to 2014.

Table 9.5 shows the Year Wise TPM Award (Various Categories) Winner Indian Organisations in the Year 1995–2015.

9.10 CONCLUSION

The conclusions made in this chapter are summarised as the study of TPM, its pillars, calculation of OEE, various losses related to maintenance and its types, and case studies of the automotive and food sectors, etc. The study has demonstrated the design and development of TPM promotion organisational structure, the framework structure of a formal education and training programme for employees, and establishment of a TPM Master Plan including all eight TPM pillars.

9.11 CASE STUDIES

9.11.1 CASE STUDY 1: THE AUTOMOTIVE SECTOR

Aim: Reduction of costs through the implementation of Total Productive Maintenance.

History: The firm produces electrical component of two main types. These are mostly used in lighting of streets, greenhouses, shops, buildings, and public places. Both types of product have a high output and are energy-efficient also. The producer used a technique called injection moulding, which is also used in plastics, to create complex shaped ceramic components. Due to increase in global demand for energy-efficient products, demand has increased for these products. As a result, there should be a check on quality too.

Challenges: To improve the productivity, delivery, and quality of the product. To reduce costs with sustainability in competitive market.

TABLE 9.3
TPM Award-Winner Countries

Country Name	2005	2006	2007	2008	2009	2010	2011	2012	2013	2014	2015	Total
Arabia	–	–	1	–	–	–	–	–	–	1	–	2
Argentina	6	5	2	3	2	9	3	–	–	–	–	30
Bangladesh	1	–	–	1	–	–	–	–	–	–	–	2
Belgium	4	3	5	4	1	–	–	1	–	–	–	17
Bolivia	–	–	–	–	–	–	–	–	–	–	–	1
Bosnia and Herzegovina	–	–	–	1	–	–	–	–	–	–	–	1
Brazil	3	–	3	7	2	13	7	6	2	4	1	48
Canada	–	–	–	–	1	–	–	–	–	–	–	1
Chili	–	–	1	–	–	–	2	–	–	–	–	3
China	2	6	5	1	7	6	4	10	2	6	3	52
Colombia	–	3	1	3	1	1	1	1	1	–	–	12
Ecuador	–	–	–	–	1	–	1	1	–	–	–	3
Egypt	3	–	–	–	1	1	–	–	–	–	–	5
France	12	12	8	7	–	1	–	1	2	–	–	43
Germany	5	2	4	3	5	1	1	1	1	1	–	24
Greece	–	–	1	–	–	–	–	–	–	–	–	1
Hungary	–	–	1	–	1	–	1	–	2	–	–	5
India	30	16	21	20	9	20	20	19	18	28	26	227
Indonesia	1	–	–	1	–	1	1	–	1	1	–	6
Israel	–	–	–	–	1	–	–	–	–	–	–	1
Italy	6	5	–	1	–	–	1	–	1	3	1	19
Japan	54	46	47	41	27	24	23	17	21	32	26	358

(Continued)

TABLE 9.3 (CONTINUED)
TPM Award-Winner Countries

Country Name	2005	2006	2007	2008	2009	2010	2011	2012	2013	2014	2015	Total
Kenya	–	1	–	–	–	–	–	–	–	–	–	1
Kingdom of Denmark	–	–	–	–	–	–	1	–	–	–	–	1
Korea	–	1	1	–	–	–	1	1	–	–	–	4
Luxembourg	1	–	1	–	–	–	–	–	–	–	–	1
Malaysia	–	–	1	1	1	–	–	–	–	–	–	1
Mexico	3	–	4	1	1	–	–	2	–	–	–	11
Morocco	–	–	2	1	–	–	–	–	–	–	–	3
Netherlands	–	2	–	1	1	2	3	3	2	3	2	19
New Zealand	1	–	1	2	–	–	–	–	1	–	–	4
Pakistan	2	1	3	–	1	–	–	–	–	–	–	8
Philippines	1	1	2	2	–	–	–	1	2	–	2	11
Poland	–	3	1	–	1	–	1	–	–	3	–	9
Portugal	1	1	–	–	–	1	–	–	1	–	–	3
Romania	–	1	–	–	–	1	–	–	1	–	–	3
Russia	1	2	1	1	–	1	–	1	–	1	–	8
Saudi Arabia	–	–	–	1	–	1	–	1	–	–	–	2
Serbia	1	–	–	1	–	1	–	1	–	–	1	5
Singapore	1	–	1	–	–	–	–	1	–	–	–	2
South Africa	3	2	3	–	–	–	3	–	–	–	–	9
Spain	–	2	3	–	2	–	1	1	–	2	–	10
Sri Lanka	–	2	–	–	–	–	2	–	–	–	1	3
Sweden	–	–	1	–	1	2	2	1	3	1	1	12

(Continued)

TABLE 9.3 (CONTINUED)
TPM Award-Winner Countries

Country Name	2005	2006	2007	2008	2009	2010	2011	2012	2013	2014	2015	Total
Switzerland	–	–	1	–	–	1	–	–	–	–	–	2
Taiwan	10	8	4	6	5	6	5	6	3	3	3	59
Thailand	5	8	7	8	18	13	11	26	12	17	23	148
Turkey	4	2	7	7	8	5	2	10	–	8	4	57
UAE	1	–	–	–	–	–	–	–	–	–	–	1
UK	4	1	–	1	–	1	–	–	–	–	–	7
USA	1	–	2	4	3	2	4	2	2	1	–	21
Other	1	–	–	1	–	1	–	1	4	5	5	18
Total	**168**	**136**	**142**	**130**	**100**	**115**	**99**	**114**	**81**	**120**	**99**	**1304**

Source: *International Journal of Lean Six Sigma,* Vol. 5, Issue 3, 2014.

TABLE 9.4

TPM Award-Winning Indian Organisations in the Years 1995–2001

S. No.	Company Name	Plant Name	Year	Category	Remarks
1	Vikram Cements		1995	Award for TPM	
2	Sundram Fasteners Ltd	Padi, Krishnapuram, Pondy, Hosur	1998	Excellence – First Category	
3	Tanfac Industries Ltd		1999		
4	Birla Tires		2000		
5	Hindustan Lever Ltd	Sumerpur			
6	Indo Gulf Fertilizer Ltd				
7	Aditya Cements		2001		
8	Hindustan Lever Ltd.	Chindwara			
	Hindustan Lever Ltd.	Yavatmal			
	Hindustan Lever Ltd.	Silvassa			
9	Orient Cements				
10	Vikram Cements			Award for Excellence in Consistent TPM Commitment – First Category	

Objectives: The introduction of TPM and to identify and eliminate the losses. To get effective production costs with a maintained level of quality.

Solution: Firms focused on training modules for initial implementation of TPM in 2010 (initially for Autonomous and Planned Maintenance).

In 2011, the firm conducted training on the TPM pillars and made a structure for activities by keeping in view the vision and mission of the firm. The improved structure of TPM has eight TPM pillars, with two additional special pillars that are lean and supply chain.

The activities based on the introduction and sustainability of TPM were conducted throughout the following three years. As a result, the firm was able to apply for an award for very first level of TPM in 2014.

The firm set the examples of zero failures, zero breakdown, and zero defects.

The firm also improved the use of OEE, method of delivery, and quality of products.

9.11.2 Case Study: Food Processing Sector

Aim: Implementation of TPM for the food processing sector.

History: A well-recognised firm of food producers implemented TPM in 2010. The factory was an individual business unit and also played a Change Agent role and reported to a central steering group.

The point to be noticed was the lack of activities in linking back or feedback chain planning.

TABLE 9.5

Annual TPM Award-Winning (Various Categories) Indian Organisations in the years 1995–2015

Award Category/ Year	Award for Excellence in Consistent TPM Commitment –First Category	Award for TPM Excellence –First Category	Award for TPM Excellence –Second Category	Special Award for TPM Achievement	Total
1995–2001	1	9	–	–	10
2002	3	8	–	–	11
2003	1	13	4	–	18
2004	5	19	2	–	26
2005	14	16	–	–	30
2006	3	12	–	1	16
2007	2	12	–	7	21
2008	6	11	–	3	20
2009	2	7	–	–	9
2010	19	–	–	1	20
2011	3	17	–	–	20
2012	8	9	1	1	19
2013	7	11	–	–	18
2014	8	18	1	1	28
2015	10	9	4	3	26
Total	91	162	12	17	292

Challenges: To carry out the TPM activities, such that the benefits would be reflected in the culture of the firm.

There was a lack of linking between the planning and delivery of the business plan that meant there was a lack of connectivity.

The change agents' problems were neglected and the problems came into the picture with the arrival of a new workload and new equipment.

Solution: The firm has reorganised a TPM cell so that managers can easily decide what activities have been done to meet their objectives.

With the new TPM, a clear plan of activities is there in the form of a matrix structure.

The new activities structure works in a top-down structure to give a clearer picture of instructions and the focus of work for change agents.

POINTS TO REMEMBER

TPM: TPM is a system of maintenance covering the entire life of the equipment in every division including planning, manufacturing, and maintenance.

Breakdown Maintenance: Breakdown maintenance is unplanned maintenance which is performed on equipment that has failed or broken down.

Preventive Maintenance: Preventive maintenance (PM) is a maintenance strategy which is done on a daily routine like cleaning, inspection, oiling, tightening, etc. to keep the equipment in good condition and reduce the depreciation rate as well.

Predictive Maintenance: Predictive maintenance works on the principle that 'Prevention is better than cure.'

SELF-ASSESSMENT QUESTIONS

1. What is Total Productive Maintenance?
2. What is the need for TPM in a manufacturing company?
3. What are the pillars of TPM?
4. How many pillars are in TPM?
5. What are the 5S in kaizen?
6. What is the OEE calculation?
7. What is the goal of TPM?
8. What are the benefits of TPM?
9. How many types of TPM are there?
10. What is total quality maintenance?
11. What is autonomous maintenance?
12. What do you mean by preventive maintenance?
13. How does preventive maintenance impact productivity?
14. What is breakdown maintenance?
15. What is a good OEE score?

BIBLIOGRAPHY

Agrawal, V. K., & Gandhi, O. P. (1997). Reliability-centered maintenance. *Proceedings of SERC School on RAM*, April, 14–25.

Ahuja, I. P. S., & Khamba, J. S. (2007). An evaluation of TPM implementation initiatives in an Indian manufacturing enterprise. *Journal of Quality in Maintenance Engineering*, *13*(4), 338–352.

Ahuja, I. P. S., & Khamba, J. S. (2008). Total productive maintenance: Literature review and directions. *International Journal of Quality & Reliability Management*, *25*(7), 709–756.

Bhadury, B. (2000). Management of productivity through TPM. *Productivity*, *41*(2), 240–251.

Chan, F. T. S., Lau, H. C. W., Ip, R. W. L., Chan, H. K., & Kong, S. (2005). Implementation of total productive maintenance: A case study. *International Journal of Production Economics*, *95*(1), 71–94.

Hansson, J., Backlund, F., & Lycke, L. (2003). Managing commitment: Increasing the odds for successful implementation of TQM, TPM or RCM. *International Journal of Quality & Reliability Management*, *20*(9), 993–1008.

Hartmann, E. (1992). *Successfully Installing TPM in a non-Japanese Plant: Total Productive Maintenance*. TPM Press, Pittsburgh, PA.

Jain, A., Bhatti, R., & Singh, H. (2014). Total productive maintenance (TPM) implementation practice. *International Journal of Lean Six Sigma*, *5*(3), 293–313.

Jeong, K. Y., & Phillips, D. T. (2001). Operational efficiency and effectiveness measurement. *International Journal of Operations & Production Management*, *21*(11), 1404–1416.

JIPM, T. (1996). For every operator: Japan Institute of Plant Maintenance.

Majumdar, N. (1998). TPM: The philosophy of the zero. *Business Today*, *7*, 60–73.

McKone, K. E., Schroeder, R. G., & Cua, K. O. (1999). Total productive maintenance: A contextual view. *Journal of Operations Management*, *17*(2), 123–144.

Moubray, J. (2001). *Reliability-Centered Maintenance*. Industrial Press Inc., New York.

Nakajima, S. (1988). *Introduction to TPM: Total Productive Maintenance*. (Translation). Productivity Press, Inc., Cambridge, MA, p. 129.

Rausand, M., & Vatn, J. (2008). Reliability centred maintenance. In: *Complex System Maintenance Handbook* (pp. 79–108). Springer, London.

Sangameshwran, P., & Jagannathan, R. (2002). Eight pillars of TPM. *Indian Management*, *11*, 36–37.

Seth, D., & Tripathi, D. (2005). Relationship between TQM and TPM implementation factors and business performance of manufacturing industry in Indian context. *International Journal of Quality & Reliability Management*, *22*(3), 256–277.

Seth, D., & Tripathi, D. (2006). A critical study of TQM and TPM approaches on business performance of Indian manufacturing industry. *Total Quality Management & Business Excellence*, *17*(7), 811–824.

Shirose, K. (Ed.) (1995). *TPM Team Guide*. Steiner Books, Productivity Press, Portland, OR.

Steinbacher, H. R., & Steinbacher, N. L. (1993). *TPM for America: What It Is and Why You Need It*. Productivity Press, Portland, OR.

Willmott, P. (1994). *Total Productive Maintenance: The Western Way*. Butterworth-Heinemann, Oxford.

Wireman, T. (2004). *Total Productive Maintenance*. Industrial Press Inc., New York.

Yeomans, M., & Millington, P. (1997). Getting maintenance into TPM. *Manufacturing Engineer*, *76*(4), 170–173.

10 Quality Management Systems

10.1 QUALITY MANAGEMENT SYSTEMS

Quality management systems or quality systems may be defined as techniques/ methodologies a manufacturer must follow to ensure that all the products manufactured meet the specifications.

Discussing a quality system means 'talking about a standard.' Initially, there are two quality systems:

- Military Quality System.
- ISO 9000 Quality System.

10.2 MILITARY QUALITY SYSTEM

The Department of Defence approved this quality system and made it mandatory to be used by the departments of the Army, Navy, Air Force, and Defence Supply Agency. The military quality system helps in establishing the requirements for a contractor's inspection system. The various requirements of this system are:

- Contractor responsibilities.
- Inspection and testing documentation.
- Records.
- Corrective actions.
- Drawings and changes.
- Measuring and testing equipment.
- Process controls.
- Indication of inspection status.
- Government-furnished material.
- Non-conforming materials.
- Quality products.
- Sampling inspection.
- Inspection provisions.
- Government inspection at subcontractor or vendor facilities.

ISO 9001 replaced this standard, but it may still be required for some contracts.

10.3   ISO 9000 QUALITY SYSTEM

The ISO 9000 quality management system was first published by the International Organisation for Standardisation in 1987. ISO 9000 can be defined as a group of international quality management standards which was developed to ensure that organisations fulfil the needs of clients and partners while meeting legal and administrative requirements associated with a product or service.

ISO 9000 is not limited to any specific industry and it is applicable to all the organisations willing to maintain the quality in their products. The national standards body of the United Kingdom, known as the British Standards Institution (BSI), proposed the BS 5750 series of standards to ISO in 1979. So, the BS 5750 series of standards were the basis for ISO 9000. However, around 20 years prior to BS 5750 series of standards, there were some standards for procurement by government, e.g., the MIL-Q-9858 standard in 1959 used by the US Defence system.

For supplying to government procurement agencies, there was a requirement for organisations to have a quality assurance certificate from different quality management systems as per the requirements of the contract. This situation required receiving shared acknowledgment of different quality management frameworks like NATO AQAP, MIL-Q, and Def Stan guidelines. So, ISO 9000 received global adoption as it resolved all the problems of adopting multiple and often similar requirements of different standards. Along with this, there are a number of factors responsible for the global adoption of ISO 9000. Organisations started using the ISO 9001, 9002, and 9003 requirements as the basis while signing any contract with suppliers. Adopting ISO 9000 as the basis for signing a contract limited the need for supplier development. It was so flexible that its requirements could be prepared as the agreement conditions based on the type of business, complexity of product, and risk to the buyer. ISO 9000 resulted in a reduction in the administrative burden of handling several quality management standards, as it was adopted globally.

Numerous analysts worked to recognise the effect of ISO 9000 certification on an organisation, and most of them have identified significant financial benefits for ISO 9000 certified organisations. The British Assessment Bureau conducted a survey in 2011, and found that 44% of ISO certified organisations had won new business. ISO 9000 certified organisations achieved better returns when compared with the similar organisations without certification.

Implementing ISO 9000 in any organisation is thought to be a guarantee of better financial performance, but a few researchers reported that while there is some evidence of this, the improvement is somewhat driven by the fact that the better performing companies have a tendency to pursue an ISO 9000 certificate.

10.3.1   ISO 9000 vs ISO 9001

ISO 9000 is a group of international quality management standards, whereas ISO 9001 is a member standard within the ISO 9000 family. Also there is a standard named ISO 9000 within the ISO family. This standard establishes the basics and terminology for quality management systems.

10.4 EVOLUTION OF THE ISO 9000 QUALITY MANAGEMENT STANDARDS

Professionals implementing the ISO 9000 quality management standards give their feedback and based on their feedback, standing technical committees and advisory groups revise the ISO 9000 standard. The various editions of ISO 9000 are given below.

10.4.1 ISO 9001:1987 EDITION

ISO 9000:1987 was developed on the basis of UK Standard BS-5750. It has three 'models' for quality management systems based on the activities of the organisation. The three models of this edition are given here:

10.4.2 ISO 9001:1987 MODEL

This model was used for assuring quality in design and development, production, installation, and after-sales servicing. So the organisations involved in developing new products were best suited for this model.

10.4.3 ISO 9002:1987 MODEL

This model was used for assuring quality in production, installation, and servicing. So the organisations involved in production, installation, and servicing work, but not involved in the creation of new products, should register under this model.

10.4.4 ISO 9003:1987 MODEL

This model was used for assuring quality during final inspection and testing. So this model was concerned only with the inspection of finished products, without focusing on the production process.

10.4.5 ISO 9000:1994 EDITION

ISO 9000:1994 was focused on assuring quality through preventive actions, rather than inspecting the final product. As per this model, organisations must work for a quality product and improve quality by taking preventive action.

10.4.6 ISO 9000:2000 EDITION

ISO 9001:2000 changed all the standards of the ISO 9000:1994 model. The organisations involved in the creation of new products were in need of a quality standard focused on design and development. The 2000 edition changed the focus to the concept of process management. ISO 9000:2000 edition also demanded participation by high officials to incorporate quality into the business system and to prevent junior administrators from delegation of quality works.

Another goal of this standard was to enhance effectiveness by continuous monitoring of effectiveness of actions and activities. Monitoring and improving the routine process and tracking the customer's satisfaction were made integral parts of this standard. The requirements of this standard include:

- Documents should be approved before delivery.
- The appropriate version of documents should be available when required.
- Proper records should be maintained to prove that all the needs have been fulfilled.
- A process should be developed that maintains all the records.

There were five goals in the ISO 9000: 2000 revision as given below:

- Meet the need of stakeholders.
- Useable by all types of organisations.
- Useable by all areas.
- To make it simple to understand.
- Connect the quality management system for business processes.

10.4.7 ISO 9000: 2008 EDITION

ISO 9001:2008 is simply a re-narration of ISO 9001:2000 with explanations of the current requirements of ISO 9001:2000. There were no new requirements, for example, if any organisation upgrades its quality management system, then it should be observed whether the explanation given in the revised version is being followed by the organisation.

10.4.8 ISO 9000: 2015 EDITION

ISO-TC176, which was responsible for development of ISO 9001, celebrated 25 years of implementing ISO 9001 in 2012. In that celebration, it was concluded that creating a new QMS model for the next 25 years was necessary, so they started revising ISO 9001 with the new quality management principles. This moment was considered as 'beginning of a new era in the development of quality management systems' by specialists in the field. This work of revising ISO 9001 resulted in publication of ISO 9001:2015 on September 23, 2015. In the revised version, restructuring has been done, with some modification in main terms, but the scope of the standard has been kept unchanged. This will make integration of this standard with other international management systems easier.

The new ISO 9001:2015 quality management system ensures that consumers get efficient and reliable products of the required quality with better service. It will result in increased profits for a business.

The 2015 edition of ISO 9000 was focused on performance. It adopted the 'Plan – Do – Check – Act' cycle at all the levels in the organisation. Key changes in ISO 9001:2015 quality management system include:

- It will be a high-level structure in all the new standards issued by the ISO, as the high-level structure of ten clauses has been implemented.

- It is focused on developing a management system for addressing the special needs of an organisation.
- It ensures the full involvement of all top-level management.
- It makes top-level management accountable for integrating quality in their business.
- It is focused on risk analysis, which makes the whole system a preventive tool instead of a corrective tool and results in improvement.
- Now the organisations can decide which information should be documented, and in what format it should be documented, so there is less requirements for documentation.
- Integration with other management system with the use of a general structure and core text.
- Addition of principles of knowledge management.
- Management representatives and quality manual are not compulsory.

10.5 PRINCIPLES OF QUALITY MANAGEMENT OF ISO 9000 SERIES

The seven principles of quality management of ISO 9000 series are given below.

10.5.1 CUSTOMER FOCUS

The growth of every organisation depends on its customers, so the needs of customers must be understood. Organisations should work to fulfil customer's needs and strive to exceed customer expectations. The various aims of an organisation towards customers are:

- To understand the requirements of existing and future clients.
- To set objectives of organisation that fulfil all the needs and expectations of customers.
- To focus on customer needs.
- To measure customers' satisfaction levels.
- To maintain good relationships with customers.
- To take feedback about experience of customers with the product.
- To take feedback to check the satisfaction levels of customers.

10.5.2 LEADERSHIP

Leadership is the quality that gives direction to the organisation. Leaders should set some goals for the organisations and they should motivate their employees to achieve all those goals. A good leader must:

- Set a vision and mission of the organisation.
- Set challenging but achievable goals.
- Develop trust among employees.
- Work for employees' empowerment.
- Recognise employee commitments.

10.5.3   ENGAGEMENT OF PEOPLE

Engagement of people reflects the success of an organisation. If the people are fully involved in an organisation, then it will benefit by utilising the full capacity of these people. For better results, an organisation must:

- Ensure that the abilities of people are fully utilised.
- Set accountability of people.
- Enable participation in continual improvement.
- Evaluate the performance of individuals.
- Motivate the employees for learning and knowledge-sharing.
- Discuss the problems and constraints with the employee in an open environment.
- Learn more ways to improve employee involvement.

10.5.4   PROCESS APPROACH

Managing activities and related resources as a process can give efficient results. The various activities are:

- Treat all the activities as procedures.
- Evaluate all the activities.
- Establish relationships among the various activities.
- Find out the scope for improvement.
- Use all the resources efficiently.
- Try to learn more tools used for process analysis.

10.5.5   IMPROVEMENT

Improvement in performance should be the core objective of any organisation. For overall performance in an organisation, some actions are given below:

- Improve the performance of organisation.
- Enhance the capabilities of the organisation.
- Introduce the activities resulting in improvement.
- Motivate people to improve.
- Continuously evaluate the improvement.
- Always celebrate if improvement is observed anywhere.
- Try to learn about the methods that result in improvement.

10.5.6   DECISION-MAKING BASED ON EVIDENCE

Decisions must be based on the information and data available for improving the effectiveness of the decisions. The various requirements for such decisions are:

- To ensure the availability of correct and reliable data.
- To use the best-suited method for analysing the data.

- To make decisions on the basis of the data and information available.
- To analyse data with practical experience.
- To find tools for decision-making.

10.5.7 Relationship Management

It is the relationship between an organisation and its suppliers and service providers which holds them all together and enhances the ability of all to create value. So, organisations must focus on managing a good relationship with each other. The various activities in managing a relationship are:

- To find suppliers to optimise resources and create valuable products.
- To build up long-term relationships.
- To share information, technology, resources, and plans with collaborators.
- To work together for continuous improvement.
- To ensure the success of suppliers.
- To know more about suppliers and managing the relationship with suppliers.

10.6 IMPLEMENTATION OF ISO 9001

ISO 9000-based quality management systems can be implemented through four phases, as given below:

- Planning and designing.
- Documentation.
- Implementation.
- Assessment and registration.

The following phases contain certain steps involved in the implementation of ISO 9001:

10.6.1 Phase 1: Planning and Designing

10.6.1.1 Decision-Making and Commitment

For implementing ISO 9000 in any organisation, the first step is decision by top management that the organisation should register for ISO 9001. The top management should be committed to adopting ISO 9000, and for this they must have in-depth knowledge of ISO 9001.

Top management must understand that they have to demonstrate their best commitment and determination towards adoption of the ISO 9000 quality management system within the organisation, as in the absence of a firm commitment from top management, it is not possible for any organisation to implement any quality management system. To show its full commitment towards adopting a quality management standard, top management should implement the following steps:

- Have a formal conversation with the organisation and communicate to them the significance of meeting the needs of customers.

- Draft the quality policies of the organisation and ensure that they are clearly understood by every worker.
- Ensure that all the objectives of quality standards have been adopted by all the departments at all levels.
- Make sure of the availability of all the resources which are necessary for implementing the quality management system.
- Conduct meetings for review.
- Lead the organisation from the front.
- Have an active involvement in all the activities for the improvement of processes.
- Motivate the employees towards active positive involvement.

Top management must identify the goals of implementing the quality system. Some important goals can be understood as:

- Improving the effectiveness and efficiency.
- Improved working to become more profitable.
- To produce products and services on a consistent basis which meet customers' needs and expectations.
- Work towards improving customer satisfaction.
- Increase the overall market share.
- Reduce costs and liabilities involved.

10.6.1.2 Implementation Team and Management Representative

The second step is to build a team, responsible for all implementation activities, and select a coordinator to head this team. This head of the team will act as the Management Representative (MR) and will handle all the implementation activities. This team must include representatives from all the departments, i.e. design and development, production, marketing, and quality control, etc.

The management representative is an integral part of an organisation. The MR should be a specialist in ISO 9001. With regard to the standard, the MR will work as a link between the top management of the organisation and the registrar of ISO 9001. The MR is a person who is supposed to be a quality system champion of an organisation.

The MR must be an individual:

- With the complete trust and total support of the CEO.
- Who is passionate and committed to quality in general, and specifically to the ISO 9001 quality management system.
- Who is a respectable person having a position at the organisation that can allow him to influence other employees at all levels of the organisation.
- Who has a good understanding of various quality methods, particularly ISO 9001.

There are three major responsibilities that are held by the MR, as given below:

10.6.1.3   Quality System Maintenance

The MR of any organisation will be responsible for proper implementation of all the processes of the quality management system. The MR will also be responsible for the maintenance of the quality system.

10.6.1.4   Reporting on Quality System Performance

It is the responsibility of the MR to give a performance report on the quality system to the top management. This also includes reporting any scope for further improvement.

10.6.1.5   Promoting Customer Requirements

All the employees of an organisation must know about their customers' needs. It is their primary objective to know about their customer requirements. They should also know the effect of these requirements on the company and how effectively the organisation fulfils the needs of their customers.

10.6.1.6   Employee Awareness Training

All the employees must be given information well in advance about the implementation of a quality management system. They must be told the concept of ISO 9000 and the impact of adopting ISO in their work. This will help in getting support from all the employees in a positive manner. There should not be any delay in passing information, as delay may cause rumours and gossip among the employees, which may increase the effort required for implementation.

All the departments and all the employees are affected by the implementation of ISO, so the training programme should also be categorised based on the hierarchy of employees. The training programme should cover:

- All the objectives and concepts of the quality management standard.
- The impact of implementing the quality standard on the strategic objectives of the organisation.
- The changes in work culture after implementation of the quality standard.

There is also a requirement of initial training for writing quality manuals, procedures writing, and work instructions writing. When the company itself is not able to provide this type of training, the employees must take part in training courses run by external training organisations. It is also possible to call an external training organisation into the organisation itself for in-house training.

10.6.1.7   Perform a Gap Assessment

A gap assessment is an important step to be performed while implementing a quality system. In this process, the existing quality management system is compared with the requirements of the ISO 9001 standard. The gap assessment is done with the objective of determining:

- The existing processes and procedures of the organisation, which are in accordance with ISO 9001 requirements.

- The existing processes and procedures of the organisation, which are required to be restructured to match ISO 9001 requirements.
- Additional processes and procedures, which are required to be formed to match ISO 9001 requirements.

If the required resources for gap assessment exist in the organisation, then it can be performed in the company itself, but in the absence of the required resources, a consultancy advisory can also be gathered through an ISO 9000 consulting firm.

10.6.1.8 Implementation of Planning

Once the gaps in the existing quality system compared to the ISO 9000 standard have been finalised, a detailed plan is required for its implementation. This detailed plan describes all the activities required for the proper implementation of the ISO 9000 quality standard. This detailed implementation plan should include:

- Development of quality documents and procedures.
- Selection of the required ISO 9000 standard section.
- The list of team members responsible for proper implementation.
- All the approvals from various authorities.
- Details of training needed.
- Details of various resources needed.
- Deadlines for various tasks.

All these details must be arranged in the form of a chart and should be checked and approved by top management officials. The final approved plan must explain the duties of every employee and every department. It should also mention the deadlines for finishing the tasks. All these activities should be undertaken with the observation of the management representative.

10.6.2 PHASE 2: DOCUMENTATION DEVELOPMENT

10.6.2.1 Documentation Development

Documentation is an important phase of implementing the ISO 9000 quality standard. A high-level document should include:

- A report describing the capacity of quality management system.
- Information about the various stages of quality management system.
- The quality objectives and guidelines of the organisation.
- The organisational structure chart, reflecting the interdependence and answerability of people whose actions have an impact on quality.
- An analysis of various policies at system level.

10.6.2.2 Analysis and Release Documents

Once all the documents are ready to use for proper implementation, before implementation, all these documents should be analysed and reviewed. After corrective revisions, the authority gives approval to release the documents for use.

10.6.3   PHASE 3: IMPLEMENTATION

10.6.3.1   Implementation and Employee Training

In this step, a newly documented quality management system is implemented in the organisation. Many training programmes based on hierarchy are organised to train the management and other workers to work with newly implemented quality management system.

10.6.3.2   Quality System Registrar Selection

In the initial stage of the implementation of the project, it is suggested to choose a registration body which is appropriate for issuing Quality System certifications. The Quality System certificate is issued by the registrar after auditing the company's quality system.

The following are the selection criteria to authorise the certification body to approve ISO 9001:

- Is the authorisation body recognised by a national accreditation body? If yes, by whom?
- Is the authorisation body recognised by the customers of organisation?
- Do the authorisation body auditors have expertise in the business area of the organisation?
- Is the organisation working suitably with its auditors, as each side has to work together for a definite period?
- If the auditors of an organisation are based in an area near the organisation or not, as with an increase in distance, travel expenses may be very high.

10.6.3.3   Internal Auditor Training and Commence Internal Audits

To check the performance of the Quality System, ISO 9001 and related standards require that the firm carry out an internal audit annually and reviews it to ensure that it adheres with the ISO 9001 needs along with detailed work practices of an organisation.

In any organisation, internal audits play important role in analysing quality. For getting pass in any registration audit, an organisation requires a full internal audit report. Internal audit helps in planning various processes and activities according to the quality system.

Two or more members of the organisation should be given training for internal audits. The eligibility for the review, opportunity, repetitions, and approach must be defined. Any individual from the team of internal auditors must not be partial. The only constraint is that internal auditors won't be able to review their own work.

10.6.3.4   Management Review

Management should review all the processes and should take corrective actions if required. Conducting a review guarantees and ensures the adequacy, effectiveness, and suitability of continuing the organisation's quality system. Assessment opportunities must be included in the review for the desired changes needed and improvement of the quality system, in addition to the quality policy and quality objectives. The below-mentioned points should be included as input for the management review.

- Results coming from audits.
- Feedback of customers.
- Performance of process and products.
- Report of actions both preventive and corrective.
- Various check points based on prior reviews.
- Various changes that can affect the quality system.
- Management review must focus on downfalls to effective quality system implementation.

10.6.4   PHASE 4: ASSESSMENT AND REGISTRATION

10.6.4.1   Stage 1 Registration Audit

After operating the quality system for a duration of a few months, and when it has been stabilised, it is the peak time to conduct a registration audit.

The selected registration body will audit the documentation and if everything matches with the requirements of the quality system, a visit will be made by the registrar to the company for the audit.

10.6.4.2   Corrective Actions

Management will review the result of the Stage 1 audit. Management will further try to implement corrective actions for the activities which are not matching or are off-grid with the standard's requirements.

10.6.4.3   Stage 2 Registration Audit

For ensuring that all the requirements of ISO 9001 have been met, a second stage registration audit will be performed by the registrar. He will also check if all the corrections found in the Stage 1 audit have been implemented or not.

An organisation will be certified with ISO 9001, generally for a period of three years after successful completion of the Stage 2 audit. During an interval of this three-year time period, periodic audits will be carried out by the registration body, which is to ensure that the system is continuing to operate in a satisfactory condition.

10.6.4.4   Continual Improvement

The certification of ISO 9000 that any organisation obtains should not be the end. Even after the certification, an organisation should continuously seek to improve the quality system with the help of:

- An improved quality policy.
- An objective of improved quality.
- Results from audits.
- Analysis of information and data available.
- Actions taken (both corrective and preventive actions).
- The report of the management review.

10.7   CASE STUDIES BASED ON ADOPTION OF ISO 9001

10.7.1   US Air Force Earns High Flying Results

US Air Force Programme Management Squadron adopted ISO 9001 in 1995, as a sourcing criterion in its supplier selection process. After two years, they called the management representative of each supplier and asked them to become an ASQ Certified Quality Auditor. The Air Force saved millions of dollars from these supplier contract specifications and also eliminated critical defects in supplier products and services. This also resulted in improved communication between the Air Force and its key suppliers and hence increased mission effectiveness.

10.7.2   ORKIN Results

This case study is based on a company, named 'ORKIN,' operating in pest control, which expanded its operations rapidly in the middle 1990s. With the expansion, this company faced the challenges of maintaining quality and consistency of service. As a solution to these challenges, the company decided to work to get ISO 9001 certification. To attain ISO 9001 certification, a new department, the 'Quality Assurance Department' was set up in the company in 2002. The whole company became ISO 9001 certified by issuing a manual detailing processes in the QA department. Then the company asked them to conduct a full audit. In the initial stage of the audit, local management opposed the audit, but the QA department kept on working to make them understand the benefits of the process. In 2005, ISO 9001 was earned by company's quality management system. This resulted in shifting the responsibility of quality assurance to the QA department and saving nearly $125,000 per year by removing the requirement of the external ISO 9001.

10.8   OTHER QUALITY SYSTEMS

Some other quality management systems are given below:

- QS/TS 16949 Quality System for the Automotive Industry.
- ISO 13485 Quality System for Medical Devices.
- AS 9100 Quality System for the Aerospace Industry.
- ISO 14000 Environmental Management System (EMS).
- ISO 26000 Quality System for Ensuring Social Responsibility.

10.8.1   QS/TS 16949 Quality System for the Automotive Industry

The TS 16949 quality system is a refined edition of ISO 9000, which is focused on quality assurance in the automotive industry. All the top-level suppliers of automobile manufacturers require this certification. TS 16949 is aimed at developing a quality system which results in continuous improvement, reduced wastage, reduced variation, and defect prevention. This was developed to:

- Remove the need for multiple certification audits.
- Use as a common quality system for the automobile manufacturing industry and automobile service part industry.
- Use all through the automotive production network.

10.8.2   ISO 13485 Quality System for Medical Devices

ISO 13485 was first published by ISO in 1996 for assuring quality in the design and manufacture of medical devices. Accepting the FDA's good manufacturing practices, this standard gives the definitions of various terms, such as medical device, sterile medical device, and many more.

The aim of this edition is to create easy harmonious medical device regulatory requirements for quality management systems. This standard has excluded some of the requirements of ISO 9000, as they were inappropriate for this standard. Because of this exclusion, one cannot claim conformity to ISO 9001.

10.8.3   AS 9100 Quality System for the Aerospace Industry

AS 9100 is a quality system specially developed for meeting the requirements of the aerospace industry. It is the highest level quality system available up to now. This quality system was developed to meet the common objective of ensuring quality within the aerospace industry.

Companies should produce reliable and safe products that match the needs of consumer and regulatory requirements. This will result in total customer satisfaction. The challenge of delivering products to consumers with varying quality expectations and requirements is also faced by aerospace suppliers and processors. Such situations can be handled wisely by adopting a quality system like AS 9100.

10.8.4   ISO 14000: Environmental Management System

ISO 14000, a global series of standards focused on environment management, was published in 1996 and was updated in 2004. ISO 14000 standards have been developed along with the development of the ISO 9000 quality standard. The main aim of ISO 14000 standard is to motivate the organisations to incorporate environmental concerns in their operations and product standards. The beauty of this standard is that it is not forced, but it is adopted by organisation voluntarily to control the impact of various activities on the environment. The organisations are free to adopt ISO 14000 series standards, partially or fully. ISO 14000 does not recommend any environmental performance targets; however, it equips the organisations with such tools, which helps in surveying and controlling the effect of their work, products, and services on the environment. The various aspects of environment management addressed by ISO 14000 are as follows:

- To investigate environment-related issues.
- To audit the impact of the operation of an organisation on the environment.

- To develop various terms and conditions for the safeguarding of the environment.
- To analyse the life cycles of the various products and their impact on the environment.
- To implement standards for controlling impacts on the environment.
- To evaluate the performance of standards adopted for environmental management.

10.8.4.1   Benefits for Compliance with an ISO 14000 EMS

The benefits for compliance with an ISO 14000 EMS results:

- Helps improve the relationship of the organisation with its customers.
- Helps improve the relationship of the organisation with the government.
- Improves the image of the organisation.
- Helps in establishing the organisation as a brand working with concern for the environment and society.
- Attracts customers as a producer of sustainable products.
- Results in improved value in the market and hence improves access to capital.
- As value increases in the market, market share also increases.
- High-value organisations get insurance at a reasonable cost.
- Wastage is minimised, which results in reduced costs.
- Consumption of resources and materials is reduced.
- As an environmentally conscious organisation, it becomes easier to get permits and authorisations.

10.8.4.2   ISO 14000 Registration

Registration is certification of an organisation that confirms that organisation has adopted an environment management standard and the organisation has a concern about sustainable development. Though an organisation can simply declare that they follow all the requirements of an EMS, most of the organisations go for registration of their EMS. Organisations register their EMS to assure their customers and other authorities that the organisation is fully concerned about the environment and society.

10.8.4.3   Principles behind the ISO 14000 Series

The key principles behind the development of ISO 14000 standards and documents are:

- To help in managing environmental issues in a better way.
- To focus on the various aspects related to the environment.
- To increase the applicability in all countries.
- To involve customers and the public by promoting the concept of environmental management.
- To reduce wastage and faster consumption of natural resources. It will result in reduced cost of products.

- EMS along with reduced product costs will also help in expanding the business worldwide.
- To be experimentally proven.
- To be practical, valuable, and usable.

10.9   MAJOR GROUPS OF ISO 14000 SERIES

The ISO 14000 series can be divided into two major groupings:

10.9.1   ORGANISATION-ORIENTED STANDARDS

The standard gives full guidelines required for establishing, maintaining, and evaluating an EMS. This system contains the various guidelines for environmental auditing. It is used for auditing of environmental management systems. It is also focused on environmental systems and functions of other organisations. The various organisation-oriented ISO 14000 standards are as follows:

10.9.1.1   ISO 14001:2004

This is an environmental management system. It includes various specifications with guidelines for use.

10.9.1.2   ISO 14004:2004

This is an environmental management system. It includes guidelines on principles, systems, and supporting techniques.

10.9.1.3   ISO 14010:1996

This system includes general principles and guidelines for environmental auditing.

10.9.1.4   ISO 14011:1996

This system contains the various audit procedures and guidelines for environmental auditing. It is used for auditing of the EMS.

10.9.1.5   ISO 14012:1996

This system includes guidelines for environmental auditing and qualification criteria for environmental auditors.

10.9.1.6   ISO 14031:1999

This system is used for environmental management. It contains environmental performance evaluation guidelines.

10.9.1.7   ISO/TR 14032:1999

This system is used for environmental management.

10.9.1.8   ISO/TR 14061:1998

This system contains information to assist forestry organisations in the use of an environmental management system

10.9.2 PRODUCT-ORIENTED STANDARDS

These standards are focused on the impacts of a product on the environment throughout its life cycle. In this standard, a study is done to measure the impacts made by any product on the environment. After measuring these impacts, this information is attached to the products in the form of levels and declarations. These standards help organisations in gathering the information required for decision-making. This information can be communicated to consumers of the product so that they may understand its impact on the environment.

10.10   BENEFITS OF ENVIRONMENTAL MANAGEMENT SYSTEMS

Most of the benefits of environmental management systems are the savings made by an organisation, increased profitability, and better sales opportunities. The savings may result in millions of dollars in the form of reduced penalties and fines. Other savings can be achieved by waste reduction, resource use reduction, etc. Any organisation can measure its positive impact on the environment. Some of the benefits of an EMS are given below.

a) **Better Regulatory Compliance:**
   Running an Environment Management System will help organisations in ensuring that it fulfils all the environmental legal responsibilities and all these responsibilities are easily managed.

b) **More Effective Use of Resources:**
   For sustainable development, natural resources must be used very wisely. Resources should be used more effectively without wastage. EMS will help in making some policies and procedures that will ensure a reduction in wastage of resources. This reduction in wastage will also result in reduced costs.

c) **Marketing:**
   An organisation can highlight the credibility of its business as an environmentally conscious operation, which has made a commitment to continuous environmental improvement, through advertising or annual reporting.

d) **Finance:**
   An organisation can find it easier to get investments from banks and other financial institutions, which are increasingly keen on businesses that control their environmental impact.

e) **Increased Sales Opportunities:**
   Running an EMS may help organisations by increasing sales opportunities, as some government departments and some large business houses may impose a condition of dealing with organisations that have an EMS system.

f) **Lighter Regulation:**
   EMS is not a regulatory requirement, but an organisation that runs an EMS shows its concern for the environment. For such environmental concerns, an organisation may get a benefit in the form of lower fees from environmental regulators.

g) **Certification to Recognised Standards:**
   Getting certification for running an EMS through ISO 14001, BS 8555, or
   EMAS can help any organisation in increasing its business credibility with
   customers and stakeholders.

Apart from this, with increasing awareness about the environment, it is becoming
essential for organisations to adopt an EMS for maintaining their position in the
market.

10.11 ISO 26000: QUALITY SYSTEM FOR ENSURING SOCIAL RESPONSIBILITY

Businesses and organisations cannot be separated from society. To run a business or
an organisation efficiently, their relationship with society and the environment play a
major role. Their attitude towards society and the environment play a significant role
in their success and it defines their ability to continue to operate effectively. These
days, their overall performance is measured by these relationship factors.

ISO 26000 provides guidelines for organisations to perform in socially responsible ways. This gives a direction to the organisations on working in an ethical and
transparent way for the welfare of society. ISO 26000 is an international standard
providing guidance on social responsibility to any organisation, regardless of its
place of operation, types of operations, and the size of the organisation.

ISO 26000:2010 is focused on providing guidance rather than requirements, so it
cannot be certified, unlike some other well-known ISO standards. Instead, it helps in
understanding social responsibility and shares best practices related to social responsibilities with organisations so that these organisations can translate their principles
into effective actions. It is applicable for all types of organisations regardless of their
activity, size, or location.

This Standard was launched in 2010 after five years of interaction between several
different stakeholders worldwide. Representatives of governments, non-governmen-
tal organisations, industry, consumer groups, and labour organisations across the
world were involved in its development, which shows that it represents an international consensus. On the basis of surveys and other sources, ISO 26000 has already
been adopted by 80 countries out of 160 ISO member countries as the national standard and there are still 21 countries in the adoption process. ISO 26000 is available
in more than 31 languages.

10.11.1 PRINCIPLES OF ISO 26000

The key principles of ISO 26000, which are given as the roots of socially responsible
behaviour, are discussed as below.

10.11.1.1 Accountability
An organisation should take responsibility for all its decisions and activities. It
should feel the accountability of all its decisions and their impact on society.

10.11.1.2 Transparency

The decisions and activities of an organisation have a great impact on society, so all the activities and decisions must be transparent. A transparent operation does not mean sharing commercially sensitive information. It means to communicate openly with stakeholders about both corporate and CSR vision, goals, and objectives.

10.11.1.3 Ethical Behaviour

The behaviour of an organisation should be based on the ethics of honesty, equity, and integrity. These ethics contain a commitment to addressing the interests of people, the environment, and stakeholders. An organisation must have ethical behaviour all the time.

10.11.1.4 Respect for Stakeholder Interests

Stakeholders are individuals or groups who are affected by, or have the ability to influence, the actions of the organisation. An organisation should respect and respond to the interests of its stakeholders.

10.11.1.5 Respect for the Rule of Law

It is essential to have respect for the rule of law and an organisation must accept this fact.

10.11.1.6 Respect for International Norms of Behaviour

An organisation should also respect the international norms of behaviour, while following the rules and regulations.

10.11.1.7 Respect for Human Rights

'Human rights' is a broad term which means respectful treatment of all individuals, without focusing on their personal characteristics, because they are human beings. Organisations should understand the importance and universality of human rights, and they must give respect to human rights.

10.12 CONCLUSION

Quality systems may be defined as techniques/methodologies a manufacturer must follow to ensure that all the products manufactured meet the specifications. In this chapter, various quality management systems have been covered. Gap assessment is also covered in the chapter. Evolution, implementation, and case studies of ISO 9001 standards have been explained in detail. Further, some other standards such as ISO 14000, TS 16949, and ISO 26000 are also explained in brief.

POINTS TO REMEMBER

Quality systems: Quality systems may be defined as techniques/methodologies a manufacturer must follow to ensure that all the products manufactured meet the specifications.

ISO 9001:2015: The new ISO 9001:2015 quality management system ensures that consumers get efficient and reliable products of the required quality with better service. It will result in increased profit for a business.

Gap assessment: Gap assessment is an important step to be performed while implementing a quality system. In this process, the existing quality management system is compared with the requirements of the ISO 9001 standard.

ISO 14000: The main aim of the ISO 14000 standard is to motivate organisations to incorporate environmental concerns into their operations and product standards.

ISO 26000: ISO 26000 provides guidelines for organisations to perform in a socially responsible way.

SELF-ASSESSMENT QUESTIONS

1. What do you understand by quality systems?
2. Explain the military quality system.
3. Write a short note on the ISO 9000 quality system.
4. What are the requirements of ISO 9000?
5. Explain the various editions of ISO 9000.
6. What are the seven quality management principles of the ISO 9000 series?
7. What are the various steps for implementation of ISO 9001?
8. 'Implementing quality management standards improves the effectiveness of the result.' Validate this statement with a case study.
9. Explain the QS/TS 16949 Quality System for the Automotive Industry.
10. Explain the ISO 13485 Quality System for Medical Devices.
11. Explain the AS 9100 Quality System for the Aerospace Industry.
12. Explain the ISO 14000: Environmental Management System (EMS).
13. Explain the ISO 26000: Quality System for Ensuring Social Responsibility.
14. List the various benefits of EMS.

BIBLIOGRAPHY

Bacivarov, I. C. (2015). The standard ISO 9001: 2015-a milestone in the evolution of quality management. *Asigurarea Calitatii-Quality Assurance, 21*(83), 2–4.

Benefits of ISO 14001. Online Available at: https://14000store.com/articles/iso-14000-info-benefits-of-iso-14001/.

BSI obtains first global accreditation from ANAB to certify organisations to the new Quality Management standard ISO 9001:2015. *BSI.* Retrieved 4 September 2015. BSOL Academic - BSI Group. Bsieducation.org.

Case study based on adoption of ISO 9001. Online Available at: http://asq.org/quality-progress/2012/03/customer-satisfaction-and-value/eradicating-inconsistency.html.

Case study based on adoption of ISO 9001. Online Available at: https://secure.asq.org/perl/msg.pl?prvurl=http://asq.org/2006/11/iso-9000/air-force-specifications-for-suppliers.pdf.

Chow-Chua, C., Goh, M., & Wan, T. B. (2003). Does ISO 9000 certification improve business performance? *International Journal of Quality & Reliability Management, 20*(8), 936–963.

Corbett, C. J., Montes-Sancho, M. J., & Kirsch, D. A. (2005). The financial impact of ISO 9000 certification in the United States: An empirical analysis. *Management Science, 51*(7), 1046–1059.

Environment management system. Online Available at: https://www.nibusinessinfo.co.uk/content/advantages-and-disadvantages-environmental-management-systems-ems.

Heras, I., Dick, G. P., & Casadesus, M. (2002). ISO 9000 registration's impact on sales and profitability. *International Journal of Quality & Reliability Management, 19*(6), 774–791.

High Commission of Canada & Reed Consulting BD Ltd. (2013). International standard social responsibility (Implementing ISO 26000 in Bangladesh), CanCham, Dhaka.

Infographic: ISO 9001:2015 vs. 2008 revision – What has changed? *Maritime Cyprus*. Retrieved 9 October 2018.

ISO 14000: Environmental management systems. Online Available at: https://www.omnex.com/members/standards/iso14000/iso_14000.aspx.

ISO 26000: Social responsibility. Online Available at: https://www.iso.org/iso-26000-social-responsibility.html.

ISO 9001 proven to help win new business. *British Assessment Bureau*, 25 May 2011. Archived from the original on 28 July 2013.

SO 9001 quality management. *ISO*. Retrieved 18 December 2018.

ISO 9001:2015 - Just published!. *ISO*. Retrieved 2 October 2015.

ISO quality management principles (PDF). Iso.org. Retrieved 16 December 2016.

Laskurain-Iturbe, I., Arana-Landín, G., Heras-Saizarbitoria, I., & Boiral, O. (2020). How does IATF 16949 add value to ISO 9001? An empirical study. *Total Quality Management & Business Excellence*, 1–18. Taylor and Francis, UK.

Lee, T. Y. (1998). The development of ISO 9000 certification and the future of quality management. *International Journal of Quality & Reliability Management, 15*(2), 162–177.

Moratis, L., & Widjaja, A. T. (2019). The adoption of ISO 26000 in practice: Empirical results from the Netherlands. In: *ISO 26000-A Standardized View on Corporate Social Responsibility* (pp. 47–61). Springer, London.

Naveh, E., & Marcus, A. (2005). Achieving competitive advantage through implementing a replicable management standard: Installing and using ISO 9000. *Journal of Operations Management, 24*(1), 1–26.

Naveh, E., & Marcus, A. (2007). Financial performance, ISO 9000 standard and safe driving practices effects on accident rate in the US motor carrier industry. *Accident Analysis & Prevention, 39*(4), 731–742.

Poksinska, B., Dahlgaard, J. J., & Antoni, M. (2002). The state of ISO 9000 certification: A study of Swedish organizations. *The TQM Magazine, 14*(5), 297–312.

Prajogo, D. I. (2011). The roles of firms' motives in affecting the outcomes of ISO 9000 adoption. *International Journal of Operations & Production Management, 13*(1), 78–100.

Sartor, M., Orzes, G., & Moras, E. (2019). ISO 14001'. *Quality Management: Tools, Methods, and Standards*. Emerald Publishing Limited, UK, 199–216.

Stamatis, D. H. (1995). *Understanding ISO 9000 and Implementing the Basics to Quality* (Vol. 45). CRC Press, New York.

Standards, training, testing, assessment and certification - BSI Group. Bsigroup.com.

Tarí, J. J., Molina-Azorín, J. F., Pereira-Moliner, J., & López-Gamero, M. D. (2020). Internalization of quality management standards: A literature review. *Engineering Management Journal, 32*(1), 46–60.

Tummala, V. R., & Tang, C. L. (1996). Strategic quality management, Malcolm Baldrige and European quality awards and ISO 9000 certification. *International Journal of Quality & Reliability Management, 13*(4), 8–38.

Index